ECONOMICS
AND IDEOLOGY
AND OTHER ESSAYS

ECONOMICS AND IDEOLOGY AND OTHER ESSAYS

Studies in the Development of Economic Thought

RONALD L. MEEK

Tyler Professor of Economics
at the University of Leicester

CHAPMAN AND HALL LTD

11 NEW FETTER LANE LONDON EC4

First published 1967
© *Ronald L. Meek* 1967
Printed in Great Britain by
T. H. Brickell and Son Ltd,
Gillingham, Dorset

CONTENTS

7/852

PREFACE

Most of the essays included in this book are based more or less directly on articles which have appeared over the past 10 to 15 years in a variety of publications. My choice of these particular articles was based primarily on the fact that they all seemed to make some sort of contribution to the general theme of the relation between economics and ideology which I wanted the book as a whole to develop. Another criterion of choice, although a secondary one, was the relative inaccessibility of the publications in which some of the articles appeared.

I have tried in a number of ways to prevent the book from becoming merely another volume of "collected essays". Some of the pieces contain sections which are substantially new, and in almost all of them I have done an appreciable amount of rewriting. So far as possible, I have tried to bring the views expressed into conformity with those which I hold today. I venture to hope that the essays as they now stand will be found to tell a reasonably clear and continuous story.

In Part One, I have included five essays in which a particular method of historical analysis – based largely on that of Marx – is applied to certain key problems in the development of Classical economics. The essays in Part Two are best interpreted as tentative efforts to apply this method of analysis to the work of Marx himself. In Part Three, the emphasis shifts to certain recent trends in modern economics, and an attempt is made to evaluate them with the aid of methods and criteria worked out in the earlier sections.

I am obliged to the editors of *Science and Society, Scottish Journal of Political Economy, Economica, Review of Economic Studies, The New Reasoner, Modern Quarterly*, and *The Economic Journal*, for allowing me to reproduce material published in these periodicals, and to the publishers of *Democracy and the Labour Movement* for allowing me to reproduce the article on "The Scottish Contribution to Marxist Sociology".

R.L.M.

PART ONE
CLASSICAL ECONOMICS

THE REHABILITATION
OF SIR JAMES STEUART[1]

I

The phenomenon of "rehabilitation" is a peculiarly modern one, at any rate in the field of economic theory. In this field, indeed, one could almost say that prior to the 1930's there were no real "rehabilitations" at all: the different schools which followed one another as the science developed usually contented themselves with demolishing their immediate predecessors, and made little attempt to claim affiliation with the earlier schools which these predecessors had in their day themselves supplanted. There were, of course, cases where writers unknown to, or misunderstood by, their contemporaries were rediscovered: Boisguillebert was in a sense "rehabilitated" by the Physiocrats and von Thünen by the Marginalists; and Marx was diligent in tracking down anticipations of his theory of surplus value in the work of earlier writers. List, in a rather different sense, can be said to have "rehabilitated" the Mercantilists – though in the sphere of economic policy rather than of theory. But cases where basic elements in the theoretical work of a once-famous author were discovered to have relevance and importance to a later era were very rare indeed.

During the last twenty-five years or so, however, there has been something of a swarm of rehabilitations – dating, perhaps, from Keynes's well-known essay on Malthus and the kind words which he subsequently spoke on behalf of the Mercantilists and that "brave army of heretics" which included Mandeville, Gesell and Hobson.[2] The beginnings of general equilibrium theory have been found in the mediaeval Schoolmen, and of input-output analysis in Quesnay's *Tableau Economique*. Mrs Robinson sees her own work on the problems of overall growth of the economy as being in a sense "a revival of the classical theory".[3] And Dr Sen, in an interesting book[4] which is my point of departure in the present essay, suggests that Sir James

---

[1] This essay is an amended version of an article originally published (under another title) in *Science and Society*, Fall 1958.

[2] J. M. Keynes, *Essays in Biography* (London, 1933), pp. 95 ff., and *General Theory* (London, 1936), pp. 333 ff.

[3] Joan Robinson, *The Accumulation of Capital* (London, 1956), p. vi.

[4] S. R. Sen, *The Economics of Sir James Steuart* (Cambridge, Mass., 1957).

Steuart should properly be regarded as a pioneer of our modern "economics of control".

What has caused this remarkable contemporary increase in the propensity to rehabilitate? Partly, no doubt, a sense of insecurity. Theory rarely keeps pace with history: serious lags develop and accumulate, but they remain more or less unnoticed by the orthodox until some shattering event (the slump of 1929, Keynes's *General Theory*, Khrushchev's speech on Stalin) forces recognition of the fact that theory has got out of touch with reality. Then follows a period of profound intellectual questioning, in which the reign of complacency and dogmatism begins to come to an end, and people start asking themselves whether certain earlier ideas rejected by current orthodox theory may not have had something in them after all.

But the reappraisals of past systems of thought which occur during such periods of questioning tend to be *ex post* rather than *ex ante*. Parallels with the past are usually drawn after, rather than before, the orthodox theory begins to be decisively developed in new directions. Consider, for example, some of the main changes which have taken place in economic theory in our own times.

Take value theory. Most historians of economic thought would probably agree that the long period of development in this field prior to Adam Smith was marked by two basic features – first, a transition from the idea that the "value" of a commodity was the price at which it *ought to* sell on the market to the idea that it was the price at which it *actually did* sell; and second, the working out of a fairly rudimentary supply-and-demand theory to explain how this market price was fixed. Then came the Classical economists, who, while accepting the notion that prices were fixed by supply and demand, sought for a more fundamental explanation of the *level* at which supply and demand fixed them in the normal case. Here their main emphasis was placed, of course, on the cost which lay behind supply. The Marginalists posed the general problem of value in similar terms, but placed their main emphasis on the utility which lay behind demand. But then a new tendency began to develop – towards a general equilibrium theory of price which in effect by-passed the whole problem of value as it was conceived by the Classical and Marginalist economists, and endeavoured to explain prices (to put it very crudely) in terms of the mutual interaction of supply and demand. Once this new approach had become respectable, it was only a question of time before the pre-Classical economists began to be rehabilitated as its progenitors. In Schumpeter's great reinterpretation of the history of economic analysis, for example, the salient feature of the whole period up to 1790 appears as the development of the elements of a "full-fledged theory of demand and supply",[5] and the work of Adam Smith and Ricardo appears as a sort of "detour"[6] from the historical line of economists' endeavours.

Then again, take the theory of economic development. The problem of growth and development had been one of the leading preoccupations of the later Mercantilists, and had also constituted the basic subject-matter of Classical political economy. So much so, indeed, that the very concept of a distinction between static and dynamic analysis (which was later to be popularized by J. S. Mill) was quite alien to Smith and Ricardo. Gradually, however, interest in the problem of "scarcity" – *i.e.*, the question of how scarce means could most efficiently be allocated between competing ends – came to co-exist with, and eventually almost to replace, interest in the problem of development. Criteria of economic welfare were evolved with more or less exclusive reference to the degree of efficiency displayed in the allocation of a given set of scarce means, and the problem of the factors determining the rate of increase in these scarce means themselves was discussed only by Marxists and those (like Schumpeter) who had been stimulated to supply alternative answers to the questions which Marx had propounded. Then, with remarkable suddenness, the problem of economic development, in both mature capitalist economies and under-developed countries, was placed on the agenda once again. And following on this resurgence of interest in "the nature and causes of the wealth of nations", the work of the Classical economists in the dynamic field has begun to be reconsidered. No doubt it will not be very long before a new reinterpretation of the history of economic thought appears in which the work of all the post-Ricardian theorists who ignored the problem of development is claimed to be a "detour" from the historical line of economists' endeavours.

Finally, take the so-called "economics of control". The economics of the pre-Classical schools usually rested on the assumption that an economy could not possibly work effectively if left to itself. A greater or lesser degree of intervention by the State was regarded as necessary if an economy was to grow and develop, and political economy was visualized as the art of guiding economic policy. This assumption gradually gave way to the revolutionary idea that under a regime of free capitalist competition private vices could be automatically transmuted into public benefits: allow each man to use his labour and his capital in the manner which seemed most profitable to him, and the net result could be the maximization of society's economic welfare. The division was not in

---

[5] J. S. Schumpeter, *History of Economic Analysis* (New York, 1954), p. 98.

[6] *Ibid.*, p. 474. This view is criticized in the essay on *Economics and Ideology* which appears below, pp. 196 ff.

fact quite as clear-cut as this, of course: interventionists can quote Smith's *Wealth of Nations* and anti-interventionists Steuart's *Political Oeconomy* for their purposes. But the break with the older ideas was none the less a real one for that. The role of the State was in effect reduced from that of actually guiding economic affairs to that of providing a suitable legal and political framework within which economic affairs might safely be left to guide themselves. In our own times, however, bitter experience has led the great majority of economists to question a number of the basic assumptions of *laissez-faire*, and all but a few last-ditchers are now prepared to advocate certain important measures of State interference with the free market mechanism. As a result, some of the pre-Smithian economists are now being rehabilitated, and the history of economic thought is once again being reinterpreted. "Two divergent paths", writes Dr Sen, "were pointing outwards from the milieu of Mun and Petty and Locke. Steuart followed the one which was later to lead to economic socialism. Adam Smith followed the other, leading to economic individualism."[7]

So, after a long period in which scarcely anyone was rehabilitated, we pass to a relatively short period of a quarter of a century or so in which scarcely anyone has *not* been rehabilitated. We are reminded of the Dodo, who, on being asked who had won the race, replied after a great deal of thought: "*Everybody* has won, and *all* must have prizes." But do they really deserve them? Let us consider first the particular case of Sir James Steuart, and then, in the light of this, some of the more general problems which are involved.

II

Steuart was surely the unluckiest of men: seldom has one great work been so completely and so soon eclipsed by another as Steuart's *Inquiry into the Principles of Political Oeconomy* was by Smith's *Inquiry into the Nature and Causes of the Wealth of Nations*. Smith, it must be confessed, seems to have been rather patronizing about Steuart. In a letter to Pulteney, written in 1772, he says: "I have the same opinion of Sir James Steuart's book that you have. Without once mentioning it, I flatter myself that any fallacious principle in it will meet with a clear and distinct confutation in mine."[8] This was hardly cricket. As Dr Sen correctly points out, however, Smith was not playing cricket but "fighting a grim crusade the success of which depended on the effectiveness of his slogan".[9]

[7] Sen, *op. cit.*, p. 185.
[8] J. Rae, *Life of Adam Smith* (London, 1895), pp. 253–4.
[9] Sen, *op. cit.*, p. 3.

Smith was a better strategist and a better stylist than Steuart, which no doubt partly accounts for his victory. But he also had a better theory – or at any rate a theory which corresponded better with the *zeitgeist* of his time. Mercantilism, however enlightened – and Steuart's Mercantilism was very enlightened indeed – had had its day. An illuminating extract from Luigi Cossa's *Introduction to the Study of Political Economy* admirably sums up the verdict on Steuart delivered by subsequent generations:

> Could Adam Smith have a more preposterous precursor than this defender of the omnipotence of the State, whose one idea is to combine privileged corporations with unrestricted competition, and who will allow free banking if only all banks will issue unconvertible scrip? More than an ordinary allowance of pedantry must be thrown into the balance, before Adam Smith and the physiocrats can be so much as weighed in the same scales with a writer who, like Steuart, confuses money with capital, value with price, and wages with profits.[10]

Amid a chorus of abuse of this type, the still small voice of Marx, proclaiming Steuart as "the first Briton who elaborated the general system of bourgeois economics",[11] and praising him for standing "more firmly on historical ground" than most of his eighteenth-century contemporaries,[12] remained unheeded.

Nevertheless Cossa was not entirely wrong. There was indeed an important sense in which Steuart did "confuse money with capital, value with price, and wages with profits". The important thing to appreciate, however, is that these three "confusions", in so far as they were in fact present, all sprang from one and the same source: Steuart's failure to take proper account of the emergence in agriculture and manufacture of a new social class – the class which used capital in the employment of wage labour, and as a result gained a profit bearing a more or less regular proportion to the amount of capital laid out. The "two principal Classes of a People" which Steuart distinguishes are the "farmers", who produce enough for their own subsistence plus a surplus, and the "free hands", who in effect "live upon the surplus of the farmers".[13] The class of "free hands" is divided into two sub-classes: "The first, those to whom this surplus directly belongs [*i.e.*, the landlords], or who, with a revenue in money already acquired, can purchase it. The second, those who purchase it with their daily labour or personal service."[14] The essential point to be noted here is that the class of "farmers" and the second sub-class of "free hands" may clearly include

---

[10] Cossa, *op. cit.* (tr. Louis Dyer, London, 1893) pp. 234–5.
[11] Marx, *Critique of Political Economy* (Chicago, 1904), p. 65.
[12] *Ibid.*, p. 267.
[13] Steuart, *Political Oeconomy* (1767 ed.), Vol. I, pp. 50 and 48.
[14] *Ibid.*, p. 48.

both capitalists and wage-earners, but the distinction between these latter classes is not recognized by Steuart as being relevant to the economic problems under consideration. In particular, Steuart tends to regard "profit" merely as a synonym for "gain", or at best as a sort of superior wage which may accrue under certain circumstances to *any* "farmer" or member of the second sub-class of "free hands". Broadly speaking, any net reward (over and above the cost of raw materials, tools of trade and personal subsistence) received by anyone engaged in production or trade is classified as "profit", whether its recipient happens to be an employer, a wage-earner, or a worker on his own account.[15] We look in vain in Steuart for any definite formulation of the new concept of profit which Smith was to popularize – the concept of profit as an income accruing exclusively to employers of wage-labour and bearing a regular proportion to the amount of their capital. This is no doubt what Cossa was referring to when he spoke of Steuart's "confusion of money with capital" and "wages with profits". Steuart was hardly alone in this "confusion", of course: the model of the economy which he used was not essentially different from that of Cantillon, or Quesnay, or Hume, or indeed from that of the Smith of the *Glasgow Lectures*. But the gulf between Steuart's concept of profit and that of the *Wealth of Nations* is certainly a deep and important one.[16]

Steuart's concept of profit leads directly to that "confusion of value with price" of which Cossa spoke. The prices of goods, says Steuart, are made up of two component parts – the "real value" and the "profit upon alienation".[17] The "real value" (roughly the average physical cost of production) is known when the quantity of labour required to produce the commodity, "the value of the workman's subsistence and necessary expence", and "the value of the materials" are known. "These three articles being known," concludes Steuart, "the price of manufacture is determined. It cannot be lower than the amount of all the three, that is, than the real value; whatever it is higher, is the manufacturer's profit. This will ever be in proportion to demand, and therefore will fluctuate according to circumstances." Given his concept of profit, this was as far as Steuart could possibly have gone in showing "how trade has the effect of rendering [prices] fixt and determined". Given the Smithian concept of profit as a class income accruing solely to those who used capital in the employment of wage-labour, however, a

---

15 This comes out very clearly in *ibid.*, pp. 317 ff., where Steuart discusses the circumstances which may "extend profits beyond the physical-necessary". This is one of the very few passages in which Steuart specifically mentions the distinction between employers and wage-earners.

16 Smith's concept of profit is discussed in the next essay in the present volume.

17 Quotations in this paragraph from *Political Oeconomy*, Vol. I, pp. 181–2.

further important analytical advance could be made. A high degree of competition, it could be said, did not eliminate profits, but merely reduced them to an average or "natural" level. Profit on capital at this "natural" rate could then be postulated as a constituent of the supply price of the commodity concerned, to which its market price would in the long period tend to conform. No longer was there a sort of floating element which "fluctuated according to circumstances" in the prices of commodities: older theories of price like Steuart's began to appear not only as relatively indeterminate but also as involving a "confusion of value with price".[18]

Nevertheless, Steuart was not quite as far removed from the Classical position as he is usually made out to have been. He insists that although the "profit upon alienation" may vary with the degree of competition, the "real value" never can,[19] provided that we estimate its three constituent elements "upon an average".[20] In several places, too, he recognizes that under competition profits will be reduced to the "proper standard",[21] to a "reasonable" level,[22] and so on. "While the balance [of supply and demand] stands justly poised," he says in one place, "prices are found in the adequate proportion of the real expence of making the goods, *with a small addition for profit to the manufacturer and merchant.*"[23] And in his interesting comments on what he calls the "consolidation of profits" he seems to visualize a situation in which profits are incorporated into the supply prices of commodities – "transformed into the intrinsic value of the goods", as he puts it.[24] All in all, then, it seems wrong to regard Steuart purely as a "supply and demand" theorist: he was clearly feeling his way forward from a mere supply and demand theory towards the Classical approach to the value problem. This view is reinforced by another feature of Steuart's work to which Dr Sen correctly draws attention – the fact that his theory of prices was intended as an integral part of a general theory of social dynamics,[25] just as were the value theories of Smith, Ricardo and Marx.

Steuart's "one idea", said Cossa, was "to combine privileged corporations with unrestricted competition". This is of course a rather absurd

---

[18] See pp. 202–3 below.

[19] *Political Oeconomy*, Vol. I, p. 199.

[20] *Ibid.*, p. 182. Here Steuart comes very close to the concept of socially-necessary labour.

[21] *Ibid.*, p. 490.

[22] *Ibid.*, p. 199.

[23] *Ibid.*, p. 217 (my italics).

[24] *Ibid.*, p. 221. It should be noted that Steuart deplores this "consolidation of profits", and claims that it can only come about if a monopoly situation arises which the statesman fails to correct.

[25] Sen, *op. cit.*, pp. 70 ff.

exaggeration, but the remark does point to another significant feature of Steuart's work which most commentators prior to Dr Sen tended to neglect. By Steuart's time "unrestricted competition" was coming more and more to dominate the economic scene, although it was still alloyed to a considerable extent with various elements of monopoly. Because of this, Steuart felt himself obliged to conduct his enquiry into "Trade and Industry" on the basis of the assumption that "the principle of self-interest" was the "ruling principle" of his subject,[26] and to give a full analysis of the working of competition, both restricted and unrestricted. He was obliged to recognize, too, that when the "scales" of supply and demand were evenly balanced there was no need for the statesman to interfere. Up to this point he is at one with the Classical economists. Where he differs from them is in his estimate of the capacity of the system to readjust itself after the balance has for some reason been disturbed. Even in the case of a short-run tendency for one of the "scales" to preponderate, Steuart maintained, it was the duty of the statesman to interfere – not, indeed, by taking anything out of the heavy scale, but rather by "gently ... load[ing] the opposite scale". For example, "when the scale of demand is found to preponderate, he ought to give encouragement to the establishment of new undertakings, for augmenting the supply, and for preserving prices at their former standard".[27] And in the case of long-run maladjustments it was even more incumbent upon the statesman to interfere, since long run maladjustments were both more certain to occur and more serious in their effects than short-run maladjustments. Steuart's *Political Oeconomy* is in essence a book of advice to the statesman on the appropriate measures of intervention which he ought to adopt when the economy deviates – as in Steuart's view it must inevitably and constantly tend to do – from the ideal of free competition. Many of the measures which he recommends are formally similar to those which Keynesians have recommended for dealing with the business cycle, such as public works, fiscal measures, and changes in the rate of interest; and the comparison which Dr Sen makes between Steuart's *Political Oeconomy* and A. P. Lerner's *Economics of Control* is perhaps not too far-fetched. But such comparisons should not be pushed too far. Whereas modern Western welfare economists usually take the view that deviations from the optimum exist in spite of the general tendency of the system to return to a balanced position, Steuart usually takes the view that deviations from the optimum exist because of the general tendency of the system to move away from a balanced position.

[26] *Political Oeconomy*, Vol. I, p. 162.
[27] *Ibid.*, p. 491.

To Steuart, in other words, the balance of supply and demand is more an *ideal* position than an "equilibrium" position in the Classical and modern sense of the word.

There is another point which should be borne in mind before we claim Steuart as a pioneer of modern interventionist theory and say with Dr Sen that "had not the brilliance of Adam Smith and the *laissez-faire* spirit of the nineteenth century combined to cast him into oblivion, it is quite possible that the school of thought which Malthus, List and Keynes took so long to build up might have been more rapidly developed".[28] I think there is little doubt that if Steuart had in fact won out over Smith in the eighteenth century the result would have been most unfortunate for both economic practice and economic theory. In the field of practice, it can probably be said that at that time progress demanded an extension of economic freedom for the individual capitalist and a minimization of measures of State control over economic life. In the field of theory, progress demanded improvements in the analysis of the actual working of a free exchange economy and further attempts to discover the basic laws underlying its operation and development. A victory for Steuart would surely have inhibited progress in both these fields. A century and a half later, when capitalism had passed from its competitive to its monopolistic stage and was beginning to show ominous signs of decrepitude, the times did indeed become ripe for a sort of "revival" of certain pre-Smithian ideas, including those of Steuart. But the revival of these ideas did not mean that economics had simply gone round in a circle: the ideas were revived on a higher plane, precisely as a result of the crucial analytical work which the anti-interventionists had carried out in the intervening period.

A doctor examines an infant, and declares that it is suffering from a serious disease which requires a particular type of treatment. Other doctors examine the child, and find that it seems to be developing in a reasonably healthy way and that the treatment recommended by the first doctor would be likely to inhibit its development. They therefore neglect pathological considerations, and proceed to investigate the general principles of the child's bodily structure and the laws of its growth. Eventually, much later, when the child has grown into an old man, it begins to develop the very disease which the first doctor diagnosed, and it becomes clear that the germs of this disease had in fact been present in it from infancy. The remedies originally prescribed by the first doctor are therefore applied, but owing to the knowledge of bodily structure and growth which has been acquired in the meantime as a result of the work of other doctors, these remedies can now be greatly

[28] Sen, *op. cit.*, p. 153.

improved and applied much more effectively. Steuart can be called a pioneer of modern interventionist theory only in the sense that the first doctor can be called a pioneer of the modern methods of treatment.

One of the most interesting features of Steuart's work is what Dr Sen aptly describes as his "historical, institutional and on the whole evolutionist approach".[29] Steuart does not merely postulate the existence of a society divided into "farmers" and "free hands": he also shows in some detail how such a society came into being and developed. Broadly, he argues that population must always be in proportion to the produce of the earth. At first, man lives on the spontaneous fruits of the soil; then the pressure of population and the desire for improvement lead him to "add his labour and industry to the natural activity of the soil".[30] Gradually individuals are either compelled (by means of the institution of slavery) or induced (by means of the multiplication of human wants and the encouragement of exchange) to produce a surplus of food over and above their own subsistence, thus providing a material foundation for the growth of a class of "free hands" who live on the surplus produce. It is only with the emergence of this new class that a "free society" comes into being. The main motive forces in each stage of social development are conceived by Steuart as being basically economic in character,[31] and this emphasis on the primacy of economic factors is retained throughout the whole work – as, for example, in the following characteristic passage:

> The great alteration in the affairs of Europe within these three centuries, by the discovery of America and the Indies, the springing up of industry and learning, the introduction of trade and the luxurious arts, the establishment of public credit, and a general system of taxation, have entirely altered the plan of government every where.
>
> From feudal and military, it is become free and commercial.[32]

The same general attitude can be found in Steuart's discussions of the territorial division of labour and localization of industry, the effect of the influx of precious metals from America, and "the general principles of *subordination* and *dependence* among mankind".[33] All these, Dr Sen says, "indicate an attempt at an economic interpretation of history

---

[29] *Ibid.*, p. 19. "In this respect," Dr Sen remarks (pp. 18–19), "he may be regarded as one of the earliest exponents of that school of thought which Saint-Simon and Sismondi in France and Richard Jones and Karl Marx in England were to develop in the next century. As such he may also be regarded as a pioneer writer on the theory of economic growth."

[30] Steuart, *Political Oeconomy*, Vol. I, p. 21.

[31] Cf. Sen, *op. cit.*, p. 49.

[32] Steuart, *Political Oeconomy*, Vol. I, p. 10.

[33] *Ibid.*, p. 238.

which is certainly unusual for the times when Steuart lived and wrote".[34]

"Unusual", however, only up to a point. The most striking fact which emerges from a reading of Steuart is surely his close intellectual kinship in this respect with the members of the Scottish Historical School of the eighteenth century.[35] This kinship, curiously enough, is not recognized by Dr Sen, who in fact goes so far as to say of the members of the Scottish Historical School that "every characteristic feature of their general outlook differed from that of Steuart".[36] But it can hardly be denied that the *most* "characteristic feature of their general outlook" was precisely a "historical, institutional and on the whole evolutionist approach", coupled with a bias towards an "economic interpretation of history". Men like Hume, Smith, Kames, Robertson, Ferguson and Millar may have objected to Steuart's political views and thought little of his economics, but in the field of "theoretical or conjectural history" which they were opening up they must surely have recognized him as something of a kindred spirit. In this respect at any rate Steuart was much more in tune with his times than Dr Sen appears to suspect.[37]

III

Dr Sen, then, makes out a good case for regarding Steuart as a thinker of considerable calibre whom subsequent generations have unjustly neglected, and whose basic ideas make rather more sense in the economic context of the twentieth century than they did in that of the eighteenth. If the "rehabilitations" of the present day went no further than this, no objection could properly be made to them. Unfortunately, however, few of the modern rehabilitators have been able to resist the temptation of using their rehabilitation as the basis for a complete reinterpretation of the history of economic thought, and it seems to me that as a result we are in grave danger of losing all sense of perspective when we look at past theoretical systems.

The trouble is that reinterpretation is too easy a game to play. A new theory becomes fashionable – a new theory of value, say, or a new theory of employment. Now since the problems of value and employ-

---

[34] Sen, *op. cit.*, p. 49.

[35] For an account of the work of the Scottish Historical School, see the essay on *The Scottish Contribution to Marxist Sociology* which appears below, pp. 34 ff.

[36] Sen, *op. cit.*, p. 183.

[37] Since the appearance of the article upon which this essay is based, Mr A. S. Skinner, of Glasgow University, has published a number of pieces on Steuart in which proper emphasis is laid on this point. See in particular his article "Sir James Steuart: Economics and Politics", in the *Scottish Journal of Political Economy*, February 1965.

ment have been looked at from so many different angles during the two or three centuries of the existence of economics as we know it today, the chances are that the new theory will turn out upon investigation to be not entirely new. A similar type of approach will be found to have been adopted (albeit in a very different context) by economists X, Y and Z at various periods in the development of economic thought. If we now abstract these theories of X, Y and Z from their historical context, we are ready to make our reinterpretation. We can, if we like, adopt what might be called the teleological approach, and visualize the new theory as "the divine event to which the whole creation moves", judging the performances of individual economists "according to whether they hastened or retarded its arrival".[38] The emphasis here will be on continuity, so that the work of any of the opponents of X, Y and Z who managed to get the whip hand over them for any length of time will have to be described as a detour from the historical line of economists' endeavours. Or alternatively, if X, Y and Z all lived a sufficiently long time ago we can adopt what might be called the apocalyptic approach. X, Y and Z can be represented in the guise of ancient and rather primitive prophets, whose ideas were rejected and whose followers were driven underground for a long period, at the end of which the theory they had espoused suddenly burst forth upon an astonished world. The number of new patterns in the development of economic thought which can be disclosed by the use of these and other methods of reinterpretation is quite surprising.

I do not deny, of course, that the use of these methods may have some pedagogical value (as in the case of Keynes's redefinition of the term "Classical"), or that it may throw fresh light on neglected fields of study (as in the case of Schumpeter's rehabilitation of the Schoolmen). Nor do I deny that each generation must to some extent rewrite the history of economic thought in the light of its own theoretical discoveries. But before reorientating the whole history of economic thought towards these discoveries, one must be certain that they *are* genuine and important discoveries and not mere changes of fashion; and when estimating the place of past theories in the general stream of thought one must be careful not to abstract them from the particular historical context in which they were put forward. The latter point is especially important. If we abstract the views of an economist like Steuart from the general economic and intellectual milieu in which they were formulated, and then compare them with some of the views which are fashionable today, we will certainly discover a number of interesting formal parallels. But

[38] G. B. Richardson, in a review-article on Schumpeter's *History of Economic Analysis* in *Oxford Economic Papers*, June 1955, p. 142.

if we attempt to make a complete reinterpretation of the history of economic thought on the basis of these parallels the result is not likely to be very useful.

The essential point is this: Economics, in the form in which it has come down to us, has always been primarily concerned with the analysis of the system of market exchange. But however much an individual economist may think that he is laying down laws of market exchange which will be valid at all times and places, his analysis will almost inevitably be relative (in some significant sense of that word) to the particular historical stage of development through which the market exchange system happens to be passing at the time he writes. The general approach which he makes to the phenomena of market exchange will largely depend upon his general attitude to the socioeconomic environment of his own time. This attitude will determine (*inter alia*) the answers which he gives to two all-important questions: (i) From what angle can exchange phenomena most usefully be analysed?; and, (ii) Does the free exchange system maximize economic welfare?

Take the first question. When production for the market was still a comparatively rare and localized institution, the analysis of exchange phenomena was naturally conducted from the angle of "supply and demand". Gradually, however, as feudalism disappeared and capitalism began to advance, production for the market came more and more to dominate the economic scene, and the concept of a society which was in effect bound together by this type of production began to emerge. The economic tie which linked men to one another as producers of different commodities for the market came to be viewed as the "chief cement"[39] binding society together. People who looked at the society of their times in this new light began to take the view that exchange phenomena should properly be analysed not only from the angle of "supply and demand", but also (and indeed primarily) from the angle of the relations which men entered into with one another in production. The development of the Classical labour theory of value was closely associated with the emergence of this new viewpoint, and the Classical economists carried on the same tradition in so far as they can be said to have analysed the distribution of income in terms of class relations. After Ricardo's death, however, when capitalism went over from an offensive position against the landlords to a defensive position against the newly-

---

[39] The phrase is that of Joseph Harris, *An Essay Upon Money and Coins* (1757), p. 15, footnote. Steuart had much the same idea when he spoke of "the reciprocal wants which the statesman must create, in order to bind the society together" (*Political Oeconomy*, Vol. I, p. 28).

organized working class, this way of looking at society came to appear distinctly dangerous to the more conservative economists, who began in effect to suggest that exchange phenomena could not be analysed "scientifically" unless abstraction were made of the relations of production.[40] Inevitably this line of thought led (through very tortuous paths) to the resurrection of something like the old "supply and demand" type of approach which had characterized the pre-capitalist period of development. The other type of approach was taken over from the Classical economists by Marx, whose general attitude to the socio-economic system of his time was of course radically different from that of the orthodox economists.

The views of economists on the second question have also been quite largely determined by their general attitude towards the particular stage of development through which the market exchange system happened to be passing at the time they wrote. The idea that a free exchange system will maximize economic welfare is of course a comparatively recent one: it could scarcely have been put forward prior to the eighteenth century, when this new system began rapidly to rise to a position of predominance. The first opponents of the idea were men like Steuart and Malthus, "reactionaries" in the technical sense, who tended to look back in longing towards certain institutions of the past which the new system was rapidly destroying. Steuart was suspicious of the advance of unrestricted competition and Malthus of the advance of unrestricted accumulation, and both advocated various measures of government intervention to alleviate the difficulties which they believed the new developments would entail. Their opponents, Smith and Ricardo respectively, took an entirely different view of the new system and its prospects, and their ideas won out largely because they were more in line with the demands of economic progress at the time. Then came those who turned away from the new system in revulsion because of the "dark satanic mills" spawned by the industrial revolution, or because of the cyclical tendencies which the system was coming increasingly to display, and who looked forward to a more rational system which would eventually replace it. Finally in our own times there has been a revolt against certain aspects of the system from within the ranks of the orthodox economists themselves – a revolt motivated not by a desire to return to some older system or to advance to a new one, but rather by a wish to make the existing system work. And inevitably this latter development has led to a revival of interest in the measures of control advocated by men like Steuart and Malthus, and in the theoretical analyses which lay behind their proposals.

[40] See the essay on *The Decline of Ricardian Economics in England* which appears below, pp. 51 ff.

Economics, then, has grown up hand in hand with the system of market exchange, particularly in its capitalist stage of development. Conflicts between schools of thought have arisen partly because the different phases of development of the system require different modes of analysis (a Physiocratic world is different from a Smithian world; a Marshallian world is different from a Keynesian world), and partly because in each phase of development group struggles have emerged in which economists, like everyone else, have taken sides. Similarities and continuities can be detected partly because it is at bottom one and the same system (in its different phases of development) which economists have been analysing, and partly because certain attitudes expressed for a particular reason in a particular phase of development are sometimes expressed again for a very different reason in a very different phase of development. The point I have been trying to make in this essay is simply that it is wrong to interpret the history of economic thought on the basis of similarities of the latter type. An *interpretation* of the history of economic thought, if it is to be worthy of the name, must surely start by relating the major theories which have been put forward to the different phases of development through which the system of market exchange has passed. We cannot postulate the existence of a "path" leading from Mercantilism to socialism merely on the basis of certain formal similarities between Steuart's work and the "economics of control". If we do so, we will certainly escape the Scylla of relativism, but we will do so only to drown in the Charybdis of teleology.

ADAM SMITH AND THE CLASSICAL THEORY OF PROFIT[1]

I

"The whole annual produce of the land and labour of every country," wrote Adam Smith in the *Wealth of Nations*, "or what comes to the same thing, the whole price of that annual produce, naturally divides itself . . . into three parts; the rent of land, the wages of labour, and the profits of stock; and constitutes a revenue to three different orders of people; to those who live by rent, to those who live by wages, and to those who live by profit. These are the three great, original and constituent orders of every civilized society, from whose revenue that of every other order is ultimately derived."[2]

We today have grown so accustomed to the postulation of this basic social pattern of landlords, labourers and capitalists, living respectively on rent, wages and profit, that it is sometimes difficult for us to imagine that it is less than two hundred years old. Yet Adam Smith seems to have been the first, if not to discern the existence of this pattern in the society around him, at least to appreciate its enormous significance. We look in vain for any real understanding of its importance in other places where we might perhaps have expected to find it – in Steuart,[3] Hutcheson and Ferguson, for example. Even in Cantillon, and even, what is more surprising, in the Smith of the *Glasgow Lectures*, we find little more than a few educated inklings of it. Adam Smith's predecessors certainly supplied various elements of the pattern, but he himself seems to have been the first to grasp it in its entirety and to attempt consciously to analyse its complex internal relationships.

The special feature of the pattern which marked it off from those put forward by earlier economists was the inclusion of *profit on capital* as a general category of class income which accrued to all who used "stock" in the employment of wage-labour, and which was qualitatively distinct both from the rent of land and from the wages of labour. Many of

---

[1] This essay is a slightly amended version of an article published in the *Scottish Journal of Political Economy*, June 1954.

[2] *Wealth of Nations* (ed. Cannan, London, 1930), Vol. I, p. 248. Cf. Vol. II, p. 412.

[3] Cf. above, pp. 8–9.

Smith's predecessors had recognized, of course, that those who employed stock in mercantile pursuits generally received a net reward which was proportioned not to the effort, if any, which they expended, but rather to the value of the stock employed. In Smith's new model it was recognized that net gains similar in this respect to mercantile profit were now also being earned on capital employed in other economic pursuits, such as agriculture and manufacture. But, even more important, it was also recognized that the *origin* of these gains was now very different from what it had formerly been. To Smith's predecessors, generally speaking, profit had appeared as "profit upon alienation" – *i.e.*, as the gain from buying cheap and selling dear. To Smith, on the other hand, profit began to appear as an income uniquely associated with the use of capital in the employment of wage-labour. Profit was primarily derived from the value which the wage-labourers employed added to the original value of the raw materials, etc., upon which they worked. "The value which the workmen add to the materials," said Smith, ". . . resolves itself . . . into two parts, of which the one pays their wages, the other the profits of their employer upon the whole stock of materials and wages which he advanced."[4]

And not only this. In Smith's model, the "constituent order" whose income consisted of profit on capital was regarded in a certain sense as the *leading* economic order, in so far as the mainspring of the economic mechanism was conceived in terms of the desire of individual capitalists to maximize the rate of profit on their capital and to accumulate as rapidly as possible. In his lectures at Glasgow, Smith had already gone a considerable distance towards understanding the importance of capital,[5] but he had apparently still tended to visualize the equilibrating movements of effort and resources in the economy in terms of "the concurrence of different labourers".[6] In the *Wealth of Nations*, on the other hand, the drive to maximize profit and to accumulate capital is presented as the essential precondition and basic cause of the growth of opulence. The urge to accumulate leads not only to the optimum

---

[4] *Ibid.*, Vol. I, p. 50.

[5] See, for example, *Lectures on Justice, Police, Revenue and Arms* (ed. Cannan, Oxford, 1896), p. 220. This is perhaps a convenient place to mention that another set of student's notes of Smith's lectures at Glasgow – much fuller than, and in some ways much superior to, the set discovered by Cannan – was found a few years ago by Professor Lothian, of Aberdeen University. It has recently been acquired by Glasgow University, and an edited version will be published in due course in the definitive edition of Smith's *Works and Correspondence* which Glasgow University is now preparing. For obvious reasons, however, all references to the *Glasgow Lectures* in the present volume will continue to be to the Cannan edition, and interpretations made by me in the past on the basis of the latter edition will be reproduced here unaltered.

[6] *Lectures*, p. 179.

allocation of resources within each employment[7] and between different employments,[8] but also to a substantial increase in real income over time. Smith was, indeed, quite prepared to suggest that the secular increase in real income was and always had been uniquely correlated with the increase in capital.[9] It was Smith's great emphasis on the economic role of profit on capital and capital accumulation which more than anything else gave unity and strength to the structure of the *Wealth of Nations*.

The emergence of profit on capital in the Classical sense as a new category of class income was not merely a conceptual but also a historical phenomenon. As Engels once remarked in a somewhat similar connection: "We are dealing here not only with a purely logical process, but with a historical process and its explanatory reflection in thought, the logical pursuance of its inner connections."[10] Profit on capital and the social classes which came to receive incomes of this type were of course the ultimate products of several centuries of economic development. But it was apparently not until the third quarter of the eighteenth century that profit on capital, as a new generic type of class income, became so clearly differentiated from other types of income that economists were able to grasp its full significance and delineate its basic characteristics. There were a number of obstacles which had to be overcome before this could be done.

In the first place, there were certain difficulties connected with the differentiation of profit from *rent of land* and *interest on money*. Profit formally resembled these other types of income in so far as they all appeared to stand in a more or less regular proportion to a capital sum – rent to a sum of money invested in the purchase of land, interest to a sum of money lent out to a borrower, and profit to a sum of money used directly or indirectly in the employment of wage-labour. During the century prior to the appearance of the *Wealth of Nations*, the vital distinction between *money* (*i.e.*, money as a hoard) and *capital* (*i.e.*, money utilized in order to secure a revenue) began to be recognized by a number of economists. "No Man is richer for having his Estate all in Money, Plate, &c. lying by him," wrote North in 1691, "but on the contrary, he is for that reason the poorer. That man is richest, whose Estate is in a growing condition, either in Land at Farm, Money at Interest, or Goods in Trade."[11] And at the same time a further im-

---

[7] *Wealth of Nations*, Vol. I, p. 259.

[8] *Ibid.*, p. 419.

[9] *Ibid.*, pp. 325-8. Cf. Vol. II, p. 414.

[10] Engels, *Engels on "Capital"* (London, n.d.), p. 100.

[11] *Discourses upon Trade* (1691), reprinted in *A Select Collection of Early English Tracts on Commerce* (1856). The quotation appears on p. 525 of the *Select Collection*. Cf. Marx, *Theories of Surplus Value* (ed. Bonner and Burns, London, 1951), p. 32.

portant distinction came to be made between capital which was more or less passively utilized (as in the case of "Land at Farm" or "Money at Interest") and capital which was more actively utilized (as in the case of "Goods in Trade"). It had become evident that whereas those who utilized capital passively would normally receive as revenue only the ordinary rate of interest or its equivalent, those who utilized it actively in "trade" would normally make a net gain, or "profit", over and above the ordinary rate of interest. The way was then laid open for the development of the Classical concept of interest as a derivative form of income which was paid out of gross profit and ultimately regulated by it. Smith, like Locke and Cantillon and Hume before him, emphasized the fact "that wherever a great deal can be made by the use of money, a great deal will commonly be given for the use of it; and that wherever little can be made by it, less will commonly be given for it".[12] And just as the differentiation of profit from interest in the sphere of "trade" was possible only with the emergence of a separate class of "traders", so the clear differentiation of profit from rent in the sphere of agriculture was possible only with the emergence of a separate class of agricultural capitalists. A clear distinction between rent-earning capital invested in the purchase of land and profit-earning capital invested in the actual farming of the land could not be made (unless by way of analogy with other spheres of production) prior to the fairly widespread development of capitalist methods of organization in agriculture.

In the second place, there were certain difficulties connected with the differentiation of profit from *wages*. As capitalism developed in industry and agriculture, the objective conditions were gradually established for the recognition of the fact that the essential common feature of all active uses of capital was its utilization in the employment of wage-labour, and thus for the postulation of profit as a new type of class income born of the capital-labour relationship. But it very often happened at this time that the employers of labour had risen from the ranks of the direct producers and still participated actively in the actual process of production. Therefore they naturally persisted in regarding the difference between their paid-out costs and the price they received for their commodities as a sort of superior "wage" for their own personal efforts rather than as a "profit" on the capital, often very meagre, which they had supplied. Even when such "undertakers" came to confine themselves to merely supervisory functions, it might still seem plausible to speak of their net reward, as so many economists at this time actually did speak of it, as the "wages of superintendence". How difficult it was at this time to appreciate the nature of the difference between wages

[12] *Wealth of Nations*, Vol. I, p. 90.

and profits is shown clearly enough by the emphasis which Smith himself felt obliged to place upon the point. Obviously aware that he was to some extent breaking new ground, Smith went out of his way to insist that the profits of stock were *not* "the wages of a particular sort of labour, the labour of inspection and direction", but were "altogether different", being "regulated by quite different principles". The owner of capital, said Smith, even though he was "discharged of almost all labour", still expected that "his profits should bear a regular proportion to his capital".[13]

Finally, there were certain obstacles standing in the way of the introduction of the concept of an *average* rate of profit. Before the profits of stock could come to be regarded as standing in a regular proportion to the amount of capital, *in whatever sphere it happened to be employed*, it was clearly necessary that the field covered by capitalist methods of organization should be considerably enlarged, that competition in both internal and external trade should be reasonably free, and that capital should be relatively mobile between different places and occupations. Only then could it be plausibly said that profit at the average rate was a constituent element in the "natural" price of all commodities.

It was the emergence of profit on capital as a new category of class income, sharply differentiated from other types of income, which cleared the way for the full development of Classical political economy. As the conditions I have described were gradually fulfilled in the real world, the older accounts of "profit" necessarily began to seem more and more inadequate. "Profit" could no longer be treated under the heading of rent, where Petty had tended to place it; it could no longer be identified with wages, as with Cantillon and Hutcheson; and its origin could no longer be sought in the sphere of exchange, where Steuart had claimed to find it. The relationship between capital and wage-labour was becoming the dominant socio-economic relationship in Western society, and this fact necessitated a complete revision of certain fundamental economic concepts and the postulation of a new basic social pattern.

II

It is here that we come face to face with something of a mystery. The postulation of a basic social pattern such as that put forward by Smith clearly cannot precede the emergence of the real socio-economic phenonema of which it is designed to be a generalization. These phemonena must at least be sufficiently dominant in certain key spheres to make it apparent (even if only to more perceptive observers)

[13] *Ibid.*, Vol. I, pp. 50–51.

that they are *becoming* dominant in all. Smith's division of society into landlords, labourers and capitalists would appear to presuppose quite a considerable infiltration of capital and capitalist methods of organization into agriculture and manufacture. Yet if we look at Britain, and still more if we look only at Scotland, at the time when Smith's basic ideas were formed, we are forced to the conclusion that this process of infiltration had not then proceeded far enough to render Smith's basic pattern plausible as a delineation of the *general* state of affairs in these countries.

Consider, for example, the position of Scottish agriculture. In the 1750's and 60's, taking the country as a whole, the area covered by farms where the functions of landlord, labourer and capitalist were actually exercised by three separate individuals must still have been relatively small. It is certainly true that capital was beginning to flow from commerce into agriculture (some of it from the profits of the tobacco trade, either directly or through the newly-established banks), and that the results were sufficiently spectacular to attract a considerable amount of attention.[14] The improving movement, which had begun much earlier in the century in some districts, started to gather momentum during its second half. But the bulk of the capital laid out in improvements was being invested by the landowners rather than by their tenants. Even in the 1770's, when Andrew Wight made most of his celebrated tours, the crying need in most districts was still for substantial capitalist tenants, "men of stock" as Wight called them,[15] who would be "encouraged by long leases to follow the improvements of their landlord".[16] This fact is perhaps reflected in those passages in the *Wealth of Nations* where Smith suggests that although improvements are "sometimes" made by tenants, they are in general more likely (for reasons which Smith examines at some length) to be made by the landlords.[17]

It would be wrong to conclude from this, however, that there were not distinct signs in certain districts of the emergence of a new class of capitalist farmers. In the more progressive regions – and particularly in those which Smith had special opportunities to study – capitalist methods of agricultural organization had already become quite widespread. As the improving movement began to extend during the second half of the century, ". . . small holdings were being thrown into large farms. Farming for profit was taking the place of subsistence farming . . .

---

[14] This process was, of course, particularly evident in the vicinity of cities such as Glasgow. Cf. *Wealth of Nations*, Vol. I, pp. 129–30, 356 and 382–3.

[15] A. Wight, *Present State of Husbandry in Scotland* (Edinburgh, 1778–84), Vol. IV, p. 365.

[16] *Ibid.*, Vol. III, p. 549. Cf. Vol. III, pp. 521, 708; Vol. IV, p. 119; etc.

[17] *Wealth of Nations*, Vol. I, pp. 145–6, 367, 369–70, etc. Cf. p. 354.

In the Lowlands the early improving landlords grasped the importance of security for their tenants, and so there the lease system spread rapidly ... The security thus offered called into existence a class of professional farmers, carefully chosen by the improving landowners, who were able and willing to keep abreast of the latest advances in agriculture."[18] This process was particularly evident in the Lothians. In East Lothian, Wight noted:

> Improvements in agriculture are chiefly owing to the tenants. East Lothian is a fine country, and agriculture has been long carried on there to greater perfection than in any other county in Scotland. This has made a good deal of money to circulate among the tenantry, or yeomanry, as termed in England, who are fond of their country, and never willing to desert it. By this means there are always substantial tenants at hand to bid for every spot that is vacant; and the money and credit they have, enable them to make the most of their possessions. In other parts of Scotland, gentlemen have no other method to improve their estates, but by taking farms into their own hand, improving them, and letting them out to tenants. As this is unnecessary in East Lothian, the gentlemen are few in number who apply themselves to agriculture.[19]

Smith was no doubt kept in close touch with these important developments as a result of the agricultural discussions held by the Select Society in Edinburgh, whose members were "largely connected with the landed interest" and to which "a certain number of practical farmers" were admitted in 1756.[20] And it is possible that certain passages in the *Wealth of Nations* owe their origin to these developments – for example, that in which Smith speaks of the "great stocks" which are employed in farming in some places in Great Britain and of the "rich and great farmers" who are in every country, after small proprietors, the "principal improvers".[21]

It is evident, then, that Smith's basic pattern could in fact have been observed in the agricultural field, even in Scotland, by someone who knew where to look. But in the majority of cases, even in the more advanced districts, the pattern must have been far from clear. As Smith himself pointed out, the three different sorts of revenue are commonly "confounded" with one another, particularly in agriculture. Rent is often confounded with profit, as in the case of "a gentleman who farms a part of his own estate"; wages are often confounded with profit, as in the case of "common farmers"; and sometimes rent and profit are confounded with wages, as in the case of "a gardener who cultivates his

18 Hamilton, *The Industrial Revolution in Scotland* (Oxford, 1932), pp. 5 and 55–6.
19 Wight, *op. cit.*, Vol. II, p. 275.
20 Rae, *Life of Adam Smith*, pp. 111 and 115.
21 *Wealth of Nations*, Vol. I, p. 370; cf. p. 316.

own garden with his own hands".[22] It is no doubt true that the parallel between contemporary developments in the agricultural and the industrial spheres would be very likely to impress itself on one who was a frequent attender both of the meetings of the Select Society in Edinburgh and of those of the Political Economy Club in Glasgow during the decade prior to 1764. But the emergence of the capital-labour relation to a position of dominance must have been more apparent in industry in Glasgow than in agriculture in the Lothians, and it was probably the study of developments in Glasgow which exercised the more decisive influence on the evolution of Smith's thought.

Smith, looking at the economic organization of industry in his day, was apparently able to observe as something like a norm what many economic historians of today, looking back at the same period, have been able to observe only as an exception. Mantoux, for example, has emphasized that before the Industrial Revolution "those capitalists who gained so much from the gradual concentration of the means of production were hardly industrialists . . . They were solely merchants, and industry for them was only a form of trade."[23] The exceptions – those early forms of industrial organization which Marx called "manufacture" – were no doubt significant, but they remained exceptions.[24] It was only when the Industrial Revolution was fairly well under way, according to Mantoux, that the master manufacturer managed to raise himself "so high above his workmen that he found himself on the same level as those other capitalists, the banker and the merchant".[25] Yet in the *Wealth of Nations*, which was written before the Industrial Revolution had properly begun, the master manufacturer is fairly clearly distinguished on the one hand from the merchant and on the other hand from the wage-earner. In Smith's main theoretical statements, the industrial sphere, broadly speaking, is regarded as separate from the mercantile, and the capital-labour relationship is regarded as being dominant in both. This fact is so important that it would seem useful to enquire how far Smith's account was the result of actual observation and how far of prescience or prophecy.

It was in "manufacture", of course – in Marx's sense of the word – that the process whereby the master manufacturer was separating himself from the merchant on the one hand and from the wage-earner on the other could be seen most clearly. In "manufacture" the great

---

[22] *Ibid.*, Vol. I, p. 55.
[23] Mantoux, *The Industrial Revolution in the Eighteenth Century* (rev. edn., London, 1961), p. 90.
[24] *Ibid.*, pp. 374–5.
[25] *Ibid.*, p. 376.

potentialities of the capitalist form of productive organization,[26] and in particular the considerable extent to which this form allowed the division of labour to be carried,[27] were most readily apparent. Adam Smith was evidently very greatly impressed with the large manufactories of his time.[28] The typical master manufacturer of the *Wealth of Nations* is one who has invested a fairly large proportion of his capital in machines and the "instruments of his trade" – for example, "the furnace for melting the ore, the forge, the slitt-mill" which are found in a "great iron-work",[29] or the shafts, "engines for drawing out the water", and "roads and waggon-ways" constructed by the "undertaker of a mine".[30] "The expence which is properly laid out upon a fixed capital of any kind," Smith observed, "is always repaid with great profit", and this is especially the case when the labourers are "assisted with the best machinery".[31] It is this investment in fixed capital which constitutes, as it were, the undertaker's stake in the manufacture, and broadly speaking it is this investment in fixed capital which marks him off as a manufacturer rather than as a merchant.

At this time, particularly in Glasgow, a great deal of capital was flowing from the profits of commerce into manufacture. A number of the most spectacular of the Glasgow manufactories were founded on the initiative of merchants – some of them merely in order to find an outlet for funds seeking investment, and others in order to facilitate the production of goods for sale to the American colonists.[32] But not all the capital for these new projects came from the merchants. Much of it

[26] Even in the manufactory, of course, the method of organization was much less advanced than in the new type of production unit which began to spring up as the Industrial Revolution proceeded. (Cf. Dobb, *Studies in the Development of Capitalism* (London, 1946), p. 260.) It is significant in this connection that Smith normally included raw materials along with wages in the "advances" which the capitalist made to his labourers.

[27] Smith recognized, of course, that the division of labour was often carried just as far, if not farther, in industries like "the linen and woollen manufactures" (*Wealth of Nations*, Vol. I, p. 7), where "every different branch of the work employs so great a number of workmen, that it is impossible to collect them all into the same workhouse" (*ibid.*, Vol. I, p. 6). He also recognized very clearly that the division of labour was essentially dependent upon "the accumulation of stock" (*ibid.*, Vol. I, pp. 258–9).

[28] For interesting contemporary accounts of the Glasgow manufactories, see John M'Ure, *The History of Glasgow* (1736), pp. 227–30 and 257–8, and John Gibson, *The History of Glasgow* (1777), pp. 236–59.

[29] *Wealth of Nations*, Vol. I, p. 262.

[30] *Ibid.*, Vol. I, p. 290.

[31] *Ibid.*, Vol. I, p. 270.

[32] See, e.g. Rae, *Life of Adam Smith*, pp. 88–90, and James Gourlay, "The Tobacco Period in Glasgow, 1707–1775", in *A Glasgow Miscellany* (n.d.), *passim*. There is some useful information on the relation between the Glasgow tobacco trade and the establishment of local manufactories in *Scotland and Tobacco*, an unpublished thesis by T. D. J. Wilkinson, formerly of Glasgow University.

came from rich master craftsmen who broke free from the restrictions imposed by their craft organizations, entered into partnership with groups of merchants, and became managers of the new manufactories which the partnerships set up. Developments such as these, generally speaking, tended in the long run to increase rather than to diminish the growing distinction between the merchant and the master manufacturer, since they encouraged the setting up of large manufactories which required a substantial investment in fixed capital, and also facilitated the rise of master craftsmen to the status of industrial capitalists. The difference between the case of the "undertaker of a great work" and the master craftsman who employed a few journeymen and servants was clearly regarded by Smith as one of degree rather than of kind. They were both master manufacturers.

The rise of a new class of industrial capitalists, who were soon to develop into the entrepreneurs or "captains of industry" so characteristic of modern capitalism, had as its natural correlative the rise of a propertiless urban working class – the "labourers, journeymen, servants of every kind"[33] whom Smith included in the "constituent order" which lived by wages. Once again it was in the manufactories, where the workers were generally divorced from the ownership of the means of production, that the distinction between the capitalist master manufacturer and the wage-labourer was most apparent. Smith was impressed by the fact that in Glasgow (as distinct from Edinburgh) "the inhabitants are chiefly maintained by the employment of capital".[34] And "the quantity of industry which any capital can employ," he noted, "must, evidently, be equal to the number of workmen whom it can supply with materials, tools, and a maintenance suitable to the nature of the work."[35] Smith obviously regarded the typical worker in a manufactory as being largely dependent upon his master for the provision of "instruments of trade".[36] The supply of propertiless labourers, he

[33] *Wealth of Nations*, Vol. I, p. 70.
[34] *Ibid.*, Vol. I, p. 319.
[35] *Ibid.*, Vol. I, p. 279.
[36] Cf. the passage in the so-called "Early Draft of the *Wealth of Nations*" where Smith speaks of the "master of the work" in the famous pin factory affording his workers "the wire the tools and the employment" (Scott, *Adam Smith as Student and Professor* (Glasgow, 1937), p. 331). Some economists – e.g., Beer, *A History of British Socialism* (London, 1920), Vol. I, p. 197, and Stark, *The History of Economics in its Relation to Social Development* (London, 1944), pp. 26–7 and 30–31 – have noted that Smith often omits the "tools" and refers only to materials and wages when he is describing the "advances" made by the capitalist to the labourer, and have taken this fact as evidence that in Smith's time "the labourer and the means of labour were not yet separated" (Stark, *op. cit.*, p. 26). In certain cases (the spinners and the weavers, for example), this was no doubt largely true, and it is also true that there are many survivals in the *Wealth of Nations* of the old habit of describing manufacture as if it

recognized, was generally increased "in years of scarcity", when "poor independent workmen frequently consume the little stocks with which they had used to supply themselves with the materials of their work, and are obliged to become journeymen for subsistence".[37] Once again, the distinction between the status of a worker in a large manufactory and that of a journeyman employed by a small master craftsman was regarded by Smith as one of degree rather than of kind.

If, then, we look at one of the great commercial and industrial centres of Smith's time, such as Glasgow, where capital was flowing at a considerable rate into manufacture, the basic pattern put forward in the *Wealth of Nations* becomes a much closer approximation to reality than if we look at Scotland, or even at Britain, as a whole. In these centres, the extension of capitalist methods of organization was leading to the emergence of a new class of capitalist master manufacturers, who were separating themselves more and more both from their own employees and from the merchants. These master manufacturers were coming to receive an income which was related not to their personal efforts but to the size of their capital – an income which was apparently derived from the value which the wage-labour employed by this capital added to the raw materials which it worked up. Smith, observing the growing dominance of the capital-labour relationship in this sphere, and foreseeing its eventual dominance in all, grouped the profit on agricultural and commercial capital with that on industrial capital as different species of the same new genus.

III

In our discussion of the factors contributing to the formation of the new social pattern, however, we should not emphasize the part played by the contemporary economy to the exclusion of that played by contemporary economists. By Smith's time, quite a number of economists were coming to realize that the social class whose income took the form of "profit" no longer consisted entirely of merchants. When earlier eco-

---

were carried on entirely by more or less independent "manufacturers". But Smith's frequent omission of "tools" from the "advances" made by the capitalist to the labourer is not evidence that this state of affairs was still general. Smith usually regarded that portion of capital which was fixed in "useful machines and instruments of trade" as affording its owner a profit by "remaining with him", while that portion which consisted of raw materials and wages afforded a profit to him by being "advanced" or "circulated". The capitalist's "advances" to his labourers, therefore, consisted only of materials and wages for the simple reason that these were the only items which he could properly be said to have "advanced" to them. As I have already suggested, it is the inclusion of raw materials in the "advances", rather than the omission of tools and machines, which is significant.

37 *Wealth of Nations*, Vol. I, p. 85. Smith also mentioned, however, that the reverse might happen in "cheap years".

nomists like North and Locke thought of capital in its active use, they almost invariably thought in terms of commercial capital. But some of Smith's contemporaries, when they used words like "trader", "dealer" or "broker", probably meant to include in these categories not only merchants properly so-called but also those whose roots were in industry and agriculture rather than in commerce. For example, in a pamphlet by William Temple, a clothier of Trowbridge, dated 1758, we find the following interesting anticipation of Smith's "natural price" doctrine: "I can most clearly perceive that the value of all commodities, or the price, is a compound of the value of the land necessary to raise them, the value of the labour exerted in producing and manufacturing them, and of the value of the brokerage which provides and circulates them."[38] By "brokerage", as the ensuing passage shows, Temple clearly meant something very like "profits" in Smith's sense of the word. "If the broker's gains do not please him," Temple proceeded, "he will withhold his sales. The farmer will not sow, the manufacturers will leave off their trades, if their employments and occupations produce a loss instead of a profit." As another example, we may take the following extract from a letter written by David Hume to Turgot in September 1766:

I beg you also to consider, that, besides the Proprietors of Land and the labouring Poor, there is in every civilized Community a very large and a very opulent Body who employ their Stocks in Commerce and who enjoy a great Revenue from their giving Labour to the poorer sort. I am perswaded that in France and England the Revenue of this kind is much greater than that which arises from Land: For besides Merchants, properly speaking, I comprehend in this Class all Shop-Keepers and Master-Tradesmen of every Species. Now it is very just, that these should pay for the Support of the Community, which can only be where Taxes are lay'd on Consumptions. There seems to me no Pretence for saying that this order of Men are necessitated to throw their Taxes on the Proprietors of Land, since their Profits and Income can surely bear Retrenchment.[39]

[38] *A Vindication of Commerce and the Arts* (1758), reprinted in *A Select Collection of Scarce and Valuable Tracts on Commerce* (1859). The quotation, which appears on p. 522 of the *Select Collection*, is referred to by Patten in *The Development of English Thought* (New York, 1910), pp. 237–8. See also the appendix to Temple's pamphlet (not reprinted in the *Select Collection*), in which "brokerage" appears as an important constituent of the "national income". Temple's pamphlet, which was dedicated to Charles Townshend's father, was brought to the notice of Lord Kames by Josiah Tucker, who, in a letter of 6th July 1758, described Temple as one "who has immense erudition in his way, – understands the principles of commerce extremely well, but pushes some of them too far" (Lord Woodhouselee's *Memoirs of the Hon. H. Home of Kames* (2nd edn., Edinburgh, 1814), Vol. III, p. 161.)

[39] *The Letters of David Hume* (ed. J. Y. T. Greig, Oxford, 1932), Vol. II, p. 94. I am indebted to Professor A. L. Macfie for drawing my attention to this interesting passage. Cf. also the remarkable soliloquy of Mr Jonathan Wild the Great in Chapter XIV, Book I, of Henry Fielding's *Life* of that gentleman (1743).

Nor should we neglect the important part played by that brilliant circle of thinkers, headed by Lord Kames, with whom Smith was so closely associated. Indeed, it seems possible that Smith's attention may have been specifically drawn to this new way of looking at the economic organization of society by his friend James Oswald. Dugald Stewart, discussing in his lectures Smith's analysis of the component parts of the price of commodities into rent, wages and profit, mentioned that "it appears from a manuscript of Mr Smith's, now in my possession, that the foregoing analysis or division was suggested to him by Mr Oswald of Dunnikier".[40] This statement may well be essentially true. Oswald, as appears from the letters which survive of his correspondence with David Hume, could argue very intelligently on matters of political economy – and was also, incidentally, fully seized of the importance of accumulation.[41]

The discovery of the so-called "early draft of the *Wealth of Nations*" has led to speculations concerning the approximate date at which Oswald's views on this subject were communicated to Smith. Professor Scott, the discover of the "early draft", tentatively placing its date at 1763, claimed that it contained much more on distribution than was to be found in the *Lectures*, and, indeed, that the distributive division of rent, wages and profit was quite explicit in it. From this (*inter alia*) he concluded that Oswald's views were probably communicated to Smith and used by him prior to his departure for France early in 1764.[42] It is true that the manuscript contains one passage dealing with distributive questions – but as far as I can see only one – of which there can perhaps be said to be no really definite trace in the student's notes of the *Lectures*, and that in this passage a division of the produce between the "profit" of the master and the wages of the artisans whom he employs is fairly clearly envisaged.[43] But however this may be, it is surely obvious from the manuscript as a whole that Smith, at the time of its compilation, was not yet thinking in terms of the basic pattern of the *Wealth of Nations*. This is made clear from Smith's sketch of the section dealing with the circumstances which regulate the prices of commodities, which follows more or less exactly the scheme of the *Lectures*. The natural price

---

[40] Stewart, *Collected Works*, Vol. IX (1856), p. 6. Cf. Vol. X (1858), p. 81.

[41] *Memorials of James Oswald* (1825), pp. 65–71. See particularly pp. 67–8, and cf. pp. 122–3.

[42] *Adam Smith as Student and Professor*, pp. 117–18 and 319–20.

[43] The passage appears on p. 331 of Professor Scott's book. Even here, it might very well be argued that the last four lines on p. 164 of the *Lectures* were intended by the student as a summary of the passage which appears in the first thirteen lines on p. 331 of Professor Scott's book, and that the student simply omitted the arithmetical illustration, as students often do.

reappears as "that price which is sufficient to encourage the labourer",[44] and there is no trace of any suggestion that profit at the average rate should be regarded as one of the constituents of the natural price. If Oswald's views were in fact communicated to Smith prior to the composition of the "early draft", and if they were really as important as Stewart's note would seem to indicate, then it seems fairly clear that Smith did not immediately realize their implications. Making the best guess which seems to be possible under the circumstances, I would suggest *either* that Oswald's communication did not reach Smith until after his return from France, *or* that if it reached him before he left for France he did not come to appreciate its real significance until during or after his conversations with the French Physiocrats.

This does not mean that we must revert entirely to the old beliefs about the degree of Smith's dependence on the Physiocrats. On many matters he did not require any instruction from them – for example, his own basic ideas on the virtues of *laissez-faire* and free trade had apparently been formed at least as early as 1749[45] – and if he learned a certain amount from Mercier de la Rivière and Nicolas Baudeau, either as a result of personal discussion during his stay in Paris or through the books which they subsequently published, it is quite likely that they learned just as much from him. From Turgot, however, whose *Reflections* were probably being composed about the time of Smith's stay in Paris, he may have learned rather more. The central theme of the second half of Turgot's *Reflections* is the idea that "the cultivation of the land, manufactures of all kinds, and all branches of commerce depend upon a mass of capitals, or of moveable accumulated riches, which having been at first advanced by the Undertakers in each of these different classes of labours, must return to them every year with a steady profit".[46] Smith, as we have seen, had already been impressed by the importance of the "accumulation of stock" before he went to France, but he had probably not yet fully appreciated the extent to which the attainment of what he had called in the *Lectures* the "natural balance of industry"[47] was dependent upon the action of capitalists who, desiring to maximize their rate of accumulation, constantly directed their capitals into those avenues where it was expected that they would yield the highest rate of

---

[44] Scott, *op. cit.*, p. 346.

[45] Scott, *op. cit.*, pp. 53–4.

[46] Turgot, *Reflections on the Formation and the Distribution of Riches* (ed. Ashley, New York, 1898), pp. 62–3. Turgot proceeds to emphasize that "it is this advance and this continual return of capitals which constitute . . . that useful and fruitful circulation which gives life to all the labours of the society, which maintains movement and life in the body politic".

[47] *Lectures*, p. 180.

profit. His discussions with Turgot in Paris in 1766 may have assisted him to develop his own views on this point.[48] But he must have been struck at least as much by the limitations of Physiocratic thought as by its positive features. Was it in fact true, as most of the Physiocrats were then maintaining, that there was no "disposable" element in the rewards normally received by the master manufacturer, the capitalist farmer and the merchant? Certainly, in Britain at any rate, a substantial portion of these rewards did appear to be "disposable" in the Physiocratic sense. This seemed evident from the fact that the classes mentioned appeared to be already accumulating capital at a far greater rate than would be possible according to the Physiocratic "privations" theory. The Physiocrats' attitude on this point, which must have seemed to Smith quite arbitrary and dogmatic, may well have assisted substantially in persuading him of the importance of the phenomenon they sought to deny, and may possibly have led him further along the path towards the classification of the rewards of the manufacturer, the farmer and the merchant as different species of the same genus.

IV

The danger of any enquiry such as the present is that so many factors will be found to have influenced the formation of the new doctrine which is being examined that no room seems to be left for genius. Research of this character is sometimes apt to leave the investigator somewhat disenchanted: he begins to marvel, not at the genius of the first begetter of the doctrine, but at the stupidity of all the other thinkers of the time who failed to beget it.

But the important point is surely that whereas to discern what is actually typical may require only acuteness of observation, to discern what is *becoming* typical often requires the addition of genius. Smith was no doubt greatly influenced by what was happening in Glasgow during his residence there, but the basic social pattern which he finally adopted was rather more than a simple generalization of these phenomena. What he saw, with remarkable clarity, was that the further extension of those capitalist methods of production which had produced such spectacular results in and around Glasgow could transform and was in fact transforming the whole of Western society. What he saw, too, was that this rise of the capitalist form of organization to the status of a norm

---

[48] It seems also quite probable that Smith had actually read Turgot's *Reflections* before writing the *Wealth of Nations*. On this contentious point, see the excellent survey of the evidence in Viner's *Guide to John Rae's "Life of Adam Smith"* (New York, 1965), pp. 128 ff.

could produce and was in fact producing such a bountiful crop of new economic regularities that it had become possible for the first time to work out a *science* of political economy, analogous to the physical sciences. Smith's thought, as J. M. Clark has pointed out, was "progressive" in the sense that it emphasized "those forces which are now in existence but to which prevailing institutions give inadequate outlet and recognition in proportion to their present importance and force". Such a theory "must emphasize the things the age does not yet see, not those on which its institutions are consciously founded".[49] The basic social pattern which Smith put forward in the *Wealth of Nations* was of this type, and we need have no fears that a thinker who could so accurately summarize "the manifest destiny of the time", at a period when it was by no means immediately manifest, will suffer a loss in stature merely through an analysis of the contemporary phenomena upon which his genius fed.

[49] J. M. Clark, "Adam Smith and the Currents of History", in *Adam Smith, 1776–1926* (Chicago, 1928), pp. 55 and 57.

THE SCOTTISH CONTRIBUTION
TO MARXIST SOCIOLOGY[1]

The first necessity in any theory of history, wrote Marx and Engels in *The German Ideology*, is to accord its due importance to a certain fundamental fact – the fact that "men must be in a position to live in order to be able to 'make history' ". The production of the means to satisfy the needs of life is "a fundamental condition of all history". The French and the English, said Marx and Engels,

even if they have conceived the relation of this fact with so-called history only in an extremely one-sided fashion, particularly as long as they remained in the toils of political ideology, have nevertheless made the first attempts to give the writing of history a materialistic basis by being the first to write histories of civil society, of commerce and industry.[2]

The present essay sets out to commen: upon certain "attempts to give the writing of history a materialistic basis" which were made by a group of eighteenth-century Scottish writers – the so-called "Scottish Historical School" – of whom Professor Pascal reminded us in an important article in *The Modern Quarterly* in 1938.[3] My contention is, broadly, that the sociological work of these writers has been seriously underestimated. When it is valued at its proper worth, the British contribution (taken as a whole) to the making of Marxist sociology begins to appear greater in degree, and to some extent different in kind, from what has commonly been imagined.

The British contribution to Marxist thought is often virtually identified with what has come to be called Classical political economy. Adam Smith and David Ricardo, it is sometimes said, laid the foundations of the labour theory of value and the theory of distribution which was associated with it, and Marx continued and completed their work. This is true enough so far as it goes, but it does not go nearly far enough. For Classical political economy grew up in close association with a more

[1] This essay is an amended version of an article published in *Democracy and the Labour Movement* (ed. Saville, London, 1954).

[2] *The German Ideology* (ed. Pascal, London, 1938), p. 16.

[3] Roy Pascal, "Property and Society: The Scottish Historical School of the Eighteenth Century", *The Modern Quarterly*, March 1938. My own considerable debt to this article will be apparent from what follows.

general system of ideas about the structure and development of society which we can perhaps call Classical sociology. And it is the contention of this article that in the latter half of the eighteenth century the Scottish Historical School developed this Classical sociology to a stage where it was becoming remarkably similar, at least in its broad outlines, to Marxist sociology.

The main members of the Scottish Historical School were four university professors. First, there was Professor Adam Smith, of Glasgow. It is now more than two centuries since Adam Smith was appointed to the Chair of Moral Philosophy at Glasgow University, and during that time the sociologist in Smith has tended to become somewhat obscured. The more narrowly economic views of the *Wealth of Nations* have usually been emphasized at the expense of the general sociological system of which they were essentially a part. The elements of that sociological system can, indeed, be easily enough detected in the *Wealth of Nations* – just as the elements of Marx's sociological system can be easily enough detected in *Capital* – but for a more complete outline of it we have to go back to Smith's *Glasgow Lectures* and to his *Theory of Moral Sentiments*. In other words, we have to try and reconstruct the elements of that great sociological treatise on the development of law and government which Smith always intended to write but never managed to finish.[4] Second, there was Professor Adam Ferguson, of Edinburgh, whose remarkable *Essay on the History of Civil Society*, his chief claim to fame, first appeared in 1767.[5] Ferguson's views do not have to be reconstructed: they are quite clearly expressed in this book, and, in a rather watered-down version, in two later works.[6] Third, there was Professor William Robertson, the Principal of Edinburgh University, and one of the foremost historians of the day. Robertson's general approach is discernible in all his historical studies, but particularly in his history of Scotland[7] and in

[4] At the end of his *Theory of Moral Sentiments* (1759), Smith said: "I shall in another discourse endeavour to give an account of the general principles of law and government, and of the different revolutions they have undergone in the different ages and periods of society, not only in what concerns justice, but in what concerns police, revenue, and arms, and whatever else is the object of law" (*Works* (ed. Dugald Stewart, London, 1812), Vol. I, pp. 610–11). And in a letter of 1785, published in *The Athenaeum*, 28th December 1895, Smith said: "I have likewise two other great works upon the anvil; the one is a sort of Philosophical History of all the different branches of Literature, of Philosophy, Poetry and Eloquence; the other is a sort of theory and History of Law and Government. The materials of both are in a great measure collected, and some Part of both is put into tollerable good order. But the indolence of old age, tho' I struggle violently against it, I feel coming fast upon me, and whether I shall ever be able to finish either is extremely uncertain."

[5] The references below are to the 6th edn. of 1793.

[6] *Institutes of Moral Philosophy* (1769), and *Principles of Moral and Political Science* (1792).

[7] *The History of Scotland, etc.* (1759).

the introductory volumes of his histories of America[8] and the reign of
Charles V.[9] Fourth, there was Professor John Millar, who occupied the
Chair of Law at Glasgow University from 1761 until his death forty
years later. It is the comparative neglect of Millar's remarkable contribution which more than anything else has hindered general recognition
of the true significance of the work of the School as a whole. Professor
Pascal in this country, and Professor Lehmann[10] in the United States,
seem to have been – at any rate up to a few years ago[11] – the only
modern investigators to have taken a really serious interest in Millar
and his work. Finally, mention should be made of a number of other
authors who, if they cannot properly be said to have been actual
members of the School, at least worked on its fringes. These included
Lord Kames and Gilbert Stuart (both comparative lawyers), Lord
Monboddo, Hugh Blair and James Dunbar. The work of all these men,
taken together, forms what is perhaps the most striking manifestation of
that great cultural renaissance in eighteenth-century Scotland whose
extent and significance are only now coming to be properly appreciated.

The Scottish Historical School, like all other such schools, had of
course its predecessors. Among these the greatest common influence
was probably that of Montesquieu, with his insistence on the importance of the fact that "man is born in society, and there he remains",[12]
and his central interest in the evolving relationships between law and
environment.[13] All the members of the School regarded Montesquieu
with the greatest admiration. For example, Smith's *Glasgow Lectures* on
jurisprudence, as Millar noted, "followed the plan that seems to be

---

[8] *The History of America* (1777), Vol. I.

[9] *The History of the Reign of the Emperor Charles V* (1769), Vol. I.

[10] W. C. Lehmann, *Adam Ferguson and the Beginnings of Modern Sociology* (New York,
1930); "John Millar, Historical Sociologist", in *The British Journal of Sociology*, March
1952; and *John Millar of Glasgow* (Cambridge, 1960).

[11] Since the appearance of the article on which the present essay is based, and an
article by Duncan Forbes which appeared at about the same time ("Scientific Whig-
gism: Adam Smith and John Millar," *Cambridge Journal*, August 1954), there has been
something of a resurgence of interest in John Millar and the Scottish Enlightenment.
The major event has been the publication of Lehmann's *John Millar of Glasgow* (see
previous footnote), which has helped to stimulate interest in the subject among a
number of other writers. Among the various articles which have recently been published, two in particular deserve special mention: A. L. Macfie's "John Millar",
Scottish Journal of Political Economy, October 1961, and A. S. Skinner's "Economics and
History – The Scottish Enlightenment", *Scottish Journal of Political Economy*, February
1965. Mr Skinner's current work on Sir James Steuart, which draws attention to certain interesting parallels between Steuart's ideas and those of the Scottish Historical
School, has already been referred to above (p. 13). See also my *Economics of Physiocracy*
(London, 1962), pp. 38, 65–71, and 376–7, where further parallels are drawn with the
ideas of the Physiocrats.

[12] Ferguson, *Essay*, p. 27.

[13] *De L'Esprit des Lois* (1748).

suggested by Montesquieu";[14] and Robertson spoke of Montesquieu's "usual discernment and accuracy".[15] Hume, with his interest in the origins and foundations of society, his rejection of speculative fictions such as the social contract, and his realistic evolutionism, was another obvious influence, both personally and through his writings. Dugald Stewart, indeed, had no hesitation in linking Hume's name with those of Montesquieu, Smith, Kames and Millar as men with a common interest in a new study – that of the "natural history" of society.[16] Mandeville, to go a little farther back, should also probably be counted among the predecessors, although perhaps not so directly. There were few other men at that time who had so clear a perception as he had of the fact that "the Cement of civil Society" is simply that "every Body is obliged to eat and drink".[17] And, at least so far as Millar is concerned, Harrington must also be regarded as a very important predecessor. Harrington was certainly largely responsible for Millar's remarkable "economic" interpretation of the English civil war, and may have been partly responsible for his general sociological position.[18]

The main members of the School had two basic propositions in common, both derived from empirical observation of the course of social development in different countries and different ages. Robertson's statement of them, though not quite the clearest, is perhaps the most convenient. First, "in every inquiry concerning the operations of men when united together in society, the first object of attention should be their mode of subsistence. Accordingly as that varies, their laws and policy must be different."[19] (Compare this with the early statement by Marx and Engels in *The German Ideology*: "The 'history of humanity' must always be studied and treated in relation to the history of industry and exchange," since "the multitude of productive forces accessible to men determines the nature of society.")[20] The second proposition is implied in the following statement, which is to be found in Robertson's survey of the history of feudalism: "Upon discovering in what state property was at any particular period, we may determine with precision what was the degree of power possessed by the King or by the nobility at

[14] See Dugald Stewart's *Account of the Life and Writings of Adam Smith* in his edn. of Smith's *Works*, Vol. V, p. 414.
[15] *Charles V*, Vol. I, p. 223.
[16] Stewart, *op. cit.*, pp. 447–55.
[17] *The Fable of the Bees* (ed. Kaye, Oxford, 1924), Vol. II, p. 350.
[18] See, e.g., Millar's *An Historical View of the English Government* (posthumous edn. of 1803), Vol. III, pp. 284–8. For details of the contents of this edn., see Lehmann, *John Millar of Glasgow*, pp. 55–6.
[19] Robertson, *History of America*, Vol. I, p. 324.
[20] *The German Ideology*, p. 18. In this particular context, what Marx and Engels here call the "mode of co-operation" is specifically included in the category "productive forces".

that juncture."[21] The causal connection between property relationships and the form of government which is implied in this statement is constantly emphasized by all the members of the School. As Ferguson puts it in one place, in a slightly different way, "forms of government take their rise, chiefly from the manner in which the members of a state have been originally classed."[22] These, then, were the two basic propositions which the members of the School tried, with a greater or lesser degree of consistency, to apply to the study of man in society.

The two basic principles were applied within a common framework of general attitudes about which something should now be said. In the first place, their approach (at least in intention) was "scientific" in the best sense of the word – as was implied in the description of their subject as the "natural history" of law, government, etc. They tried, with some success, to bring to the study of men's relations to one another in society the same scientific attitude which had recently been so brilliantly brought to the study of men's relations to nature. To call their work "*Theoretical* or *Conjectural History*", as Dugald Stewart did,[23] is really to miss one of the main points about it – that it tried consciously to base itself on the study of concrete historical facts, in opposition to the abstract speculation and conjecture (particularly with regard to the so-called "state of nature") which had so often been employed in the past. Second, they had in common a particular view of the *manner* of social development which to a large extent determined their method of attack. Society, they argued, developed blindly. The School consistently rejected any facile explanations of social development in terms of the activities of "great men". "Every step and every movement of the multitude," said Ferguson, "even in what are termed enlightened ages, are made with equal blindness to the future; and nations stumble upon establishments, which are indeed the result of human action, but not the execution of any human design."[24] It was Millar's leading principle, said Jeffrey in an article in the *Edinburgh Review*, "that there was nothing produced by arbitrary or accidental causes; that no great change, institution, custom, or occurrence, could be ascribed to the character or exertions of an individual, to the temperament or disposition of a nation, to occasional policy, or peculiar wisdom or folly."[25] Some of the

[21] *Charles V*, Vol. I, p. 222.
[22] Ferguson, *Essay*, p. 226. Cf. Smith, *Lectures*, p. 8: "Property and civil government very much depend on one another."
[23] Stewart, *op. cit.*, Vol. V, p. 450.
[24] *Essay*, p. 205. Cf. *ibid.*, p. 304.
[25] *Edinburgh Review*, October 1803, p. 157. Jeffrey was undoubtedly exaggerating here: Millar's basic approach, as we shall see later, was by no means as crudely mechanistic as this statement would seem to imply. But Jeffrey does at least give a fair idea of the types of approach to history which the School was mainly concerned to oppose.

members of the School, Smith for example, tended to emphasize the gradual and continuous character of social development;[26] others, such as Ferguson, stressed the importance of social conflict and drew particular attention to revolutionary changes.[27] But to all of them development was essentially blind: as Engels was later to put it, "the conflict of innumerable individual wills and individual actions in the domain of history produces a state of affairs entirely analogous to that in the realm of unconscious nature".[28] Nevertheless, great social changes did occur, and uniformities and regularities were clearly observable in the development of different societies. How were these to be explained? What laws lay behind the development of society? This was the great problem to which the Scottish Historical School brought to bear the two basic materialist principles which I have just described. They did not, of course, pose the problem in precisely these terms: they could hardly have been expected, in the conditions of their time, to anticipate Engels to that extent – although Ferguson sometimes came very near to doing so. But there is little doubt that this kind of problem was always at the back of their minds.

To illustrate their method of approach to the problem, we may outline very briefly Adam Smith's views on the development of law and government as he presented them in the *Glasgow Lectures*. Smith's views on this subject can be taken as a fair sample of those of the School as a whole, although some members of it, notably Millar, went into much more detail. There were four main stages in social development, Smith argued – hunting, pasturage, agriculture and commerce,[29] which generally followed one another in that order.[30] Each of these stages, as will be seen, is in effect defined in terms of what Robertson called the "mode of subsistence". In the first stage, hunting, there is properly speaking no government at all, because there is virtually no private property. "Till there be property", said Smith, "there can be no government, the very end of which is to secure wealth, and to defend the rich from the poor."[31] It was in the second stage of development, pasturage, that what Smith calls an "inequality of fortune" was first introduced, owing to the institution of private property in flocks and herds. It was only then that "regular government" came into being. But "property receives its greatest extension," says Smith, in the next stage – agriculture, since the land itself, which until then has been held more or less in common, now comes to be divided up among private individuals.[32]

[26] See, e.g., *Wealth of Nations*, Vol. I, pp. 389–90.
[27] For a summary of Ferguson's views on the role of conflict in society, see Lehmann, *Adam Ferguson and the Beginnings of Modern Sociology*, pp. 98–106.
[28] Engels, *Ludwig Feuerbach* (London, n.d.), p. 58.
[29] *Lectures*, p. 107.   [30] *Ibid.*, p. 108.   [31] *Ibid.*, p. 15.   [32] *Ibid.*, p. 109.

Thus, in the agricultural stage, government is further extended in scope, and altered in form. Then eventually, as Smith puts it, "the age of commerce naturally succeeds that of agriculture. As men could now confine themselves to one species of labour, they would naturally exchange the surplus of their commodity for that of another of which they stood in need."[33] And once again law and government undergo corresponding changes. Throughout all these successive stages, broadly speaking, the way in which people get their living is conceived to determine the main lines along which they think and behave;[34] and superior wealth more than any other quality "contributes to confer authority".[35] Smith was by no means consistent in his adoption of this kind of approach, of course; few pioneers can afford the luxury of consistency. But even if we cannot properly ascribe *the* materialist conception of history to Smith, we may certainly ascribe to him *a* materialist conception of history which was not without considerable influence on later writers.

But it is in the work of John Millar, more than in that of any other member of the School, that we find this new way of looking at society most explicitly formulated and most expertly applied. There is all the difference in the world between using a philosophy of history unconsciously and using it consciously, and Millar was always perfectly well aware of what he was doing. Consider the following remarkable passage, which occurs in the introduction to his book on the *Origin of the Distinction of Ranks*. How does it come about, he asks, that there is such an "amazing diversity to be found in the laws of different countries, and even of the same country at different periods"? How have mankind "been led to embrace such different rules of conduct"? "In searching for the causes of those peculiar systems of law and government which have appeared in the world," he answers,

we must undoubtedly resort, first of all, to the differences of situation, which have suggested different views and motives of action to the inhabitants of particular countries. Of this kind, are the fertility or barrenness of the soil, the nature of its productions, the species of labour requisite for procuring subsistence, the number of individuals collected together in one community, their proficiency in arts, the advantages which they enjoy for entering into mutual transactions, and for maintaining an intimate correspondence. The variety that frequently occurs in these, and such other particulars, must have a prodigious influence upon the great body of a people; as, by giving a peculiar direction to their inclinations and pursuits, it must be productive of correspondent habits, dispositions, and ways of thinking.

. . . There is . . . in man a disposition and capacity for improving his conditions, by the exertion of which, he is carried on from one degree of advancement to another; and the similarity of his wants, as well as of the faculties by which

[33] *Ibid.*, p. 108.   [34] *Ibid.*, pp. 159–61.   [35] *Ibid.*, p. 9.

those wants are supplied, has every where produced a remarkable uniformity in the several steps of his progression . . . By such gradual advances in rendering their situation more comfortable, the most important alterations are produced in the state and condition of a people: their numbers are increased; the connections of society are extended; and men, being less oppressed with their own wants, are more at liberty to cultivate the feelings of humanity: property, the great source of distinction among individuals, is established; and the various rights of mankind, arising from their multiplied connections, are recognized and protected: the laws of a country are thereby rendered numerous; and a more complex form of government becomes necessary, for distributing justice, and for preventing the disorders which proceed from the jarring interests and passions of a large and opulent community. It is evident, at the same time, that these, and such other effects of improvement, which have so great a tendency to vary the state of mankind, and their manner of life, will be productive of suitable variations in their taste and sentiments, and in their general system of behaviour.

There is thus, in human society, a natural progress from ignorance to knowledge, and from rude to civilized manners, the several stages of which are usually accompanied with peculiar laws and customs.[36]

This, then, was the master-principle which Millar believed would enable him to penetrate, as he himself put it (much in the manner of Marx), "beneath that common surface of events which occupies the details of the vulgar historian".[37] But the principle must not be interpreted mechanistically. As Millar went on to make clear, immediately following the last statement quoted above,

Various accidental causes, indeed, have contributed to accelerate, or to retard this advancement in different countries. It has even happened that nations, being placed in such unfavourable circumstances as to render them long stationary at a particular period, have been so habituated to the peculiar manners of that age, as to retain a strong tincture of those peculiarities, through every subsequent revolution. This appears to have occasioned some of the chief varieties which take place in the maxims and customs of nations equally civilized.[38]

And although Millar strongly attacked the "great man" approach to history, insisting that the "greater part of the political system of any country [is] derived from the combined influence of the whole people", he was quite prepared to admit that "a variety of peculiar institutions will sometimes take their origin from the casual interposition of particular persons, who happen to be placed at the head of a community, and to be possessed of singular abilities, and views of policy".[39]

[36] *Origin of the Distinction of Ranks* (4th edn., Edinburgh, 1806), pp. 1–4.
[37] *An Historical View of the English Government*, Vol. IV, p. 101.
[38] *Origin of Ranks*, pp. 4–5.
[39] *Ibid.*, p. 5.

In his book on the *Origin of Ranks*, Millar uses this principle to explain the changes which occur in certain important types of power-relation as society develops. He is here concerned in particular with the relations between husband and wife, father and child, sovereign and subject, and master and servant. In general he assumes throughout that the most important way in which the basic economic factors influence these power-relations is through induced changes in property relations. In his later book, *An Historical View of the English Government*, he uses the principle to explain the evolution of the English constitution; and in a posthumous volume of the same work he uses it to explain the changes which occur in manners, morals, literature, art and science as society develops. No one before Millar had ever used a materialist conception of history so consistently to illuminate the development of such a wide range of social phenomena.

Many of Millar's individual themes deserve elaboration in some detail, but a brief summary of a few of them will have to suffice here. For example, there are his attempts to delineate what might be called the "techno-economic bases" for certain great social changes which he analyses, such as the institution of private property,[40] the rise of commodity production and trade,[41] and the institution[42] and abolition of slavery. On the abolition of slavery he has this to say:

> A slave, who receives no wages in return for his labour, can never be supposed to exert much vigour or activity in the exercise of any employment. He obtains a livelihood at any rate; and by his utmost assiduity he is able to procure no more. As he works merely in consequence of the terror in which he is held, it may be imagined that he will be idle as often as he can with impunity. This circumstance may easily be overlooked in a country where the inhabitants are strangers to improvement. But when the arts begin to flourish, when the wonderful effects of industry and skill in cheapening commodities, and in bringing them to perfection, become more and more conspicuous, it must be evident that little profit can be drawn from the labour of a slave, who has neither been encouraged to acquire that dexterity, nor those habits of application, which are essentially requisite in the finer and more difficult branches of manufacture.[43]

Then again, there is that fascinating section in the *Origin of Ranks* dealing with group marriage and matriarchy in primitive society,[44] which J. F. MacLennan said almost anticipated Bachofen,[45] and which Sombart rather less cautiously said *did* anticipate Engels.[46] Then there are the interesting passages in which Millar discusses the differences in

[40] *Ibid.*, pp. 157 ff.   [41] *Ibid.*, pp. 87–8.   [42] *Ibid.*, pp. 247–8.   [43] *Ibid.*, pp. 250–51.
[44] Chapter I, section 2.
[45] J. F. MacLennan, *Studies in Ancient History* (1876), p. 420, footnote.
[46] Cf. Lehmann, *John Millar of Glasgow*, pp. 132–3.

the national characteristics of the English and the Scots, tracing them in large part to differences in the degree of development of the division of labour in these countries.[47] Then again, historians of economic thought may be interested to note the passages in which Millar quite clearly and unambiguously anticipates the "productivity" theory of profit which is nowadays usually associated with the name of Lord Lauderdale.[48] Millar was in fact a close friend of Lauderdale's, and it seems likely that they worked the theory out jointly.[49] And finally, in the field of historiography, a rather impressive paragraph may be quoted showing Millar's keen perception of the economic forces underlying the English civil war of 1640:

> The adherents of the king were chiefly composed of the nobility and higher gentry, men who, by their wealth and station, had much to lose; and who, in the annihilation of monarchy, and in the anarchy that was likely to follow, foresaw the ruin of their fortunes, and the extinction of their consideration and influence. The middling and inferior gentry, together with the inhabitants of towns; those who entertained a jealousy of the nobles, and of the king, or who, by the changes in the state of society, had lately been raised to independence, became, on the other hand, the great supporters of parliament.[50]

Those who had "lately been raised to independence" by "the changes in the state of society", as Millar's earlier analysis makes clear, were the "tradesmen, manufacturers, and merchants".[51] It is certainly true that Millar, in common with most of his contemporaries, usually tended to exaggerate the importance of 1688 at the expense of that of 1640. Nevertheless, he did see the civil war quite clearly as a class war, and as marking an important stage in a great historical process in which "the progress of commerce and manufactures" was gradually transforming what he called "the manners and political state of the inhabitants".[52]

Of course, there is still a very deep gulf between Millar, even at his best, and Marx. To appreciate this, we have only to compare Millar's statement of his master-principle in the introduction to the *Origin of Ranks* with Marx's famous summary of his in the preface to the *Critique of Political Economy*. In Marx's conception of history, there is a feeling for the dialectic of social change which was conspicuously lacking in Millar's. And, most important of all, there was no trace in Millar's work of that essentially new line of thought which Marx himself regarded as

---

[47] *Historical View*, Vol. III, pp. 89–96.

[48] Cf. Millar, *Historical View*, Vol. IV, pp. 118–22, with Lauderdale, *An Inquiry into the Nature and Origin of Public Wealth* (1804), pp. 158 ff.

[49] See the remarks by John Craig, Millar's first biographer, on p. xc of the 1806 edn. of the *Origin of Ranks*.

[50] *Historical View*, Vol. III, p. 295.

[51] *Ibid.*, Vol. III, p. 103.   [52] *Ibid.*, Vol. III, p. 1.

his own most distinctive contribution. "No credit is due to me," said Marx in his well-known letter of March 1852 to Weydemeyer,

for discovering the existence of classes in modern society nor yet the struggle between them. Long before me bourgeois historians had described the historical development of this class struggle and bourgeois economists the economic anatomy of the classes. What I did that was new was to prove: (i) that the *existence of classes* is only bound up with *particular, historic phases in the development of production*; (ii) that the class struggle necessarily leads to the *dictatorship of the proletariat*; (iii) that this dictatorship itself only constitutes the transition to the *abolition of all classes* and to a *classless* society.[53]

Millar was certainly well aware of "the existence of classes in modern society", and his work in describing the historical development of the struggle between them in terms of their "economic anatomy" was in advance of that of most of his contemporaries. He was often perceptive, too, in his treatment of "the discrepancies that frequently occur between rank-position and individual merit",[54] and in his attacks on the abuses of class power. But there is no suggestion that he ever regarded the existence of "ranks" *as such* as anything other than a natural and inescapable feature of all modern societies. Indeed, as his first biographer correctly emphasizes, his proposals for reform were always made within the framework of "those established distinctions of Rank which it is often unjust, and always hazardous, to abolish".[55] For example, even though he was a strong supporter of the French Revolution he could not be brought "to excuse the Asssembly for rashly and presumptuously abolishing all those distinctions of ranks to which the people had been habituated, and by the influence of which they might have been restrained from many excesses".[56]

The difference between Marx and Millar is particularly apparent in the latter's analysis of the economic relationship between the labourer and the capitalist. Following Smith, Millar recognized that "the whole property of a [commercial] country, and the subsistence of all the inhabitants, may . . . be derived from three different sources; from the rent of land or water; from the profits of stock or capital; and from the wages of labour: and, in conformity to this arrangement, the inhabitants may be divided into landlords, capitalists, and labourers". He recognized, too, that the labourers, "having little or no property, and earning a bare subsistence by their daily labour . . . are placed in a state of inferiority", and that the advance of trade and manufactures,

[53] Marx and Engels, *Selected Correspondence, 1846–95* (London, 1936), p. 57.
[54] Lehmann, "John Millar, Historical Sociologist", p. 41.
[55] *Origin of Ranks*, pp. lv–vi.
[56] *Ibid.*, p. cxiii.

by bringing together "large bands of labourers or artificers" into the towns and cities, had greatly increased both their opportunity and their desire to combine in their own interests.[57] But by adopting the "productivity" theory of profit mentioned above, Millar implicitly denied that the labour-capital relationship was based upon exploitation. "The profit arising from every branch of mercantile stock," he wrote, "whether permanent or circulating, is derived from its enabling the merchant, or manufacturer, to produce the same effect with less labour, and consequently with less expence than would otherwise have been required."[58] And feeling himself obliged, apparently, to comment upon the traditional view of profit as a surplus produced by the labourer and appropriated by the capitalist, he added the following revealing footnote:

Perhaps part of the profit of a manufacturer may also be drawn from the workman, who, however, will have a full equivalent for what he thus resigns. By working to a master he is sure of constant employment, is saved the trouble of seeking out those who may have occasion for his labour, and avoids the anxiety arising from the danger of being thrown occasionally idle. In return for these advantages, he willingly relinquishes to his master some part of what he can earn while employed.[59]

It has to be remembered, of course, that Millar lived at a time when, as he put it himself, "every man who is industrious may entertain the hope of gaining a fortune", and when it appeared to many that wealth, and therefore political power, would probably soon be "in some measure diffused over all the members of the community".[60] The change from feudalism to capitalism did not appear to Millar, as it was later to appear to Marx, as being essentially the substitution of a new ruling class, with a new method of exploitation, for an old one, but rather as the emergence of a state of economic and political *independence*. What impressed Millar was not so much the subordination of the labourer to the capitalist, as the capacity of the labourer to become a little capitalist himself. Nevertheless, Millar was by no means happy about the economic and political conditions of his time – a fact which revealed itself both in his writings and in his political activities. In his writings, for example, he constantly emphasized the dangers of the rapidly increasing influence which the Crown had exercised since 1688, and gave a very interesting account of the economic and social basis of this influence.[61] He warned, too, that the extension of the division of labour,

[57] *Historical View*, Vol. IV, pp. 115 and 134–5.
[58] *Ibid.*, Vol. IV, p. 122.
[59] *Ibid.*, Vol. IV, p. 120. Cf. Steuart, *Principles of Political Oeconomy*, Vol. I, p. 318.
[60] *Origin of Ranks*, p. 235.
[61] *Historical View*, Vol. IV, chapter 2, and *passim*.

by stripping the worker of his mental powers and converting him into "the mere instrument of labour",[62] was making it possible for the common people to become "the dupes of their superiors".[63] And he emphasized even more strongly than Ferguson that in modern society "the pursuit of riches becomes a scramble, in which the hand of every man is against every other".[64] And in his political life his immense concern with the problem of liberty revealed itself just as forcefully. He was a rather unorthodox left-wing Whig with republican sympathies, who in every political crisis ranged himself on the side of the angels of history. He supported the Americans in their war of independence – a highly unpopular attitude in Glasgow at that time; he took an active part in the struggle to abolish slavery; he defended the French Revolution, even in its later stages; he became a zealous member of the Society of Friends of the People when it was formed in the early 1790's; and he campaigned against the French wars with all the means at his disposal.[65] In view of the fierceness of the contemporary witch-hunt, which exiled Millar's eldest son and destroyed Thomas Muir, one of Millar's greatest pupils, these were by no means easy attitudes for a professor at a university to take up and maintain.

As an example of the sort of thing which people in Millar's position had to put up with at this time, the following extract from an anonymous attack against him which appeared in a Glasgow newspaper in 1793 may perhaps be usefully cited. Millar is not mentioned by name in it, but it is clear from the context that it is he (and possibly one or two of his colleagues at Glasgow University) who is being referred to. The writer is one "Asmodeus", and the attack occurs in the course of a series of letters entitled "Strictures on the Glasgow Democrats". It reflects the authentic – and only too familiar – atmosphere of the witch-hunt:

Every man of common sense must acknowledge the force of early impressions; and in this age of *attempts* at the establishment of detestable, impracticable theories, their baneful effects should be guarded against with the utmost caution. – Beings of my order, Mr Editor, are incapable of procreating flesh and blood; but were I a mortal and a father, I would certainly prefer finishing my son's education at a brothel, to a school where his political principles were likely to be contaminated: In the former, he would only run the risk of his nose – in the latter, of his neck. – These observations proceed from having observed, that, in some instances, the teachers in the public seminaries of this kingdom profess themselves Republicans; though, at the same time, I must admit, that nine times in ten their dislike of Monarchy arises, not from principle, but from interested motives only. Men of that description should either relinquish their

---

[62] *Ibid.*, Vol. IV, p. 152.   [63] *Ibid.*, Vol. IV, p. 156.   [64] *Ibid.*, Vol. IV, p. 249.
[65] See the biography by John Craig referred to above. Special mention should be made of his anonymous *Letters of Crito*, an attack on the French wars.

tenets or their places; for, is there not a gross inconsistency in their eating the King's bread, and at the same time vilifying his Government?

The mildness of the British Constitution is strongly exemplified, in the security in which these pests of society vomit forth their opinions. Were the like freedoms taken with the executive government in their beloved land of *Liberty and Equality*, the lamp-iron or the scaffold would soon terminate their career. But although the British Lion indignantly pisseth upon these snarling curs, is it fitting that they should continue their practices with impunity?[66]

Let me turn now to another important question. What was there about Scotland in the latter half of the eighteenth century which made it capable of producing Millar and the other members of the Historical School? Why was it that such a large proportion of the great sociologists of the time – to say nothing of the great political economists – were Scotsmen? There is no easy answer to this question, of course, and all that can be done here is to suggest what might be *one* fruitful line of enquiry. Social thinking of this type, which lays primary emphasis on the development of economic techniques and economic relationships, is not simply a function of economic advance as such. If it were, England rather than Scotland would surely have been the cradle of sociology and political economy in the eighteenth century. Rather, such thinking seems to be a function, first, of the rapidity of economic advance, and second, of the facility with which a contrast can be observed between areas which are economically advancing and areas which are in different stages of development. In Scottish cities like Glasgow in the 1750's and 60's, owing largely to the progress of the tobacco trade with the American plantations, economic development was extremely rapid. Great changes in economic techniques and basic economic relationships were taking place, and visibly transforming the whole social life of the community.[67] And the new forms of economic organization which were emerging could be fairly easily contrasted with the forms of organization which still existed, say, in the Scottish Highlands, or in feudal France, or among the Indian tribes in North America. Interest in different forms of social organization was bound to be fairly widespread in Scotland at this time, and it was no accident that attempts were made to trace the causal nexus in history to "the mode of subsistence". In the form in which it is stated here this answer to the question is, of course, far too crudely mechanistic, and any serious enquiry would also have to take account of a number of other important factors – for example, the special situation of the Scottish schools and universities at the time. But

[66] This quotation will be found on pp. 2–3 of a pamphlet entitled *Asmodeus: or, Strictures on the Glasgow Democrats* (1793), in which the original letters were collected and reprinted.

[67] Cf. above, pp. 25–8.

I do suggest that the key to the problem may well be found in the place which I have indicated.

Finally, something should be said about the manner in which the ideas of the Scottish Historical School were transmitted to the nineteenth century, and in particular to Marx and Engels. A direct connection existed, of course, in the case of Adam Smith, upon whose work Marx wrote a number of extended commentaries (without, however, having the *Glasgow Lectures* available to him), and also in the case of Ferguson, from whom Marx quotes several times (mainly in connection with the division of labour) in *The Poverty of Philosophy* and *Capital*. But in the case of Millar the connection was much less direct. Marx, it is true, made a *précis* of Millar's *Origin of Ranks*,[68] and at least two of the authors with whom Marx was very well acquainted – Hodgskin and James Mill – quoted liberally from Millar in certain of their writings.[69] I have not, however, been able to find any specific reference to Millar in the work of Marx and Engels: all one finds are acknowledgments in general terms of their indebtedness to the British and French sociologists of the eighteenth century,[70] and to "all the English historians up to 1850".[71] Part of the reason for this – but no doubt only part – may lie in the swift decline in the influence of Millar's work in the years following his death. The French Revolution and the accompanying disturbances at home, the wars against France, and, most important of all, the gradual development of organized struggle between labourers and capitalists, made it very difficult for dangerous thoughts such as Millar's to survive, at least in the middle-class milieu which had originally given birth to them.[72] There is no doubt, however, that Millar's work played an important part in the creation of that climate of opinion in which the work of men like the so-called "Ricardian socialists" and the early Chartists was able to flourish.

[68] See M. Rubel, "Fragments Sociologiques dans les Inédits de Marx", *Cahiers Internationaux de Sociologie*, January–June 1957, p. 132, footnote.

[69] On Hodgskin in this connection, see Lehmann, *John Millar of Glasgow*, p. 158. On James Mill, see the next paragraph of the present essay.

[70] See, e.g., the quotation from the *German Ideology* at the beginning of the present essay.

[71] Marx and Engels, *Selected Correspondence, 1846–95*, p. 518. Cf. *ibid.*, p. 56.

[72] Cf. Lehmann, "John Millar, Historical Sociologist", p. 45: "The tide of the time was running strongly against the acceptance of ideas like Millar's. Not only did the directly political elements in his teaching meet with strong opposition from the more reactionary of his contemporaries; but even more, even the most 'non-political' elements in his work, his historical, analytical, functional approach to the problems of law, government and society, contained a threat to the established order of things that was clearly recognized by men of insight. And those responsible for the education of future leaders did their best to provide them with another diet. . . . Under such conditions writings like Millar's would be read only by courageous men of strong convictions." Cf. *John Millar of Glasgow*, p. 148.

If Millar's ideas did continue for a while to exercise a limited amount of direct influence, notwithstanding these inhibiting circumstances, this was probably due in the main to James Mill, whose admiration for Millar's work – and for that of the School as a whole – was very considerable. By the time Mill left Scotland for England in 1802, at the age of twenty-nine, he had studied the main works of the leading members of the School, and in the subsequent years seems to have made some attempt to popularize their views in England.[73] His high opinion of Millar was expressed, for example, in a review in the *Literary Journal* of June 1806,[74] and Millar's influence is particularly apparent in some sections of his *History of British India*. In 1817, shortly before the *History of British India* was published, Ricardo asked Mill for advice regarding reading, and Mill recommended him to embark upon "the study of civil society in general", commencing with (*inter alia*) Millar's *Historical View*. This book, said Mill, "was very instructive to me; but I rather think you told me, you had not a copy of it".[75] A little over a year later Ricardo reported that he had "read Millar with great pleasure", although it is not certain whether he was referring to Millar's *Historical View* or to his *Origin of Ranks*, a copy of which was in Ricardo's library at Gatcombe.[76] And Mill apparently also managed to pass on some of his own enthusiasm for Millar to his son John Stuart.[77]

Classical sociology also influenced Marxist sociology in another way – through Classical political econony. The basic doctrines of Classical political economy, which formed the starting-point of the economic researches of Marx and Engels, in a sense embodied the materialist approach to "civil society" which was characteristic of Classical sociology. The development of the materialist approach in the eighteenth century was very closely associated with the development of political economy. A concept of civil society which lays primary emphasis on the material conditions of life will naturally be accompanied by the belief that, as Marx put it, "the anatomy of that civil society is to be sought in political economy".[78] And to a large extent this general view of society will tend to determine the form and method of the political economy which is produced, particularly in the sphere of value theory.[79]

In the eighteenth century, the writer in whose work Classical political

---

[73] See Alexander Bain, *James Mill* (1882), pp. 18–19, 34–5 and 51.

[74] *Ibid.*, pp. 56–8.

[75] Ricardo, *Works* (ed. Sraffa, Cambridge, 1952), Vol. VII, pp. 195–7.

[76] *Ibid.*, pp. 382 and 197, footnote.

[77] See, e.g., *Lettres Inédites de John Stuart Mill à Auguste Comte* (1899), p. 357; and cf. p. 162.

[78] *Critique of Political Economy*, p. 11.

[79] Cf. below, pp. 204–5.

economy and Classical sociology were most closely associated was, of course, Adam Smith. Smith, like Marx, was a whole man, who tried to combine a theory of history, a theory of ethics, and a theory of political economy into one great general theoretical system. After Smith, Classical sociology was developed by Millar, who was relatively weak in the field of political economy, and Classical political economy was developed by Ricardo, who was relatively weak in the field of sociology. After Ricardo's death, a few rather hesitant attempts to reunite political economy and sociology in a new synthesis were made by radical writers like Bray, Proudhon and Rodbertus. But it was not until 1844–5, when Marx and Engels sketched the main outlines of their general theory, that the two disciplines were really united again. And Marx's study of Classical political economy in 1844 was, I think, the decisive factor which led him forward from Feuerbachian materialism to the materialist conception of history. But however this may be, there is no doubt that Marx can properly be said to be the heir of the basic ideas of the Scottish Historical School. Marx saw the vital connections which had been forgotten, and restored the unity which had been destroyed.

THE DECLINE
OF RICARDIAN ECONOMICS
IN ENGLAND[1]

I

This essay is concerned with one of the really crucial questions in the history of economic thought: what happened to "Ricardian economics" after the death of Ricardo? Different historians, approaching the question for different reasons and with different concepts of "Ricardian economics" in their minds, have given a wide variety of different answers to it. It will be helpful, perhaps, to begin by reviewing a few of these answers.

One of the earliest interpretations of the period was that of Marx, whose knowledge of the relevant literature was more profound and extensive than that of any of his contemporaries. Writing in 1873, in an "Afterword" to the second German edition of *Capital*, Marx spoke of the period from 1820 to 1830 as having been

notable in England for scientific activity in the domain of Political Economy. It was the time as well of the vulgarizing and extending of Ricardo's theory, as of the contest of that theory with the old school. Splendid tournaments were held . . . The unprejudiced character of this polemic – although the theory of Ricardo already serves, in exceptional cases, as a weapon of attack upon bourgeois economy – is explained by the circumstances of the time. On the one hand, modern industry itself was only just emerging from the age of childhood . . . On the other hand, the class-struggle between capital and labour is forced into the background, politically by the discord between the governments and the feudal aristocracy gathered around the Holy Alliance on the one hand, and the popular masses, led by the bourgeoisie on the other; economically by the quarrel between industrial capital and aristocratic landed property – a quarrel that . . . in England broke out openly after the Corn Laws. The literature of Political Economy in England at this time calls to mind the stormy forward movement in France after Dr Quesnay's death, but only as a Saint Martin's summer reminds us of spring. With the year 1830 came the decisive crisis.

In France and in England the bourgeoisie had conquered political power. Thenceforth, the class-struggle, practically as well as theoretically, took on

[1] This essay has the same name and general theme as an article in *Economica*, February 1950, but a great deal of it has been more or less completely rewritten.

more and more outspoken and threatening forms. It sounded the knell of scientific bourgeois economy. It was thenceforth no longer a question, whether this theorem or that was true, but whether it was useful to capital or harmful, expedient or inexpedient, politically dangerous or not. In place of disinterested inquirers, there were hired prize-fighters; in place of genuine scientific research, the bad conscience and the evil intent of apologetic.[2]

This judgement was of course based on the assumption that "political Economy can remain a science only so long as the class-struggle is latent or manifests itself only in isolated and sporadic phenomena"[3] – an assumption the validity of which is questionable, at any rate so far as our own times are concerned. But leaving this aside for the moment, let us note only that Marx saw the year 1830 as marking the end of "Ricardian" economics – and, indeed, not only of "Ricardian" but also of "Classical" and even of "scientific" economics. From then on, the scientists were obliged to give way to the hired prize-fighters.

To the economists who ushered in the "marginal revolution" of the 1870's and the generation of historians who followed in their wake, Marx's view could hardly have been expected to appeal. Quite apart from its political implications, it suggested that the "great divide" in the history of economic thought had occurred round about 1830. To the marginal revolutionaries, naturally enough, this seemed half a century too early: the "great divide" was surely that which they themselves were creating. And the dead hand of authority against which they were revolting was not merely that of John Stuart Mill, but also that of his acknowledged master, David Ricardo. Jevons believed that his new theory would "overthrow many of the principal doctrines of the Ricardo-Mill Economics",[4] and spoke again and again of "the mazy and preposterous assumptions of the Ricardian School",[5] "the exclusive importance attributed in England to the Ricardian School of Economists",[6] etc. Cannan, too, in the great iconoclastic survey of production and distribution theory which he wrote in order to help clear the way for the new doctrines, frequently spoke in contemptuous terms of the "Ricardian school", and argued that from the scientific point of view the theories of production and distribution arrived at in the first half of the nineteenth century must be "visited with almost unqualified condemnation".[7]

This view was not substantially altered by the discovery that a number of pioneers of the "modern" approach had lived and worked

[2] *Capital* (Foreign Languages Publishing House, Moscow, 1954), Vol. I, pp. 14–15.
[3] *Ibid.*, Vol. I, p. 14.
[4] *The Theory of Political Economy* (4th edn., London, 1931), p. li.
[5] *Ibid.*, p. xliv.   [6] *Ibid.*, p. xviii. Cf. pp. v, xvi and 277.
[7] *Theories of Production and Distribution* (3rd edn., London, 1917), p. 383.

during the period of the allegedly overwhelming predominance of "Ricardian" economics. To Jevons, men like Gossen and Cournot were merely the exceptions which proved the rule, the stars whose brightness accentuated the paleness of the others. And when it was found that men like these were much more numerous than Jevons had suspected, it was still argued that their work had been little more than a flash in the pan. Even Seligman, who did more than anyone else to bring this work to the attention of economists, believed that it had very little influence upon the intellectual climate of the time;[8] and Professor Marian Bowley, who in 1937 called so emphatically in her book on Senior for a revision of the traditional interpretation of the period, still maintained that an orthodox Ricardian school flourished in England during the whole period from the death of Ricardo to the time of Mill's recantation of the wages-fund doctrine.[9]

Keynes's *General Theory*, with its suggestive redefinition of "Classical" economics[10] and its remarks about "the completeness of the Ricardian victory", opened the way for yet another interpretation of the post-Ricardian period. "The idea that we can safely neglect the aggregate demand function", wrote Keynes, "is fundamental to the Ricardian economics, which underlie what we have been taught for more than a century . . . Malthus, indeed, had vehemently opposed Ricardo's doctrine that it was impossible for effective demand to be deficient; but vainly . . . Ricardo conquered England as completely as the Holy Inquisition conquered Spain."[11] This virtual identification by Keynes of "Ricardian economics" with what is now often called "Say's Law" was no doubt a useful and striking pedagogical device. It was designed to emphasize one of the really significant features of Keynes's own contribution, and it succeeded admirably in its purpose. But Keynes's "solecism" has also been used for another purpose, which Keynes himself presumably never intended. Professor Checkland, in an interesting article published in 1949,[12] assumed without question that "Say's Law" was indeed "the basic premise of the New School",[13] and proceeded to discuss the propagation and ultimate victory of the doctrines of the school in terms of the tactical and strategic advantages enjoyed by those who believed in the truth of "Say's Law". If this view were correct, it would mean that the "great divide" between "Ricardian" and

---

[8] "On Some Neglected British Economists", *The Economic Journal*, 1903, pp. 534–5.
[9] *Nassau Senior and Classical Economics* (London, 1937), *passim*.
[10] *General Theory*, p. 3, footnote. Cf. below, pp. 179–80.
[11] *Ibid.*, p. 32. Cf. *Essays in Biography*, pp. 140–41.
[12] "The Propagation of Ricardian Economics in England", *Economica*, February 1949.
[13] *Ibid.*, p. 40.

"modern" economics occurred not in 1830, and not in the 1870's, but in 1936.

With Schumpeter's *History of Economic Analysis*, the wheel in a sense turns full circle. So far as the *facts* are concerned, Schumpeter agrees substantially with Marx. Speaking of James Mill, McCulloch and De Quincey – "the only unconditional adherents and militant supporters of Ricardo's teaching who gained sufficient reputation for their names to survive" – he writes:

> None of the three added anything substantial, and the touches they did add – James Mill and McCulloch especially – were mostly of doubtful value. They did not even succeed in summing up Ricardo correctly or in conveying an idea of the wealth of suggestions to be found in the latter's *Principles*. What they did convey was a superficialized message that wilted in their hands and became stale and unproductive practically at once . . . It was not their fault that Ricardo's system failed from the first to gain the assent of a majority of English economists . . . This was owing to its inherent weaknesses. Nor was it their fault that the system was not made for a long career. But it was their fault that defeat came so quickly. Ricardo died in 1823. In 1825, Bailey launched his attack that should have been decisive on the merits of the case. Actually it was not, for schools are not destroyed so easily. But the decay of the Ricardian school must have become patent shortly after, for in a pamphlet published in 1831 we read that "there are some Ricardians still remaining". In any case, it is clear that Ricardianism was then no longer a living force.[14]

Schumpeter goes on to try to account for "the prevailing impression to the contrary" – a problem to which I shall return at the end of this essay. In the meantime, let us note that there is one very important respect in which Schumpeter's interpretation differs from that of Marx. Both historians, it is true, date the defeat of the "Ricardian" school at 1830 or thereabouts, and both agree that the defeat was closely associated with a tendency to get away from "the class connotation of the categories of economic types".[15] But whereas Schumpeter strongly approves of this tendency, Marx just as strongly condemns it as "one of the symptoms of the degeneration of bourgeois economics".[16] It is also perhaps worth noting that, whereas Schumpeter blames the members of the school for the fact that its defeat came so quickly, Professor Checkland gives these same members the credit for the fact that its victory was so long-lasting.

Where then do we stand? At first sight it might seem that in the presence of guide-lines which are so constantly shifting, and judgements which are so obviously temporal and subjective, our only possible refuge

14 *History of Economic Analysis*, pp. 476–8.
15 *Ibid.*, p. 552. Cf. below, pp. 205 ff.
16 *Ibid.*, p. 553. Cf. p. 559, footnote 12.

is in some kind of arid combination of relativism and semanticism. Each generation must make its own history of economic thought; periodization can never be an exact science; each of the answers which has been given to our initial question is as right – or as wrong – as the others. I would be the last to deny that up to a point these things are true: one simply has to learn to live with them, and do the best one can without the help of absolute standards.[17]

In relation to the question at issue, however, it seems to me that there are at any rate two things which may usefully be done. First, we may try to define the role which "Say's Law" played in Ricardo's theory, in an endeavour to find out whether we can in fact say anything really useful about the development of "Ricardian" economics after 1823 merely by accounting for the survival of this one particular doctrine. Second, we may try to define those parts of Ricardo's theory which did in fact fall into abeyance after 1830, and make some estimate of the motives which led to their removal from the corpus of "Ricardian" doctrine.

II

Was "Say's Law" actually the "basic premise" of Ricardian economics? To John Stuart Mill, it is true, the idea that "a general over-supply, or excess of all commodities above the demand" is an impossibility[18] did indeed appear to be "fundamental". "Any difference of opinion on it", he wrote, "involves radically different conceptions of Political Economy, especially in its practical aspect ... Besides; a theory so essentially self-contradictory cannot intrude itself without carrying confusion into the very heart of the subject, and making it impossible even to conceive with any distinctness many of the more complicated economical workings of society."[19] Mill's testimony, however, is hardly conclusive so far as Ricardo's own system is concerned: we know that Mill carried out something of a "transformation" of that system,[20] and his ideas of what was or was not "fundamental" were not necessarily Ricardo's. To what extent, then, could "Say's Law" in one or other of its various possible interpretations be said to have been "fundamental" to Ricardo himself?

[17] This is a problem which is treated in the essay on *Economics and Ideology*, which appears below. In the present context, I wish merely to add an acknowledgement of my debt to the dignified defence of "complete rational relativism" in Professor A. L. Macfie's "Economics – Science, Ideology, Philosophy?", *Scottish Journal of Political Economy*, June 1963.

[18] J. S. Mill, *Principles of Political Economy* (Toronto edn. of the *Collected Works*, Vol. III, 1965), p. 572.

[19] *Ibid.*, pp. 575–6.

[20] Schumpeter, *History of Economic Analysis*, p. 487.

E

Ricardo was probably acquainted with "Say's Law", at any rate in the form in which James Mill put it forward in his *Commerce Defended*, from the time of publication of the latter work. John Stuart Mill tells us that the merit of having placed the question of "general over-production" in its true light

belongs principally, on the Continent, to the judicious J. B. Say, and in this country to Mr Mill; who (besides the conclusive exposition which he gave of the subject in his Elements of Political Economy) had set forth the correct doctrine with great force and clearness in an early pamphlet, called forth by a temporary controversy, and entitled, "Commerce Defended"; the first of his writings which attained any celebrity, and which he prized more as having been his first introduction to the friendship of David Ricardo, the most valued and most intimate friendship of his life.[21]

But there is no evidence that the true significance of Mill's doctrine and its relevance to his own theoretical system had been brought home to Ricardo before September 1814, when Malthus pointed it out to him – by which time, as we now know, he had already arrived at many of the basic propositions of the *Principles*. It is instructive, I think, to examine in some detail the state of the debate between Ricardo and Malthus at the beginning of 1814, and the way in which "Say's Law" – or rather "Mr Mill's theory"[22] – was brought into the picture.

Early in 1814, Ricardo wrote some "very interesting papers on the profits of Capital"[23] which have not survived. They no doubt embodied the views about the relation between the accumulation of capital and the rate of profit which Ricardo had arrived at in the course of a discussion with Malthus on the subject in the previous year[24] and which he summarized as follows in a well-known letter to Trower:

When Capital increases in a country, and the means of employing Capital already exists, or increases, in the same proportion, the rate of interest and of profits will not fall.

Interest rises only when the means of employment for Capital bears a greater proportion than before to the Capital itself, and falls when the Capital bears a greater proportion to the arena, as Mr Malthus has called it, for its employment. On these points I believe we are all agreed, but I contend that the arena for the employment of new Capital cannot increase in any country in the same or greater proportion than the Capital itself,[25] unless there be improvements in husbandry, – or new facilities be offered for the introduction of food from

[21] *Principles of Political Economy*, p. 576.
[22] An attempt is made below, pp. 60–1, to distinguish between the two.
[23] Ricardo, *Works*, Vol. VI, p. 102.
[24] See *ibid.*, Vol. VI, pp. 92–5.
[25] A footnote by Ricardo at this point reads: "the following to be inserted: unless Capital be withdrawn from the land".

foreign countries; – that in short it is the profits of the farmer which regulate the profits of all other trades, – and as the profits of the farmer must necessarily decrease with every augmentation of Capital employed on the land, provided no improvements be at the same time made in husbandry, all other profits must diminish and therefore the rate of interest must fall.

To this proposition, Ricardo goes on, "Mr Malthus does not agree". He thinks

that the arena for the employment of Capital may increase, and consequently profits and interest may rise, altho' there should be no new facilities, either by importation, or improved tillage, for the production of food; – that the profits of the farmer no more regulate the profits of other trades, than the profits of other trades regulate the profits of the farmer, and consequently if new markets are discovered, in which we can obtain a greater quantity of foreign commodities in exchange for our commodities, than before the discovery of such markets, profits will increase and interest will rise.

In such a state of things the rate of interest would rise as well as the profits of the farmer, he thinks even if more Capital were employed on the land.

And Ricardo then sums up the basic issues as follows:

Nothing, I say, can increase the profits permanently on trade, with the same or an increased Capital, but a really cheaper mode of obtaining food. A cheaper mode of obtaining food will undoubtedly increase profits says Mr Malthus but there are many other circumstances which may also increase profits with an increase of Capital. The discovery of a new market where there will be a great demand for our manufactures is one.[26]

It seems rather unlikely that Ricardo, in arriving at this position, was influenced in any really direct and fundamental way by "Say's Law", whether in Mill's version or in Say's. Within the next few months, however, the debate between Ricardo and Malthus took a turn which revealed clearly to both men the relevance of this theory to their respective positions. When Malthus expressed "doubts respecting the effects of restrictions on the importation of corn, in tending to lower the rate of interest", Ricardo replied as follows:

The rise of the price or rather the value of corn without any augmentation of capital must necessarily diminish the demand for other things . . . With the same Capital there would be less production, and less demand. Demand has no other limits but the want of power of paying for the commodities demanded. Every thing which tends to diminish production tends to diminish this power.[27]

In this last sentence one may, if one wishes, see a hint of "Say's Law" in its simplest and most truistic sense – but surely nothing much more than this.

[26] *Works*, Vol. VI, pp. 103–5 (letter of 8th March 1814).
[27] *Ibid.*, Vol. VI, p. 108 (letter of 26th June 1814).

On 6th July, Malthus replied that Ricardo was wrong in assuming that "in the case supposed, there would be less production and less demand with the *same* capital". Surely, he argued, "there would be *much less capital*". If so, "the question then seems to be whether production or demand would decrease the fastest? . . . I can by no means agree with you in thinking that every thing which diminishes produce, tends to diminish the power of paying for the commodities wanted, or as you intimate, to diminish the effective demand. If this were true, why do profits rise at the commencement of a war when stock is destroyed?"[28] Ricardo replied on 25th July as follows:

> Effective demand, it appears to me, cannot augment or long continue stationary with a diminishing capital; and your question why if this were true profits rise at the commencement of a war? does not I think bear any connection with the argument, because profits will augment under a diminution of capital and produce, if demand tho' diminished does not diminish so rapidly as Capital and produce.[29]

Malthus seized on this passage in his next letter, maintaining that in *all* cases of diminution of capital "demand tho' diminished does not diminish so rapidly as Capital and produce", and that therefore Ricardo was wrong in arguing that "effective demand . . . cannot augment or long continue stationary with a diminishing capital". "The whole amount of demand will from advanced prices diminish of course," said Malthus, "but the *proportion* of *demand* to the *supply* which is always the main point in question, as determining prices and profits, may continue to increase as it does in all countries the capital of which is retrograde."[30]

The debate continued in much the same vein during the remainder of August. In a letter dated 30th August, Ricardo put the case of two imaginary countries, in one of which "from bad government and the consequent insecurity of property" or some such cause, profits and interest were permanently high, and in the other of which, where these causes did not operate, profits and interest were permanently low. "It would surely be incorrect," argued Ricardo, "to say that the cause of the high profits was the greater proportion of demand for produce, when in both countries, the supply would be, or might be, precisely equal to the demand, and no more."[31] This remark stimulated Malthus to make the following reply, which for the first time brought "Mr Mill's theory" into the picture and raised the question of the possibility of a general insufficiency of effective demand:

> I think you would allow that when capital is scanty compared with the means of employing it, from whatever cause arising, whether from insecurity of prop-

---

[28] *Ibid.*, Vol. VI, pp. 110–11.   [29] *Ibid.*, Vol. VI, p. 114.
[30] *Ibid.*, Vol. VI, p. 117 (letter of 5th August 1814).   [31] *Ibid.*, Vol. VI, p. 129.

erty, or extravagant habits, profits will be high not only temporarily but permanently. And I cannot help being of opinion that these high profits always indicate a comparative excess of demand above supply, even though the demand and supply should *appear* to be precisely equal. Effectual demand consists of two elements the *power* and the *will* to purchase. The power to purchase may perhaps be represented correctly by the produce of the country whether small or great; but the will to purchase will always be the greatest, the smaller is the produce compared with the population, and the more scantily the wants of society are supplied. When capital is abundant it is not easy to find new objects sufficiently in demand. When capital is scarce nothing is more easy. In a country abundant in capital the value of the whole produce cannot increase with rapidity from the insufficiency of demand. In a country with little comparative capital the value of the yearly produce may very rapidly increase from the greatness of demand. In short I by no means think that the power to purchase necessarily involves a proportionate will to purchase; and I cannot agree with Mr Mill in an ingenious position which he lays down in an answer to Mr Spence, that in reference to a nation, supply can never exceed demand. A nation must certainly have the power of purchasing all that it produces, but I can easily conceive it not to have the will: and if we were to grow next year half as much corn again as usual, a great part of it would be wasted, and the same would be true if all commodities of all kinds were increased one half. It would be impossible that they should yield the expence of production. You have never I think taken sufficiently into consideration the wants and tastes of mankind. It is not merely the proportion of commodities to each other but their proportion to the wants and tastes of mankind that determines prices.[32]

Malthus's manner of reference to Mill's "ingenious position" strongly suggests that he assumed that Ricardo was ignorant of it, which can presumably be taken to indicate that Ricardo had never mentioned it – or at least never stressed it – in his discussions with Malthus. The point which Malthus was now raising was, in fact, essentially a new one so far as the debate between the two men was concerned. Ricardo dealt with it in somewhat the same way as Mill had dealt with it in his reply to Spence – by arguing first that "the desire of accumulation will occasion demand just as effectually as a desire to consume", and second that "Mr Mill's idea, that in reference to a nation, supply can never exceed demand" must indeed be held to be true unless one takes the implausible view "that with an increase of capital men will become indifferent both to consumption and accumulation". In short, Ricardo concluded,

I consider the wants and tastes of mankind as unlimited. We all wish to add to our enjoyments or to our power. Consumption adds to our enjoyments, – accumulation to our power, and they equally promote demand.[33]

[32] *Ibid.*, Vol. VI, pp. 131–2 (letter of 11th September 1814).
[33] *Ibid.*, Vol. VI, pp. 133–5 (letter of 16th September 1814).

These propositions were batted back and forth between the two men in a few more letters.[34] The appearance of the second edition of Say's *Traité*, supporting "the doctrine that demand is regulated by production", was commented upon by Ricardo,[35] but Malthus, who had then become very busy writing his pamphlet on rent, had little to say in reply,[36] and the controversy over "Mr Mill's idea" temporarily died down.

Let us pause at this stage to consider what "Mr Mill's idea" actually was, or at least what it was then conceived to be by Malthus and Ricardo. Basically, as can be seen from the above account of the debate, it was the idea that "in reference to a nation, supply can never exceed demand". Now this idea was in effect a combination of three logically separate propositions which may be stated as follows:

(i) *That "the power to purchase may . . . be represented correctly by the produce of the country whether small or great".*[37]

This is a crude formulation of what may perhaps be called "Say's Law proper". As Schumpeter puts it, Say had perceived that

under division of labour, the only means normally available to everyone for acquiring the commodities and services he wishes to have is to produce – or to take part in the production of – some equivalent for them. It follows that production increases not only the supply of goods in the markets but normally also the demand for them. *In this sense*, it is production itself ("supply") which creates the "fund" from which flows the demand for its products: products are "ultimately" paid for by products in domestic as well as in foreign trade.[38]

Now proposition (i) obviously does not in itself embody the notion that "in reference to a nation, supply can never exceed demand". In order to proceed to the latter, one must say in addition two things about the actual *exercise* of the "power to purchase". First, one must make it clear that if purchasing power is invested instead of being spent on immediate consumption this will not diminish effective demand – *i.e.*, as Ricardo put it,

(ii) *That "the desire of accumulation will occasion demand just as effectually as a desire to consume".*[39]

Second, one must make it clear that under normal circumstances there will be no hoarding – *i.e.*, that income will be fully "spent" either in accumulation or in current consumption. This was expressed by Ricardo in the form of the proposition

---

34 *Ibid.*, Vol. VI, pp. 141–2, 147–9, 155–6, 163–4 and 168.
35 *Ibid.*, Vol. VI, pp. 163–4 (letter of 18th December 1814).
36 *Ibid.*, Vol. VI, p. 168 (letter of 29th December 1814).
37 Above, p. 59.
38 *History of Economic Analysis*, p. 616.
39 Above, p. 59.

(*iii*) That it is untrue that "*with an increase of capital men will become indifferent both to consumption and accumulation*".[40]

Since (*i*) is obviously true, it appears to follow, if (*ii*) and (*iii*) are also held to be true, that "in reference to a nation, supply can never exceed demand".

Let us henceforth call (*i*) "Say's Law proper", and (*i*) plus (*ii*) plus (*iii*) "Mill's Theory". So far as Say's Law proper is concerned, it is probably true to say that Ricardo was aware of it at least from the time of publication of Mill's *Commerce Defended*, and that it formed part – although not a very important part – of the intellectual apparatus which he used when writing his "papers on the profits of Capital" at the beginning of 1814. But when Keynes described as "fundamental to the Ricardian economics" the idea that "we can safely neglect the aggregate demand function",[41] it was clearly Mill's Theory rather than Say's Law proper which he had in mind. Say's Law proper, after all, is obviously true, and Keynes would surely not have condemned Ricardo for holding to it. And it seems fairly clear from the events of 1814, as described above, that Mill's Theory was *not* in any way "fundamental" to Ricardo's system, at any rate at its then stage of development. The role of Mill's Theory at that time was simply to assist Ricardo to dispose of a particular objection which Malthus happened to have raised against his idea that "if there were no increased difficulty [in obtaining food], profits would never fall"[42] with the accumulation of capital. This basic idea had been clearly expressed in Ricardo's letter of March 1814 to Trower,[43] and it was incorporated without substantial alteration in his *Essay on the Profits of Stock* which appeared in February 1815[44] and which contained no reference whatever, whether express or (as far as one can see) implied, to Mill's Theory.

After the publication of the *Essay*, Ricardo retreated from the idea that "it is the profits of the farmer which regulate the profits of all other trades".[45] The general idea that profits "depend on the price or rather on the value of food"[46] was retained in the *Principles*, but emphasis was now laid almost exclusively on the effect which the changes in the value of food associated with accumulation would have on profits *through the*

---

[40] Above, p. 59.   [41] Above, p. 53.

[42] *Works*, Vol. VI, p. 162 (letter of 18th December 1814).

[43] Above, 56–7.

[44] Cf. Sraffa, in *Works*, Vol. IV, p.4: " When in February 1815, Malthus's pamphlets appeared, Ricardo was able to write within a few days his *Essay on the Influence of a Low Price of Corn on the Profits of Stock*, by using his already developed theory of profits, incorporating Malthus's theory of rent, and adding a refutation of the protectionist arguments put forward by Malthus in his *Grounds of an Opinion*."

[45] Above, p. 57.

[46] *Works*, Vol. IV, p. 26.

medium of the consequential changes in wages.[47] This new version of the theory
was related to an important general proposition which Ricardo had
laid down in a letter to Malthus as early as 26th June 1814: "The rate
of profits and of interest must depend on the proportion of production
to the consumption necessary to such production, – this again essentially
depends upon the cheapness of provisions, which is after all, whatever
intervals we may be willing to allow, the great regulator of the wages of
labour." [48] As Ricardo's theory of value was developed, it became
possible for him to express this basic proposition in the form which it
assumed in the *Principles* – that profits depended on the "proportion of
the annual labour of the country . . . devoted to the support of the
labourers".[49] If this proposition were true, it followed that nothing
could permanently lower the rate of profit which did not increase the
quantity of social labour which it was necessary to allocate to the wage-
goods industries relatively to the quantity allocated to the non-wage-
goods industries. This way of formulating the theory added a new
dimension, as it were, to Ricardo's reply to Malthus's objection to it:
changes in "the proportion of demand to the supply" would clearly not
affect the crucial ratio. At the same time, it meant that more was at
stake than before: if Malthus were proved to be right, it could plausibly
be maintained that Ricardo's theory of value would be discredited along
with his theory of profit.

It was the first of these two factors rather than the second which seems
to have been uppermost in Ricardo's mind when writing the *Principles*.
"Say's Law" is not mentioned (apart from a commendatory reference
in the Preface)[50] until Chapter XXI, where Ricardo uses it to refute
Adam Smith's theory of the falling rate of profit. At the beginning of the
chapter, Ricardo makes it clear that he believed Smith to have been
already refuted by the theory of profit outlined in the preceding chapters. "From the account which has been given of the profits of stock," he
writes, "it will appear, that no accumulation of capital will permanently
lower profits, unless there be some permanent cause for the rise of
wages . . . If the necessaries of the workman could be constantly increased with the same facility, there could be no permanent alteration
in the rate of profits or wages, to whatever amount capital might be

[47] This line was fairly clearly foreshadowed in a letter to Malthus of 18th December
1814; see *Works*, Vol. VI, p. 162.

[48] *Works*, Vol. VI, p. 108. Sraffa (*Works*, Vol. I, p. xxxii) describes this passage as the
nearest that Ricardo ever came to an explicit statement of the "corn-ratio" theory of
profit which he allegedly held in the early days of the development of his system. My
own feeling, however, is that the passage in question looks forward to the mature theory
of profit of the *Principles* much more than it looks back at any early "corn-ratio" theory.

[49] *Works*, Vol. I, p. 49. Cf. p. 126.

[50] *Ibid.*, Vol. I, p. 7.

accumulated."[51] But "Say's Law" was such a convenient weapon (and, as will be seen shortly, had such useful political connotations) that Ricardo could not resist using it as a reply to Smith's theory (and, of course, by implication, to the arguments Malthus had put up):

> Adam Smith . . . uniformly ascribes the fall of profits to accumulation of capital, and to the competition which will result from it, without ever adverting to the increasing difficulty of providing food for the additional number of labourers which the additional capital will employ . . . He does not appear to see, that at the same time that capital is increased, the work to be effected by capital, is increased in the same proportion. M. Say has, however, most satisfactorily shewn, that there is no amount of capital which may not be employed in a country, because demand is only limited by production. No man produces, but with a view to consume or sell, and he never sells, but with an intention to purchase some other commodity, which may be immediately useful to him, or which may contribute to future production. By producing, then, he necessarily becomes either the consumer of his own goods, or the purchaser and consumer of the goods of some other person . . .
>
> There cannot, then, be accumulated in a country any amount of capital which cannot be employed productively, until wages rise so high in consequence of the rise of necessaries, and so little consequently remains for the profits of stock, that the motive for accumulation ceases.[52]

The main emphasis here is on proposition (*i*) above (Say's Law proper), but propositions (*ii*) and (*iii*) are also fairly clearly implied. This conversion of Say's Law proper into Mill's Theory is confirmed in a passage which almost immediately follows:

> If ten thousand pounds were given to a man having £100,000 per annum, he would not lock it up in a chest, but would either increase his expenses by £10,000; employ it himself productively, or lend it to some other person for that purpose; in either case, demand would be increased, although it would be for different objects. If he increased his expenses, his effectual demand might probably be for buildings, furniture, or some such enjoyment. If he employed his £10,000 productively, his effectual demand would be for food, clothing, and raw material, which might set new labourers to work; but still it would be demand.[53]

These passages were not altered in the third edition of the *Principles* (1821), in spite of the fact that Malthus's *Principles of Political Economy*, with its important new contribution to the "general glut" controversy, had appeared in April 1820.[54] In the light of this fact, remembering that Ricardo considered "the most objectionable chapter in Mr Malthus' book" to be "that perhaps on the bad effects from too great

---

[51] *Ibid.*, Vol. I, p. 288.   [52] *Ibid.*, Vol. I, pp. 289–90.   [53] *Ibid.*, Vol. I, p. 291.
[54] Cf. *ibid.*, Vol. I, pp. liii–vi; and Vol. II, pp. vi–xii.

accumulation of capital",[55] and looking at the passages quoted above in their general context, it seems fair to suggest at any rate that Ricardo himself did not consider Mill's Theory to be of substantial *analytical* importance in relation to his mature system.

Analytical importance is one thing: *political* importance is another. Once admit that profits might be lowered as a result of accumulation *per se*, "without ever adverting to the increasing difficulty of providing food",[56] and the way was immediately laid open for serious criticism of the economic system. Ricardo was never particularly concerned to defend the interests of any single social class except in so far as the interests of that class happened to be bound up with an increase in production,[57] but it would hardly have been possible for his attitude towards the economic system itself not to have been to some extent apologetic. Although the institutional foundations of the system had not yet been seriously called into question in Britain, a tendency was already becoming apparent among those who defended the system to explain certain manifest defects in its working *in terms of the operation of factors external to it*. The appalling poverty among the lower orders, for example, was explained by means of the Malthusian theory of population. A more difficult problem was set by the mysterious "tendency of the rate of profit to fall". If the rate of profit tended naturally to fall as society progressed, and if capital accumulation depended upon profits, then a limit seemed to be set to the expansion of social welfare under the existing system. If accumulation were necessarily attended by the destruction of the ability and motive to accumulate, how could this state of affairs be explained without impugning the system itself?[58] Ricardo might insist that the stationary state could not properly be described as a state of stagnation,[59] and that in any event it would not be reached for a very long time, but the doubt remained. Here again an external factor – in this case Nature – was brought in by way of explanation. Not even the best of all possible economic systems, it was maintained, could overcome the obstacle of diminishing returns in agriculture. To economists thinking almost instinctively in such terms, Malthus's suggestion that the system itself was internally defective – if only in the sense that its continued progress required the existence of a vast horde of idlers – must have come as something of a shock,[60] and it is hardly sur-

---

[55] *Ibid.*, Vol. VIII, p. 181.   [56] Above, p. 63.

[57] Cf., e.g., *Works*, Vol. IV, p. 41.

[58] Cf. M. H. Dobb, *Political Economy and Capitalism* (London, 1937), pp. 82–3.

[59] *Works*, Vol. IX, p. 25 (letter to Malthus of 21st July 1821).

[60] Ricardo several times complains that Malthus sees "great evils in great powers of production" (*ibid.*, Vol. IX, p. 23). His tone in some of these passages shows how seriously his moral conscience was shocked by the nature of Malthus's critique.

prising that all the available theoretical weapons, including Mill's Theory, should have been employed against such a major heresy.

One thing which seems to require explanation is Ricardo's insistence, at any rate towards the close of his life, that Mill's Theory was fully operative even in the short period. Little damage would surely have been done to Ricardo's system by a recognition of the fact that over-accumulation might occasionally cause a temporary fall in profit – provided, of course, that the existence of effective long-run corrective tendencies was also recognized. Ricardo's advocacy of a fairly inflexible version of Mill's Theory seems to have been associated with his desire to defend certain important political conclusions suggested by his idea that profits depended solely upon the value of food. In his 1815 essay he had argued that the long-run tendency of the rate of profit to fall might be hindered by (*inter alia*) agricultural improvements and a fall in the price of imported corn.[61] But agricultural improvements (at least in the short run) and an abolition of restrictions upon importation were against the interests of the landlords, since they would each lead directly to a fall in rents. Thus the theory that profits depended solely upon the value of food implied that "the interest of the landlord is always opposed to the interest of every other class in the community",[62] since the interests of the other classes obviously lay in checking the "natural" fall in profits as far as this was possible. There is little doubt that Malthus's desire to find an alternative theory of profit which did not involve this unfor-tunate political conclusion was at least partly responsible for his contention that profits might fall, even though improvements were en-couraged and the Corn Laws repealed, if production outstripped con-sumption. The important point seems to be that Ricardo believed Malthus to have asserted, not only that this *might* happen, but also that it latterly *had* happened.[63] The question at issue, then, was not only an academic one: it was related directly to the thorny problem of the cause of the present distresses. If Ricardo were correct, it followed that the actions of those of his contemporaries who were *at that time* fighting in various ways to weaken the influence of the land-owning interests were supported by the new science of political economy. If Malthus were correct, on the other hand, it followed that they were simply wasting their time. Indeed, their actions might be positively harmful, since if the

[61] *Works*, Vol. II, p. 22. Cf. M. H. Dobb, *op. cit.*, p. 87.
[62] *Works*, Vol. II, p. 21.
[63] *Ibid.*, Vol. IX, p. 16: "You often appear to me to contend not only that produc-tion can go on so far without an adequate motive, but that it actually has done so lately, and that we are now suffering the consequences of it in stagnation of trade, in a want of employment for our labourers, &c. &c., and the remedy you propose is an increase of consumption" (letter of 9th July 1821).

existence of a class of unproductive consumers were in fact a permanent institutional necessity, then so far from the interests of the landlord being always opposed to those of the rest of the community, the economic health of the rest of the community actually depended upon the wealth and idleness of the landlord.

To sum up, then, it would seem to be very misleading to speak, as Keynes did, as if "the idea that we can safely neglect the aggregate demand function" was "fundamental to the Ricardian economics"[64] – at any rate if this be taken to imply that we can say anything very useful about the development of "Ricardian" economics after Ricardo's death in terms merely of the survival of Say's Law and Mill's Theory. Politically, there is no doubt of their importance, although this was probably greater for the immediate followers of Ricardo than for Ricardo himself. Analytically, they were important only in so far as they provided Ricardo and his followers with an effective means of counter-attack against one of Malthus's criciticisms of their basic theory.[65]

III

If Ricardo himself had been asked to note down those of his doctrines which he regarded as "fundamental" to his mature system, there is little doubt that his theory of value would have appeared high up on the list. "I confess it fills me with astonishment", he wrote to Malthus in 1818, "to find that you think . . . that *natural price*, as well as *market price*, is determined by the demand and supply . . . In saying this do you mean to deny that facility of production will lower natural price and difficulty of production raise it? . . . If indeed this fundamental doctrine of mine were proved false I admit that my whole theory falls with it."[66] By this time Ricardo was fully aware of the kind of function which a theory of value ought to fulfil in a theoretical system such as his, and had seized upon human labour as the substance and measure of that "difficulty or facility of production" [67] which in his view determined natural price. It was by no means an easy task for an economist at this time to emancipate his thought from the traditional notion that labour contributed value to its product only through the medium of wages paid to it, and Ricardo was virtually the first to fashion anything like a consistent theory of value from the notion that it was not the capitalist's expenditure on subsistence goods for his workmen but the expenditure of energy by the workmen themselves which conferred value on commodities.

[64] Above, p. 53.
[65] For some further comments on the role of "Say's Law" in the Ricardian system, see below, p. 183.
[66] *Works*, Vol. VII, pp. 250–51.   [67] *Ibid.*, Vol. IV, p. 20.

One of the most interesting features of the decade immediately following the death of Ricardo is the extraordinary speed with which this theory of value, together with certain basic concepts with which it was directly associated, was successfully dethroned. As early as 1829, Samuel Read could refer to "the almost universal rejection of labour as the standard",[68] and in 1831 Cotterill stated that he felt himself obliged to repeat the usual arguments against the labour theory only because he suspected that "there are some Ricardians still remaining".[69] Ricardo, as Read acutely observed, had believed that "the idea of value in commodities *cannot even be conceived* without being mingled with the idea of their relation to mankind and to human labour, of which *some portion* must always be employed in procuring them originally".[70] It was this vital concept which virtually vanished from English political economy after Ricardo's death. McCulloch was almost the only economist to continue to defend Ricardo's theory of value after 1826, and his defence contained a number of bizarre elements which afforded an easy target for critics.

And it was not only Ricardo's theory of value which fell into disrepute during this period, but also a number of his other fundamental doctrines. Indeed, it is hardly too much to say that by the early 1830's the most important question was not so much whether Ricardo's or Malthus's views on the general glut question were to prevail, as whether Ricardo's system as a whole was to be more or less completely abandoned to the Ricardian socialists or inoculated against misuse by these individuals by the injection of certain suitable amendments. Interesting evidence of the rapid decline of a number of Ricardian doctrines at this time is to be found in the proceedings of the Political Economy Club. If, as Professor Checkland suggests, the founding of the Club was a "political act" by which the "excellent tacticians" of the new Ricardian school sought "to consolidate their advantage", one can only say that they were not very diligent in following up this "political act".[71] Early in 1831, Torrens put forward the following question for discussion: "What improvements have been effected in the science of Political Economy since the publication of Mr Ricardo's great work; and are any of the principles first advanced in that work now acknowledged to be correct?" The question was debated on 13th January and 15th April, 1831, and Mallet has left us an account of the discussions. Torrens apparently held at the first meeting "that all the great principles of Ricardo's work had been successively abandoned, and that his theories of Value, Rent and

---

[68] S. Read, *An Inquiry into the Natural Grounds of Right, etc.*, p. 203.
[69] C. F. Cotterill, *An Examination of the Doctrine of Value, etc.*, p. 8.
[70] Read, *Inquiry*, p. viii, footnote.   [71] Checkland, *op. cit.*, pp. 50–51.

Profits were now generally acknowledged to have been erroneous".
Bailey had settled the question of value and Thompson that of rent; and
Ricardo's omission to take account of the replacement of fixed capital
"was decisive of the unsoundness of his views" on profit. McCulloch
admitted that Ricardo's theory of profit was defective in this respect,
but energetically defended his theories of value and rent. Tooke supported Ricardo only on the question of rent. At the adjourned meeting
it seems to have been generally agreed that "neither [Ricardo's]
Theories of value, nor his Theories of Rent and profits are correct,
according to the very terms of his propositions; but they are right in
principle". There follows in Mallet's account an important catalogue of
Ricardo's errors:

> He is one of the first who has treated the subject of Taxation, and he always
> reasons out his propositions, whether true or false, with great logical precision
> and to their utmost consequences; but without sufficient regard to the many
> modifications which are invariably found to arise in the progress of Society.
> One of the errors of Ricardo seems to have been to have followed up Malthus'
> principles of population to unwarrantable conclusions. For, in the first place it
> is clear from the progress of social improvement and the bettering of the con-
> dition of the people in the greater part of the civilized world, that Capital, or the
> means of Employment – the fund for labour – increases in a greater ratio than
> population; that men generally reproduce more than they consume, and the
> interest of the capital besides, which surplus goes to increase the fund for labour.
> Then he looks forward from the gradual demand for food and the use of land,
> to the gradual lowering of wages and profits till nothing remains but rent to the
> Landlords. But long before that, modification would take place in the state of
> society which would make such conclusions all wrong. First of all, it is contended
> that the interest of the Landlords does in fact coincide with those of the other
> classes; and then we see that in Ireland, where rent is absorbing everything, in
> consequence of the immense competition for land, a system of Poor Laws is like-
> ly soon to equalize the division.[72]

What were the reasons for the rapid decline which manifested itself
at this time in the influence of certain fundamental Ricardian doctrines?
One may say, of course, if one wishes, as Schumpeter did, that it was
due to the "inherent weaknesses" of the system itself.[73] But something
more than this is surely required to explain the strength, vigour and
virtual universality of the early reaction against Ricardo. These were
above all due, I suggest, to the fact that a number of elements in his
system seemed to set limits to the prospects of uninterrupted and
harmonious progress under capitalism. In particular, the work of the

[72] *Centenary Volume of the Political Economy Club* (London, 1921), pp. 35, 36 and 223–5.
I am indebted to Professor Hayek for drawing my attention to these passages.
[73] Above, p. 54.

Ricardian socialists revealed certain disharmonious and pessimistic implications of Ricardo's system so forcibly that the economists of the day could hardly avoid being influenced by them in the course of their revaluations of Ricardo.

A significant number of economists was at this time becoming conscious of the fact that the labouring classes were beginning to think for themselves and to question the moral validity of the foundations of the social structure. In his *Elements of Political Science*, published in 1814, John Craig could remark that "the fear of levelling is altogether chimerical".[74] In the first edition of Mrs Marcet's *Conversations* (1816) we find Mrs B denying that she would teach political economy to the labouring classes.[75] Yet only ten or twelve years later Mrs Marcet is to be found vying with Harriet Martineau in the composition of economic fairy tales of a wholesome moral character for the enlightenment of the proletariat. So long as the labouring classes are passive and ignorant their views on political economy can be ignored. But when it becomes no longer possible to prevent them from listening to Mr Hodgskin at a Mechanics' Institute the situation has radically changed. The fear of levelling is no longer chimerical. Evidence that the seriousness and importance of this change were widely appreciated is to be found in the works of many economists of the period, but by no one were the facts more cogently stated, and the new tasks facing political economy more admirably summarized, than by Mountifort Longfield in 1833:

It is daily becoming more important that the notions which are generally entertained should be correct, since they now lead so directly to action . . . No person can now remain altogether neutral, and avoid such topics. He must, according to the degree of pains he has taken with the subject, be a teacher of useful truth, or a disseminator of mischievous falsehood. Opinions . . . exercise immense influence on a class of people formerly removed beyond the reach of such discussions . . . I allude to the labouring orders, both agricultural and manufactural. It is no longer a question, whether these men shall think or not, or what degree of influence their opinions ought to exert over their conduct; they will follow the path where they conceive their interests to point, and it only remains to be considered, in what manner a true sense of their real interests may be most effectually brought home to them. The change has taken place, whether for the better or the worse it is useless now to enquire, since the steps which have led to it can never be retraced. The people will no longer be guided by the authority of others . . . It depends in some degree upon every person present, whether the labourer is taught that his interest will be best promoted by prudence and industry, or by a violent demolition of the capital destined to his support.[76]

[74] J. Craig, *Elements of Political Science*, Vol. II, p. 230.
[75] *Conversations on Political Economy*, p. 158.
[76] Longfield, *Lectures on Political Economy* (L.S.E. reprint, 1931), pp. 16–18.

It is evident, too, that the majority of economists were very much aware of the dangerous use to which a number of radical writers were putting certain Ricardian concepts. To the extent that the arguments of the radicals were taken up by the working-class movement, the claim to the whole produce of labour – or even to a greater proportion of the produce of labour – appeared as a monstrous assault on the very foundations of civilized society. The work of men like Charles Hall and Piercy Ravenstone might be safely ignored; but Hodgskin's *Labour Defended*, born as it was of the working-class activity which followed the repeal of the Combination Laws, could not be so easily passed over.[77] In a number of cases Hodgskin was attacked directly. The American economist Thomas Cooper wrote in 1830:

> The modern notions of Political Economy among the operatives or mechanics are stated, but not very distinctly, by Thomas Hodgskin in his treatise on *Popular Political Economy* . . . If these be the proposals that the mechanics combine to carry into effect, it is high time for those who have property to lose, and families to protect, to combine in self-defence.[78]

Charles Knight's edifying work, *The Rights of Industry*, published in 1831 under the superintendence of the Society for the Diffusion of Useful Knowledge, seems to have been aimed directly at Hodgskin, and had a very wide influence. Samuel Read obviously considers Hodgskin and others like him who flatter and persuade the workers "that they produce all" as the main enemies against whom his reasoning is directed;[79] and Scrope finds "truly unaccountable" the blindness of Hodgskin and all others who "declaim against capital as the poison of society, and the taking of interest on capital by its owners, as an abuse, an injustice, a robbery of the class of labourers!"[80]

It is hardly too much to say that every new development in economic thought in England about this time had the objective effect of cutting the ground from under the feet of writers like Hodgskin and William Thompson. And at least in some cases there can be little doubt that the critics of Ricardo knew exactly what they were doing and why they were doing it. Scrope, for example, was disarmingly frank. "At the time of the passing of the first Reform Bill," he wrote in 1873, "it became evident that the power of directing the Legislation of Britain was about to pass . . . from the hands of the few into those of the many." Wishing to

---

[77] Francis Place drew attention to the interesting fact that Hodgskin's ideas attracted large numbers of disillusioned Ownites (B.M., Place Ad. Mss., 27,791, F. 263).

[78] T. Cooper, *Lectures on Political Economy* (2nd edn.), pp. 350–53.

[79] Read, *Inquiry*, pp. 125–32, xxix, etc.

[80] G. P. Scrope, *Principles of Political Economy* (1833), pp. 150–51. See also the amusing passage in a review of Senior's lectures in the *Edinburgh Review*, Vol. 48, September 1828, pp. 170 ff.

estimate the probable results of this change upon "the social destinies of the country", Scrope endeavoured to ascertain "what were the notions likely to prevail among the masses, when they became the repositories of supreme power, with regard to the principal institutions of modern society". What lessons in this respect, he asked himself,

... were they likely to imbibe from the current doctrines of Political Economy? Were these lessons fitted to reconcile them to the hardships of a condition of almost ceaseless toil for, in many cases, but a meagre subsistence; and this in a country overflowing with wealth enjoyed in idleness by some at the expense (as might at first sight appear to them) of the labour of others? On examination of the works of the most noted Economists of the day, Messrs Ricardo, Jas. Mill, Maculloch, Malthus, Chalmers, and Whateley, I could not discover in them any answer likely to satisfy the mind of a half-educated man of plain common-sense and honesty who should seek there some justification for the immense disparity of fortunes and circumstances that strike the eye on every side. On the contrary, these works appeared to me to contain many obvious inconsistencies and errors, to inculcate many false and pernicious principles, and certainly to be little adapted to the purpose which I looked for in them.[81]

Approaching political economy in this spirit, it is hardly surprising that Scrope should have been the first British economist to propound a consistent version of the abstinence theory.[82] Samuel Read was another who understood perfectly well that Ricardian political economy could be made to lead logically to radicalism. His refutation of the "mischievous and fundamental error" of the "Ricardo economists" (*i.e.*, their doctrine that "labour is the only source of wealth") consists largely of an endeavour to put forward as many apologetic theories of profit as possible, regardless of consistency.[83] And Longfield, finally, was surely quite as fully aware of the political and ethical implications of his theory of distribution as was J. B. Clark of those of his some sixty years later. It seems not too unfair to say that economists like Scrope, Read and Longfield, in varying degrees, tended towards the view that if a doctrine "inculcated pernicious principles", if it denied that wealth under free competition was consigned to its "proper" owners, or if it could be so interpreted as to impugn the motives or capacity of the Almighty, then that doctrine must necessarily be false. Their fundamental approach, in other words, was determined by a belief that what was socially dangerous could not possibly be true.

To say that the work of Hodgskin and his fellow radicals had more to do with the innovations of the period than it is usual to admit is neither

---

[81] *Political Economy for Plain People*, Preface.
[82] *Quarterly Review*, January 1831, Vol. XLIV, p. 18.
[83] *Inquiry*, p. xxix and *passim*.

to deny the great originality and importance of some of the new contributions nor to assert that the majority of their authors were consciously indulging in apologetics. The writings of men like Bailey, West, Lloyd and Longfield possess an interest and significance which are by no means purely historical, and remain as important landmarks in a period of great anticipations. But surely something more than mere intellectual curiosity and the "inherent weaknesses" of the Ricardian system must be postulated to account for the iconoclastic attitude adopted towards that system by so many of the innovators. As I have suggested above, this attitude would seem to have been largely due to a feeling that any theory which suggested that the possibilities of uninterrupted and harmonious progress under capitalism were limited could not be true. Even Hodgskin admitted that he disapproved of certain of Ricardo's doctrines because they seemed "to set bounds to our hopes for the future progress of mankind in a more definite manner even than the opinions of Mr Malthus".[84]

It did not take very long for most of the more "pessimistic" Ricardian doctrines to fall into disuse or to be amended out of all recognition. In 1835, Mallet reports that "the whole artillery of the Club" was directed against Malthus's principle of population.[85] As early as 1831, as we have seen, the Club seems to have agreed that the interest of the landlord was not in fact in conflict with the interests of the other social classes, and also that the doctrine of the stationary state required radical amendment. In the early 30's it was widely suggested that industrial experience had proved Ricardo's theory of the inverse relationship between wages and profits to be false, since wages and profits might and often did increase together. The Ricardian concepts of value as embodied labour and profit as a kind of surplus value, which had proved so useful to the radicals, were among the first to be amended or rejected: value began to be conceived in terms of utility or cost of production, or sometimes (as with Bailey) as little more than a mere relation; and profit came to be explained not as the result of something which the labourer did but as the result of and reward for something which either the capitalist or his capital did. John Stuart Mill, growing up in this new revisionist atmosphere, found no difficulty in incorporating Senior's abstinence concept into his system and in substituting a rather superficial cost of production theory of value for Ricardo's labour theory. Ricardo's system, in short, was purged of most of its more obviously disharmonious elements, particularly those which might have been used to suggest that there was a real conflict of economic interest

---

[84] Letter to Place of 28th May 1820 (B.M., Place Add. Mss., 35,153).
[85] *Op. cit.*, p. 265.

between social classes under capitalism, or that progress under capitalism might be limited for some other reason.

IV

We are left, then, with Schumpeter's problem: if it is true that by the early 1830's "Ricardianism was . . . no longer a living force", how can we account for "the prevailing impression to the contrary"?[86] The factors which Schumpeter himself stressed – the faithfulness of the henchmen who continued to stand by their guns, the lag of public opinion, and "Ricardo's *personal* prestige" – were all no doubt quite important. The last was probably of more significance than the others, since, as Schumpeter pointed out, "J. S. Mill emphasized his early Ricardianism throughout and neither realized himself nor made it clear to his readers how far he had actually drifted away from it by the time he wrote his *Principles*".[87] But even more important, surely, was the fact that certain of the theoretical notions, attitudes and emphases which had characterized Ricardo's work did in fact survive the purge and reappear in Mill's *Principles* more or less unscathed. I am thinking here in particular of Ricardo's emphasis on "the progress of a country in wealth and the laws by which the increasing produce is distributed"[88] as one of the main problems of political economy; of his notion that the productivity of labour in agriculture governed the rate of profit on capital; of his insistence that the problem of value had to be tackled from the cost side; and of his acceptance of Say's Law proper and Mill's Theory. The indubitably "Ricardian" flavour of these ideas and emphases, put together as they were in a book which did actually effect something of a minor counter-revolution so far as "Ricardian" ideas in general were concerned, was sufficiently strong to lead contemporaries to believe that "Ricardianism" had indeed triumphed. The fact that Mill "only succeeded in upholding an *emasculated* version of Ricardo's system"[89] appeared less important than the fact that it was indeed a version of *Ricardo's* system which he upheld.

Only if one chooses to define the essence of Ricardo's system in terms of one or more of these ideas which survived, however, is it really possible to claim that "Ricardianism" won the victory. So far as Mill's Theory is concerned, I have given reasons above for the view that it cannot plausibly be described as fundamental to Ricardo's system. So

---

[86] Above, p. 54.
[87] *History of Economic Analysis*, p. 478.
[88] *Works*, Vol. VII, p. 24.
[89] M. Blaug, *Ricardian Economics* (New Haven, 1958), p. 167. (My italics.)

far as the cost approach to the value problem is concerned, I think it would be fairly generally agreed that there was nothing specifically "Ricardian" about this. This leaves only the first two ideas mentioned above. If one defines these, as Dr Blaug has recently done, as "the heart of the Ricardian system",[90] then the conclusion that "Ricardianism" won the victory naturally follows from the definition. My only real objection to this procedure is that it involves us in saying that most of Ricardo's opponents were themselves "Ricardians", since, as Dr Blaug himself points out, "most economists in the period, *including most of Ricardo's critics*, did believe that the amount of profit and, given the stock of capital, the rate of profit are governed by the efficiency of labour in agriculture".[91] Provided we recognize this, however, I see no reason why we should not use Dr Blaug's definition if the task we have in hand seems to require it. Each of the definitions of "Ricardianism" which we have considered – with the exception, perhaps, of that of Keynes – has helped to add something of importance to our knowledge of what actually happened during the period in question. It is the facts which are important, not the labels which we decide from time to time to attach to them.

[90] *Op. cit.*, p. 3.

[91] *Op. cit.*, p. 222. (My italics.) Cf. p. 226: "The Ricardian emphasis on economic growth and the changes in the distributive shares so permeated economic thinking in the period that even those who revolted against Ricardo's authority in fact accepted its essential outlook."

THOMAS JOPLIN AND
THE THEORY OF INTEREST[1]

I

Keynes's notion, that savings and investment should be regarded as determining not the rate of interest as the "Classical"[2] theory had assumed, but the volume of output and employment was no doubt the most significant feature of his contribution to economic thought.[3] Whereas the "Classical" economists thought in terms of the amount saved out of a given income, with the rate of interest as its most important determinant, we have now become accustomed to think in terms of the amount saved out of a variable income, with the effect of the rate of interest lumped together with that of the other factors upon which saving depends under the general heading of the propensity to save. Most "Classical" economists, of course, recognized that saving actually did vary with income, just as they usually recognized that income varied with investment; what they did not realize was the relevance of these facts to some of the problems (particularly the problem of employment) which their theory of interest was believed to illuminate. The "Classical" savings and investment curves were actually interdependent, but this did not become clear until the importance and relevance of changes in the level of income had been appreciated. Once the inhibiting assumption of a given income was dropped, income quite naturally began to appear as the primary variable in the savings function. The crucial step had then been taken, and the new Keynesian

---

[1] This essay is an amended version of an article which appeared in the *Review of Economic Studies*, No. 47, 1950–51. The amendments, which relate almost exclusively to the account of Ricardo's theory of accumulation in section II, have been made in an endeavour to take account of the criticism of my original views expressed by Professor Tucker in his *Progress and Profits in British Economic Thought* (Cambridge, 1960), pp. 108–10.

[2] In this essay, I use the word Classical in quotation marks in Keynes's sense, and without quotation marks in Marx's sense. (See Keynes, *General Theory*, p. 3, footnote.)

[3] This remark and those which immediately follow are not, of course, to be construed as contributions to the current "Keynes versus the Classics" controversy! They are intended merely to reflect the great liberating effect, in the years following the publication of the *General Theory*, of the simple "Keynesian savings-investment-income cross". Cf. Samuelson's 1946 comments on "the vitally important consumption function", reprinted in *Keynes' General Theory: Reports of Three Decades* (ed. Lekachman, New York, 1964), p. 330.

model began to fall into shape. If saving is a function of income, then saving decisions and investment decisions can be accommodated to one another only by means of changes in income.

But Keynes was not, of course, the first economist to insist upon the importance of the relation between saving and the ability to save: the Classical theory of accumulation also laid a considerable amount of emphasis on this relation. Nor was Keynes the first economist to assert that it was changes in the ability to save which accommodated the supply of savings to changes in the demand for loans: in this respect he had been substantially anticipated by Thomas Joplin in his *Outlines of a System of Political Economy*, which appeared in 1823. The main purpose of the present essay is to suggest that many contemporary genealogies of the Keynesian approach – which often concentrate on the Malthusian under-consumptionist doctrines and the glosses on "Say's Law" written by the early analysts of forced saving[4] – are seriously incomplete because of their neglect of Joplin's contribution and the tradition in which he wrote. The essay begins with a brief discussion of Ricardo's theory of accumulation, designed to place Joplin's work in its historical perspective; it then passes to a more detailed examination of the relevant passages in the *Outlines*; and it concludes with some speculations (inspired by one of Joplin's later works) as to the reasons for the failure of economists to follow up Joplin's line of approach in the post-Ricardian era.

II

There are two aspects of the Ricardian theory of capital accumulation which are of particular significance in the present connection. In the first place, the process of accumulation is visualized by Ricardo (as it had also been visualized by Smith) in terms of the disposition of the social labour force. "When we say that revenue is saved, and added to capital," Ricardo writes, "what we mean is, that the portion of revenue, so said to be added to capital, is consumed by productive instead of unproductive labourers."[5] The social surplus, or "net revenue", when it first comes into the hands of the landlord or capitalist,[6] is either expended by its recipient in the employment of unproductive labour

---

[4] E.g., T. Wilson, *Fluctuations in Income and Employment* (3rd edn., London, 1948), chapter I. Joplin himself, of course, was one of the most prominent of the "forced saving" writers, but I am not directly concerned with this aspect of his work in the present essay.

[5] *Works*, Vol. I, p. 151, footnote.

[6] Ricardo recognized that the labourer might also share in the net revenue (cf. *Works*, Vol. I, p. 348, footnote), but usually assumed that this fact could be neglected (cf. *Works*, Vol. II, pp. 380-1).

(menial servants, entertainers, etc.), or used by him as capital – that is, in the employment of productive labour.[7] If hoarding is regarded as an aberration which for all practical purposes can be ignored, and if full employment is assumed, then the net revenue must necessarily be used to support labour of one of these two types, and an increase in the rate of accumulation, other things being equal, will bring about an increase in the proportion of productive to unproductive labour in the social labour force.

In the second place, Ricardo more often than not seems to have taken the view that accumulation could most usefully be regarded as dependent upon the net revenue – and in particular (since "all savings are made from profits")[8] of that part of the net revenue which took the form of profits. Ricardo, like many of his contemporaries, often tended to treat the urge to accumulate on the part of those who had the power to do so rather as a datum presented by nature than as a factor which varied significantly with the rate of reward. "I consider the wants and tastes of mankind as unlimited", he wrote in a well-known letter to Malthus. "We all wish to add to our enjoyments or to our power. Consumption adds to our enjoyments, – *accumulation to our power*, and they equally promote demand."[9] If, then, the propensity to accumulate out of net revenue is given, at least up to a point, more or less independently of changes in the rate of reward, the main determinant of the volume of accumulation in an advancing economy is likely to be conceived as the *ability* to accumulate, which is measured by the volume of net revenue accruing to the saving classes. "High profits are favourable to the accumulation of capital", wrote Ricardo in the *Principles*;[10] and it seems fairly clear that when making this statement, and a large number of others like it, Ricardo was thinking primarily of the effect upon accumulation of a high volume, rather than a high rate, of profits.

It would be wrong, I think, to state categorically that Ricardo definitely conceived accumulation as a function not of the incentive but of the ability to accumulate. On a number of occasions he does seem to make reference to the existence of a functional relation between the supply of capital and the rate of reward. The great majority of these references, however, "concern the minimum rate below which no further additions would be made to capital",[11] thus strengthening the

---

[7] "Productive", speaking very broadly, was taken to mean productive of a surplus over cost. "Productive labour", again speaking very broadly, was labour employed on a capitalist basis.

[8] *Works*, Vol. IV, p. 234.

[9] *Ibid.*, Vol. VI, pp. 134–5. (My italics.)

[10] *Ibid.*, Vol. I, p. 334.

[11] Tucker, *op. cit.*, p. 109.

view that so far at any rate as English conditions were concerned
"Ricardo probably believed that a fairly substantial fall in the profit-
ability of investment would be necessary to produce a significant effect
on the supply of new capital".[12] But in two early letters,[13] and on one
occasion in the *Principles*,[14] Ricardo does make statements which are
open to the interpretation that he had in mind something like a continuous relation between accumulation and the rate of profit.[15] Nevertheless, statements of this type do seem to be the exception rather than
the rule. The situation was summed up by G. F. Shove in a well-known
article as follows:

> Ricardo's view about the supply of capital fluctuates. Sometimes his argu-
> ment seems to require the hypothesis that it is constant. Sometimes he inclines
> to treat it as depending on the rate of profit; sometimes as depending on the
> excess of aggregate output over what is required to maintain the population at
> the conventional standard of comfort. *On the whole, the last notion perhaps pre-
> dominates.* But he nowhere states that the amount of accumulation is a definite
> proportion or function of the surplus output.[16]

In view of the fact that so many of the statements relating accumulation
and the rate of profit are concerned with the situation which would
exist near the end of the descent to the stationary state, I would myself
wish to remove the word "perhaps" from the sentence I have italicized;
but apart from this the summary seems an admirably fair one.[17]

Now in so far as the supply of capital is regarded as being dependent
upon the net incomes of the saving classes, it follows that the supply of
capital can be accommodated to a change in the demand for it only
by means of a change in these net incomes. Ricardo, however, never
concerned himself with this problem; he was not particularly interested
in the process whereby savings from net revenue were transformed into
capital. The word "accumulation" in Classical political economy was
a blanket term covering both the action of saving a part of the net
revenue and the action of using the savings to employ productive

[12] *Ibid.*, p. 109.

[13] *Works*, Vol. VI, p. 121 (letter of 11th August 1814), and p. 134 (letter of 16th
September 1814).

[14] *Ibid.*, Vol. I, p. 122.

[15] In interpreting these passages, it should always be borne in mind that Ricardo
may be assuming that the supply of capital is stimulated by a rise in the rate of profit
because this rise increases the *income* of the capitalists and thus their *power* to accumulate. Cf. G. F. Shove, "The Place of Marshall's Principles in the Development of
Economic Theory", *The Economic Journal*, December 1942, p. 299.

[16] Shove, *op. cit.*, p. 299, footnote. (My italics.)

[17] The reader who wishes to arrive at his own judgement on this point may begin
by consulting the following references: *Works*, Vol. I, pp. 79, 98, 120, 122, 160, 166–7,
238, 290–91, 334 and 396; Vol. II, pp. 302, 308, 309 and 328–9; Vol. IV, pp. 35–6 and
234; Vol. VI pp. 121 and 134; Vol. VIII, p. 181; and Vol. IX, pp. 24–5.

labourers. The Classical economists were, of course, perfectly well aware that the act of saving and the act of investment were often performed by different persons and for different motives, but in general they were convinced that what happened in the money market was more or less irrelevant to the main body of economic analysis. This conviction was a natural consequence of their habit of viewing the process of accumulation in "real" terms – that is, in terms of the disposition of the social labour force. If an act of accumulation is visualized primarily in terms of the redisposition of the social labour force which results from it, there seems to be no good reason for emphasizing the distinction between the case where the man who does the saving employs his savings as capital himself, and the case where he lends them to someone else to employ as capital. In either case the saved portion of the net revenue will eventually be consumed "by productive instead of unproductive labourers". Both Smith and Ricardo assumed that it was unnecessary, at least in the main body of their analysis, to treat the two cases separately;[18] and the controversy between Ricardo and Malthus on the general glut question seems to have been conducted on the same assumption.[19] The question of the transformation of savings into capital was regarded as relevant, strictly speaking, only to the theory of money – a branch of enquiry separate from and definitely subordinate to the "real" analysis in which the

[18] Cf. Smith, *Wealth of Nations*, Vol. I, p. 320, and Ricardo, *Works*, Vol. I, p. 291.

[19] A failure to realize that the Classical economists regarded the act of saving and the act of investment simply as two facets of the single act of accumulation is responsible, I believe, for much over-valuation of Malthus's contribution. Malthus's argument was based on his belief that the amount spent out of income generated by new investment would not necessarily be sufficient to purchase all the new commodities at a profitable price, if the capitalists were committed to a policy of parsimony. The demand of the newly-employed workers would certainly increase by the amount of their wages, but the workers' demand alone was obviously insufficient to absorb the new commodities at a profitable price. And the deficiency of demand, generally speaking, could not be made up by increased consumption on the part of the capitalists, since their very decision to increase investment necessarily implied a corresponding increase in saving on their part, which was conceived by Malthus as involving a *national* diminution of consumption. Under conditions where capital was being rapidly accumulated, therefore, a general glut could only be avoided by an increase in the consumption of the "body of unproductive consumers". It is surely an exaggeration, then, to say that Malthus posed "the whole problem of the balance between Saving and Investment" (Keynes, *Essays in Biography*, pp. 146–7), or that he argued that the trouble was due to "sterile savings" (Wilson, *op. cit.*, p. 4). Some commentators speak as if Malthus visualized the general glut as resulting from a deflationary situation caused by the existence of idle savings, whereas in reality Malthus always regarded "saving" and "the conversion of revenue into capital" as two aspects of the same thing. The difference between the Keynesian and Malthusian systems is indeed striking: in the former, investment is regarded as an invigorating factor necessarily promoting and extending demand, whereas in the latter, under certain conditions, it is regarded as a depressive factor because it is believed to involve a relative diminution of effective demand.

Classical economists were chiefly interested. Ricardo's discussion of money tended to be confined to isolated passages bearing little relation to the remainder of the argument. On the one hand, there was the long-period analysis of the economy as a whole, conducted almost entirely in "real" terms on the assumption that money did not matter; on the other hand, on what was virtually a separate plane of discourse, there was the theory of money. The savings-investment problem could only interest an economist who was concerned with the examination of short-period rather than long-period equilibrium, and who was interested in the theory of the *monetary economy*. Such an economist was Thomas Joplin, who attacked the problem in his *Outlines* in the year of Ricardo's death.

III

The *Outlines* is a curious and ill-ordered medley of plagiarism, superstition and intuitive wisdom. It was written, the sub-title tells us, "with a view to prove to Government and the country, that the cause of the present agricultural distress is entirely artificial; and to suggest a plan for the management of the currency, by which it may be remedied now, and any recurrence of similar evils be prevented in future". Joplin's purpose was to advocate the establishment of English joint stock banks, on the Scottish model, and to call for an alteration of the Bank of England charter to enable this to be done. He had begun his campaign in February 1822 with an *Essay on Banking*, which apparently had a certain amount of success. His view was that the issues of the country banks, under the regime which he was attacking, "are not regulated by those of the Bank of England, but are improperly influenced by the pressure and anti-pressure of capital, independently of the Bank of England, or of the Country Bankers themselves".[20] After the publication of the *Essay on Banking*, Joplin seems to have decided that his "plan for a self-regulating system of Currency, which would prevent fluctuations in prices"[21] would possibly appear more plausible if the theory of money upon which it was based were related to the real analysis with which contemporary economists like Ricardo were primarily concerned. The *Outlines* was the result. The book, as Joplin later admitted, was "composed with a very imperfect knowledge of the writings of others, on the same subject", and did not succeed in attracting much attention. Nevertheless, it is something of a landmark in the history of economic thought. "The title was somewhat ambitious,"

---

[20] *Analysis and History of the Currency Question* (1832), pp. 120-1.
[21] *Ibid.*, p. 141.

Joplin himself said of it, "but the opinions were new, whether they were well or ill founded."[22]

The sections of the *Outlines* to which I wish to draw attention commence with a familiar proposition which Joplin calls "the fulcrum of the argument":

> The first thing necessary to the annual production of any commodity is, that there should be an annual consumption and demand for it. Its production is, in fact, a proof of its consumption. Without consumption no demand could exist, and no production would take place. Demand, on the other hand, proceeds from income. . . . This conclusion is, therefore, obvious – that if to the existence of an annual income of 430 millions, an expenditure of 430 millions be necessary, in order to cause that demand which gives rise to it, and there is no other source of income from whence this consumption can proceed, every shilling of the 430 millions must be annually spent.[23]

Four short chapters dealing with various aspects of the national income follow. The fourth, dealing with the manner in which the income of society is consumed, is the most interesting. "In whatever way a person acquires the money he receives," Joplin writes, "he must do one of three things with it. He must either hoard it, lend it at interest to others, or expend it himself."[24] If he hoards it – which, as it later appears, he is in fact very unlikely to do – reactions in the sphere of foreign trade will ensure that the "ultimate demand" for commodities is not diminished. If he lends it to others at interest, they will expend it either "commercially" or "actually" – that is, either "in building houses or ships, or digging mines, etc., . . . in the manufacture of goods, or in the purchase and sale of them", or "in the actual purchase, consumption, and enjoyment of the necessaries, conveniences, and luxuries of life". And finally, if he expends it himself, "it must be either in actual or commercial consumption as above described: so that whether he saves the money, or whether he spends it, consumption is equally produced".[25]

So far, Joplin is merely elaborating a number of propositions which had been popularized by Smith and Ricardo.[26] But the terms in which Joplin expressed them, and the purpose which motivated him, resulted in his placing unusual emphasis on a problem which the Classical approach had hitherto tended to conceal – the problem of the adjustment of the supply of savings to the demand for loans. This problem is dealt

[22] *Ibid.*, p. 141.   [23] *Outlines*, p. 33.
[24] *Ibid.*, p. 44.   [25] *Ibid.*, pp. 44–5.
[26] Cf. Smith, *Wealth of Nations*, Vol. I, p. 302, and Ricardo, *Works*, Vol. I, pp. 290–91.

with in the remarkable chapter entitled "Principles which Regulate the Saving of Money".[27]

Joplin begins as follows: "As all the income of society is, and must be, annually consumed, all the money which is borrowed, in order to be spent by one person, class, or body of individuals, must be necessarily saved by another." If nobody saved, it would be impossible to borrow, and if no one consumed more than his annual income it would be impossible to lend. It follows (if it be assumed that hoarding is "very little practised") that "the demand for money on the one hand, and supply of it on the other, must be equal. The amount of the savings by those who do spend their annual incomes, must be precisely equal to those whose expenditure exceeds them." But this is an *ex post* correspondence. How are supply and demand *made* equal?

In approaching this problem, Joplin deals in turn with the demand side and the supply side. First, why do people want to borrow? A "demand for money" (*i.e.*, for loans), Joplin asserts, is produced by four different causes:

> By the necessity which exists in an improving country for an increased stock of buildings, machinery, commodities, &c., in order to supply the increased population and consumption which its increased fertility creates. By losses in trade and commerce. By the excess of expenditure of those whose expenses exceed their incomes; and by the wants of government.

After discussing each of these four causes, Joplin proceeds to consider the supply side. First, who supplies the money which people borrow on the money market? The labourers are usually unable to save, finding their incomes in general "too small to supply their customary wants". Those whose incomes are derived from property are able to save but have little incentive to do so. "Being secure of the annual receipts of their incomes, and in consequence removed from any anxious cares respecting the future, they live in general to the full extent of them." The people who do the bulk of the saving, then – the "economists of society", as Joplin calls them – "principally consist of the mercantile classes". "The capitalists of society", he writes in another place, "are a country's greatest economists."[28] An interesting statement of the motives which induce these "economists" to save part of their incomes now follows:

---

27 Chapter X, pp. 57–70. Individual page references will not be given for quotations from this chapter. It should be noted that Joplin's analysis in these passages is based on the assumption that his "plan for a self-regulating system of Currency" has actually been put into effect, so that money plays an essentially passive role in the economy, and an increased demand for loans can only be met by an increased supply of savings.

28 *Outlines*, p. 251. Cf. Ricardo, *Works*, Vol. IV, p. 234: "As all savings are made from profits, as a country is most happy when it is in a rapidly progressive state, profits and interest cannot be too high."

Being dependant upon trades of precarious profit for their support, they learn the inclination of acquiring money from the habit of doing so. It is necessary for every tradesman who means to do well to save money, in order to provide against a future evil day, which the uncertainty of trade often produces. This necessity, the desire for independence, and the ambition to be rich, which the pursuits of trade usually generate, render this class, in general, economists, and the savings of society are principally made by them.[29]

There is no suggestion in this account that the "economists" are interested in the actual rate of reward for saving, and we are accordingly prepared for the important proposition which follows:

The amount of savings by this class must altogether depend upon their power to save. When the interest of money, and profits of trade are large, their power of saving is necessarily greater than when the profits of trade, and interest of money are small. When their income is great, they can of course save more than when it is little.

Joplin's unambiguous acceptance of this idea meant that the terms in which the problem of the adjustment of the supply of savings to the demand for loans could be discussed were fairly rigidly defined. If the demand for loans increased, the supply of savings could increase correspondingly only if the increased demand set up reactions which ultimately increased the *ability* of the "economists" to save – *i.e.*, which increased "the profits of trade, and interest of money". In other words, the supply of savings could be adjusted to a change in the demand for loans only through the medium of an induced change in the net incomes of the saving classes.

The mechanism whereby the necessary changes in net incomes occurred, as Joplin described it, was set in motion by changes in the rate of interest. Like the majority of writers in the Classical tradition, Joplin seems to have believed that the rate of interest in the short period was regulated by "the demand for money", but that the *supply* of savings was not directly dependent on the rate of interest.[30] An increase in the "demand for money", therefore, would raise the rate of interest, but, since saving was a function not of the rate of interest but of the net incomes of the saving classes, the rise in the rate of interest would not *directly* affect the volume of saving – that is, it would not affect

[29] The last part of this statement is somewhat similar to that made by Ricardo in his letter to Malthus of 16th September 1814, which is referred to above, p. 59. But whereas Ricardo treats the desire for power as an attribute of "mankind" in the abstract, Joplin realizes that it is actually generated by "the pursuits of trade".

[30] Cf. *Outlines*, p. 62: "If a person have money, and he cannot get five per cent. interest for it, he must take four; if not four, three, &c. Any rate of interest, with good security, will be better than hoarding it." Joplin elsewhere recognizes that the *demand* for loans will be increased by a reduction in the rate of interest: see the interesting statement in *Outlines*, p. 184.

it through the medium of the incentive, as it was often conceived to do in the neo-Classical model. The rise in the rate of interest could affect the volume of saving in the appropriate manner only if it initiated an economic change which eventually increased the net incomes of the "economists" to exactly the required extent.

This is precisely what Joplin believed would happen, although the exact manner in which he thought that the mechanism of adjustment would work is not very clearly stated. Suppose, he argues, that the demand for money increases, while the supply of savings remains the same. The rate of interest will then immediately rise, and the following reactions will ensue:

> Profits are raised with the demand for money, by part of that money being lent for consumption, which would otherwise have gone to replace the stock of the dealer. By this means the consumptive demand is increased, and the prices of commodities raised; while, by the diminished capital in trade, stocks are kept low, and the prices kept up. Much of the capital employed in trade is borrowed of bankers, and others, by persons in trade, at the market rate of interest; and the first effect of any increased demand for money, is to induce these bankers to abstract it from its ordinary channels, in order to lend to those who offer better terms for it.[31]

Suppose, on the other hand, that the demand for money falls while the supply remains the same. In that case a different set of reactions will occur:

> If a person in trade has saved money, and cannot obtain good employment for it otherwise, he will put it into his trade; and this being done by all persons in the same trade, who have saved money, and cannot do better with it, the competition will reduce the rate of profits in that trade; or the lowered rate of interest will drive persons into the trade, as a means of obtaining a better income, who would otherwise have lived upon the interest of their capital without trade. The general effect of this is, that less income is obtained than before; that though there is more capital in trade, less profit, upon the aggregate, is derived from it. Thus the trading part of the community are unable to save money as heretofore. . . .[32]

These influences affecting the ability to save are reinforced by others which inversely affect the ability to spend. For example, when the interest rate rises, consequent upon an increase in the demand for loans, the value of land will fall. "An estate which would be worth forty years

[31] This argument may become more comprehensible if it is remembered that Joplin is (a) placing an emphasis, now unfamiliar, on the demand for loans for consumptive purposes, and (b) assuming that the increased demand for loans can be satisfied only by an actual increase in savings.

[32] *Analysis*, p. 105. There is no comparable statement in the *Outlines*, but the passage in the *Analysis* seems to express the interpretation placed by Joplin on the quotation from Smith appearing on p. 63 of the *Outlines*.

purchase with the interest of money at $2\frac{1}{2}$ per cent., would be worth only half that with the interest of money at five, and would only have half the spending in it. For this reason, as the demand for government [*sic*] increased, the power of spending by individuals would be diminished." On the other hand, if the interest rate falls, consequent upon a decrease in the demand for loans, "temptations to expenditure are held out by the increased value of landed property".

In both cases, then, the incomes of the "economists" will vary in the right direction, so that the "annual supply of incipient capital" is increased or diminished as required. It is fairly obvious that this analysis, while its ingenuity can scarcely be denied, leaves one asking a whole number of new questions. But the conclusions which Joplin draws from it are sufficiently remarkable to deserve full quotation:

Thus, with the increase or decrease of the demand for money, do interest and profits of trade rise and fall, by which the power of economizing, in order to supply the demand, is exactly proportioned to it.

The savings of a nation, therefore, diminish the power to save. The incomes of those being reduced, who are the principal economists of the country, their power of economizing is reduced with the excessive supply of money, by which the value of it is diminished.

The Dutch are the most saving people in Europe; and with them the profits of trade, and interest of money, are always at a very low ebb. When the bulk of a nation are economists, the difficulty of making money becomes excessive; and the commercial part of it is ground down to penuriousness by the national parsimony.

Precisely opposite are the effects produced by an increase of national expenditure. The profits of trade are good, and a free stile of living pervades the mercantile classes; they not only save more money, but they also spend more.

Such an unusual increase of expenditure as to raise the interest of money, rarely, however, perhaps never, happens from the expenditure of individuals. It mostly, if not always, arises from the demands of governments.

It is important to note, however, that Joplin did not visualize the process of adjustment of the supply of savings to the demand for loans as necessarily involving a variation in the *real* income of the community. He seems to have supposed that any maladjustment would correct itself automatically without affecting "national prosperity". "The profits of trade," he writes, "which fall upon the price of commodities, must be nothing more than a tax paid by the ultimate consumers of them, and . . . just in proportion as the tradesman flourishes the consumer suffers. If the whole income of society must be consumed, it is only a different mode of arranging that consumption, and nationally there is no greater prosperity with great profits than with small ones." The idea that a general depression ever exists, Joplin maintained, was simply a figment of the capitalists' imagination. But it is clear from other passages in the *Outlines* that Joplin was well aware of the fact that the process of adjustment, under certain circumstances, might involve variations in employment. For example, in the first of his chapters on money, he describes how, "in a year of extraordinary abundance", the price of corn will not fall in proportion to the increased supply, and the farmer's profits will accordingly increase. "The surplus above what is necessary for his rent is placed in banks, or lent to those who immediately expend it in the employment of labour; by which means it makes shorter circuits, more labour is employed, and a greater consumption is created." And the effect of cheap money upon employment is summed up in the following passage:

> Money, being more abundant, creates itself employment, either by the increased facilities with which it is lent out, or by the reduced interest which is charged for it; by which means traders are induced to increase their merchant stocks, and people in general to enter into undertakings in which the employment of labour is involved; but which, with a greater scarcity of money, they would not have attempted.[33]

IV

In his *Analysis and History of the Currency Question*, published in 1832, Joplin included a summary of the doctrines I have just outlined. This summary is interesting because Joplin incorporated certain new features which did not appear in the original presentation of the theory in the *Outlines* – features which may help to account for the failure of contemporary economists to follow up Joplin's line of approach.

Joplin was concerned in the *Analysis* to make a very much sharper distinction between the monetary system he was advocating and the actual system of his own time than he had made in the *Outlines*. His own system envisaged an indestructible metal currency or "a paper currency constructed on similar principles"; under the prevailing system, on the other hand, the country banks were "issuers of the currency" as well as "dealers in incipient capital".[34] Under the projected system, Joplin argued, "there never is, for any length of time, more money than there is a demand for",[35] because any discrepancy between the supply of savings and the demand for loans is immediately adjusted by means of the mechanism described in the *Outlines*. Under the actual

---

[33] *Outlines*, p. 184. On the following pages Joplin describes the "opposite effects" produced in "years of scarcity". The analysis is still being conducted on the assumption that the banks cannot meet an increased demand for loans by an extension of their issues: cf. *Outlines*, pp. 214–5.

[34] *Analysis*, pp. 108–9.   [35] *Ibid.*, p. 107.

system, however, the rate of interest charged by the country banks bears little relation to the "true" or "natural" rate, and the adjustment of the supply of savings to the demand for loans may well be achieved only at the expense of violent fluctuations in the value of money.[36]

In the *Analysis*, then, Joplin was more concerned to emphasize the *automatic* character of the process whereby the supply of savings was adjusted to changes in the demand for loans under the "natural" system. In the *Outlines*, the whole emphasis had been laid upon the functional connection between saving and the ability to save. In the *Analysis* this emphasis is somewhat less, and Joplin is obviously looking for additional factors which will help to bring the supply of savings back into equality with the demand for loans even more smoothly and harmlessly, if one happens to get out of step with the other. Suppose, for example, that the demand for loans falls. The rate of interest will then fall, and, according to the scheme of the *Outlines*, this will ultimately induce the necessary reduction in the net incomes of the saving classes. In the *Analysis* this same effect is visualised as occurring but it is reinforced by two additional effects. In the first place, Joplin stresses the fact that a lowered rate of interest will tend to stimulate once again the *demand* for loans. He points out that a fall in the rate of interest "has a general tendency to cause an increase of stocks in all trades; it induces people to build houses; and . . . leads to the embarking capital in great public undertakings, which would otherwise not have been ventured upon". In the second place, and more significantly, Joplin for the first time mentions the fact that a lowered rate of interest will tend to reduce the *inducement* to save. When the rate of interest falls, says Joplin, the following additional reaction will occur:

The man of landed or fixed income is less tempted to save than he was before. Saving is made by a sacrifice of present enjoyment, for a future good, in the shape of an increase of annual income. But as the annual income to be derived from saving diminishes, the temptation to save is reduced. In this way, likewise, a superabundance of the savings of income, or incipient capital, and a fall of interest, will also operate in checking the future supply.[37]

Now Joplin's use of this idea that saving depends not only on the ability to save but also on the incentive was quite clearly associated

[36] It was in this connection that Joplin developed his ideas on forced saving, to which a number of writers have drawn attention. See, e.g., Hayek, "A Note on the Development of the Doctrine of 'Forced Saving' ", *Quarterly Journal of Economics*, November 1932; Viner, *Studies in the Theory of International Trade* (New York, 1937), pp. 190–92; and Niebyl, *Studies in the Classical Theories of Money* (New York, 1946), pp. 109–10.

[37] *Analysis*, p. 106. The statement is expressed to apply only to "the man of landed or fixed income", but it is otherwise perfectly general, and there is no obvious reason why Joplin should not have applied it to *all* savers.

with a desire to show that the economic system, in itself, was fundamentally sound and self-adjusting. Joplin wanted to demonstrate that
if any tendency towards disequilibrium was not swiftly[38] and painlessly
corrected, this was the fault of the irrational – and alterable – monetary
superstructure. Any trouble which was experienced must be due to
something external to the system itself.[39] Such a thesis would obviously
be rendered more plausible by any argument which gave added
emphasis to the automatic character of the process of adjustment. This
suggests one possible reason why the concept of saving as a function of
the rate of reward succeeded in becoming popular in the post-Ricardian
era – because it could be usefully employed in support of the contention
that capitalism was a stable and self-adjusting system.

It is also significant, I think, that Joplin should have associated this
new idea with the proposition that "saving is made by a sacrifice of
present enjoyment, for a future good, in the shape of an increase of
annual income". This notion, which was destined to form the foundation of the neo-Classical theory of interest, had never been emphasized
by Smith or Ricardo. It became fashionable only when economists
began to feel obliged to demonstrate that interest (or profit) was a
reward for the act of saving (or accumulation) – an obligation which
began to appear particularly pressing after the middle 20's, when the
"Ricardian socialists" had shown the unfortunate use to which the
Classical concept of surplus and the labour theory of value could be
put.[40] To demonstrate that interest was a reward for the act of saving,
rather than an income in the nature of a surplus, it was necessary, first,
to discover some aspect of the saving process which could plausibly be
presented as involving a real cost or sacrifice on the part of the saver,
and, second, to posit a direct functional relationship between the
volume of saving and the rate of interest. It is sometimes assumed by
historians of economic thought[41] that the idea of a functional connection between the supply of capital and its return (involving the
recognition of a real cost lying behind accumulation) was a necessary
element in the Ricardian theory of equilibrium. This does not appear
to me to have been the case: the idea was not in fact developed with
any degree of clarity and distinctness until it was found desirable to
stress the existence of such a cost.

[38] Some of the reactions which Joplin describes are hardly consistent with his suggestion that the process of adjustment was relatively swift. Cf. *Analysis*, p. 106, where
the reduction of rents due to an increase in house-building is conceived as an element
in the mechanism of adjustment.

[39] Cf. above, p. 64.

[40] Cf. above, pp. 68–73.

[41] E.g., Marian Bowley, *Nassau Senior and Classical Economics*, p. 140.

The tendency to think of saving as being primarily a function of the rate of interest, then, may at least in its origin have been associated with the desire to show, first, that the economic system was fundamentally stable, and, second, that it was not founded on the exploitation of the labourer. But one other factor of some importance intensified the tendency, and was largely responsible for the failure of orthodox economics to exorcize it before 1936. Professor Myint has drawn attention to the significant difference between the economic problem with which the Classical economists were concerned, and that with which we are mainly concerned today.[42] The Classical economists were chiefly interested in the problem of *increasing* the wealth of the nation – in securing abundance. Modern economists, on the other hand (at least since the 1870's), have become interested primarily in the problem of *allocating* a given pool of resources as "efficiently" as possible – in making the best of scarcity.[43] Now, for obvious reasons, the idea that saving should be regarded as a function of the rate of interest has usually been associated with theories which think in terms of the amount saved out of a given income. The idea that saving should be regarded as a function of income, on the other hand, has usually been stressed by economists who were mainly interested in the causes of variations in income. The transfer of attention from the Classsical to the modern economic problem, then, meant that the concept of saving as a function of income, upon which Joplin built his analysis in the *Outlines*, began to appear not only as inferior to its successor from an apologetic point of view, but also as actually irrelevant.

---

[42] *Theories of Welfare Economics* (London, 1948), *passim*. I have left this reference and the remarks which follow as they stood in the original article, since the kind of qualification to which they are now subject will be sufficiently obvious to readers.

[43] It is interesting to speculate on the reasons for this change of emphasis. Possibly the crucial point may be that the decade in which the new marginal techniques began to become popular was one in which it was widely believed that the rate of economic growth had at last been checked.

PART TWO
MARXIST ECONOMICS

KARL MARX'S
ECONOMIC METHOD[1]

I

Most of the great "heroic" economic models of a dynamic character which have been put forward in the course of the history of economic thought – those of Quesnay, Smith, Ricardo and Marx, for example – possess certain important characteristics in common. The model-builder usually begins, on the basis of a preliminary examination of the facts, by adopting what Schumpeter has called a "vision" of the economic process. In other words, he begins by orienting himself towards some key factor or factors which he regards as being of vital causal significance so far as the structure and development of the economic system as a whole are concerned. With this vision uppermost in his mind, he then proceeds to a more thorough examination of the economic facts both of the present situation and of the past situations which have led up to it, and arranges these facts in order on what might be called a scale of relevance. Their position on this scale will depend upon such factors as the particular vision which the model-builder has adopted, his political and social sympathies, and the extent to which the facts display uniformities and regularities which promise to be capable of causal analysis in terms of the postulation of "laws" and "tendencies".

Taking the facts which he has placed at the top of the scale as his foundation, the model-builder proceeds to develop certain concepts, categories and methods of classification which he believes will help him to provide a generalized explanation of the structure and development of the economy. In this part of his work he has necessarily to rely to some extent on concept-material inherited from the past, but he also tries to work out new analytical devices of his own. The particular analytical devices which he employs – his tools and techniques, as it were – are thus by no means arbitrarily chosen. To quite a large extent they are dependent upon the nature of his vision, the nature of the primary facts which they are to be used to explain, and the nature of the *general* method of analysis which he decides to adopt. The degree of their dependence upon these factors, however, varies from one device to

---

[1] Parts of this essay are based on an article entitled "Karl Marx's Economics", which was originally published in *The New Reasoner*, Autumn 1959.

another. Whereas some of the devices may be useless or even harmful when the facts to be analysed and the orientation, aim and general method of analysis of the model-builder are radically different, others may have a greater degree of general applicability. Some may well prove useful when applied to other forms of market economy, and some may even be "universal" in the sense in which, say, statistical techniques are "universal".

With the aid of these devices, then, the model-builder proceeds to the theoretical analysis of the particular economic facts which he has placed at the top of his scale of relevance. He endeavours to give a causal explanation of the uniformities and regularities which he has observed in these facts; he affords these explanations the status of "laws" or "tendencies"; and he gathers together these laws and tendencies into his first theoretical approximation. He then takes into account the facts next in order on the scale of relevance, from which he has hitherto abstracted, enquires into the extent to which their introduction into the picture requires a modification of the laws and tendencies of the first approximation, and thus arrives at his second approximation. He may well then proceed to a third, fourth, etc., approximation, progressively taking into account facts which he has placed lower and lower on the scale of relevance; but obviously there must come a time when it is not worth while to proceed any further down the scale. At the point where the basic laws and tendencies begin to be submerged beneath the exceptions and qualifications, he usually stops. The facts further down in the scale of relevance are simply abstracted from.

The final task is to use the model for the purpose of making concrete predictions – a task which is carried out largely by extrapolating the laws and tendencies into the future, on the express or implied assumption that the economic facts will continue to maintain their assumed position on the scale of relevance. The model which finally emerges is therefore compounded of elements not only of the past and present but also of the future.

This description of the model-building process is necessarily somewhat schematic, and I certainly do not mean to imply that all the great model-builders *consciously* adopted this intricate methodological approach. In essence, however, this was the method which most of them did in actual fact adopt, whether or not they were fully aware of what they were doing. It does help, I think, to have this general scheme in mind when we are analysing the economic work of a thinker like Marx – particularly if we are analysing it with a view to discovering whether and in what sense it is still relevant today.

II

The application of this general scheme to Marx's model is easier than in the case of most of the other great models, because Marx was more conscious of what he was doing than most of his predecessors in the field. The key causal factor towards which Marx began by orienting himself was the socio-economic production relation between the class of capital-owners and the class of wage-earners. This relation, he believed, gave birth to the main contemporary forms of unearned income and to the possibility of the large-scale accumulation of capital; and this accumulation led in turn to rapid technological progress, which interacted with the capital-labour relation to determine the main features of the structure of capitalism and the main lines of the development of the system as a whole.

This was in effect Marx's "vision" of the capitalist economic process. With this vision uppermost in his mind, he made a thorough examination of the economic facts both of the past and the present. The most relevant fact appeared to him to be the existence in all forms of class society of a mass of unearned income, which in capitalist society mainly took the form of net profit on capital, rent of land, and interest. Associated with this were certain other important facts or tendencies of a historical character which Marx's study of capitalist development in the past revealed to him – notably the progressive decline in the rate of profit; the increasing subordination of formerly independent workers to the capitalist form of organization; the increasing economic instability of the system; the growth of mechanization with its accompanying changes in the industrial structure; the emergence of various forms of monopoly; the growth of the "reserve army of labour"; and the general deterioration in the condition of the working class. It is important to emphasize that these facts, by and large, were regarded by Marx simply as the *data* of his problem. As anyone can see by glancing at his *Economic and Philosophic Manuscripts of 1844*,[2] Marx had placed these facts at the top of his scale of relevance long before he came to work out the detailed tools and techniques required to analyse them.

The next stage – conceptually if not chronologically – was the development of Marx's *general* method of analysis, which was intimately associated with his vision of the economic process. Three aspects of this general method are worthy of note in the present connection.

In the first place, Marx had begun, as Lenin put it, "by selecting from all social relations the 'production relations', as being the basic

---

[2] An English language edition of these manuscripts was published by the Foreign Languages Publishing House, Moscow, in 1959.

and prime relations that determine all other relations".[3] In *Capital*, where he sets out to deal with "one of the economic formations of society – the system of commodity production", Marx's analysis is "strictly confined to the relations of production between the members of society: without ever resorting to factors other than relations of production to explain the matter, Marx makes it possible to discern how the commodity organization of social economy develops, how it becomes transformed into capitalist economy, creating the antagonistic . . . classes, the bourgeoisie and the proletariat, how it develops the productivity of social labour and how it thereby introduces an element which comes into irreconcilable contradiction to the very foundations of this capitalist organization itself".[4] In the context of the particular range of enquiry encompassed in *Capital*, it is evident that "relations of production" must be taken to include not only the specific set of relations of subordination or co-operation within which commodity production is carried out at each particular stage of its historical development (e.g., the capitalist stage), but also the broad basic relation between men as producers of commodities which persists through-out the whole period of commodity production.[5]

In the second place, within the framework of the methodological approach just outlined and in close association with it, Marx developed a highly idiosyncratic method of enquiry – it might perhaps be called the "logical-historical" method – which was one of the more interesting and significant of the fruits of his early Hegelian studies.[6] The description which Engels gave of this method in a review of Marx's *Critique of Political Economy* in 1859 has not been bettered, and the following extract can be reproduced without apology:

> The criticism of economics . . . could . . . be exercised in two ways: historically or logically. Since in history, as in its literary reflection, development as a whole proceeds from the most simple to the most complex relations, the historical development of the literature of political economy provided a natural guiding thread with which criticism could link up and the economic categories as a whole would thereby appear in the same sequence as in the logical development. This form apparently has the advantage of greater clearness, since indeed

[3] V. I. Lenin, *Selected Works* (London, 1939), Vol. II, p. 418.

[4] *Ibid.*, pp. 420–1. Lenin adds that Marx, "while 'explaining' the structure and development of the given formation of society 'exclusively' in terms of relations of production, . . . nevertheless everywhere and always went on to trace the superstructure corresponding to these relations of production and clothed the skeleton in flesh and blood" (*ibid.*, p. 421).

[5] "Commodity production" in the Marxist sense means roughly the production of goods for exchange on some sort of market by individual producers or groups of producers who carry on their activities more or less separately from one another.

[6] Cf. below, p. 156.

it is the *actual* development that is followed, but as a matter of fact it would thereby at most become more popular. History often proceeds by jumps and zigzags and it would in this way have to be followed everywhere, whereby not only would much material of minor importance have to be incorporated but there would be much interruption of the chain of thought; furthermore, the history of economics could not be written without that of bourgeois society and this would make the task endless, since all preliminary work is lacking. The logical method of treatment was, therefore, the only appropriate one. But this, as a matter of fact, is nothing else than the historical method, only divested of its historical form and disturbing fortuities. The chain of thought must begin with the same thing that this history begins with and its further course will be nothing but the mirror-image of the historical course in abstract and theoretically consistent form, a corrected mirror-image but corrected according to laws furnished by the real course of history itself, in that each factor can be considered at its ripest point of development, in its classic form.[7]

This then was another important aspect of Marx's general method of analysis. No doubt this "logical-historical" approach was sometimes carried to excess (for reasons which Marx himself partly explained in his "Afterword" to the second German edition of *Capital*),[8] but in his hands it proved on the whole to be very fruitful. It was particularly important, as will shortly be seen, in connection with the theory of value developed in *Capital*.

In the third place, and again closely associated with the two other aspects just described, there was the important notion that if one wished to analyse capitalism in terms of relations of production the best way of doing this was to imagine capitalism suddenly impinging upon a sort of generalized pre-capitalist society in which there were as yet no separate capital-owning or land-owning classes. What one ought to do, in other words, was to begin by postulating a society in which, although commodity production and free competition were assumed to reign more or less supreme, the labourers still owned the whole produce of their labour. Having investigated the simple laws which would govern production, exchange and distribution in a society of this type, one ought then to imagine capitalism suddenly impinging upon this society. What difference would this impingement make to the economic laws which had operated before the change, and why would it make this difference? If one could give adequate answers to these questions, Marx believed, one would be well on the way to revealing the real essence of the capitalist mode of production. In adopting this kind of approach, Marx was of course following – and developing further – a long and respectable tradition which had been established

[7] Engels, *Ludwig Feuerbach*, pp. 98–9.
[8] *Capital*, Vol. I, pp. 19–20.

by Smith and Ricardo. Marx's postulation of an abstract pre-capitalist society based on what he called "simple" commodity production was not essentially different in aim from Adam Smith's postulation of an "early and rude" society inhabited by deer and beaver hunters. Neither in Marx's case nor in that of Smith was the postulated pre-capitalist society intended to be an accurate representation of historical reality in anything more than the very broadest sense. Nor was it intended as a picture of an ideal form of society, a sort of golden age of the past which the coming of the wicked capitalists and landlords was destined rudely to destroy. It was clearly part of a quite complex analytical device, and in its time a very powerful one. I am accustomed to tell my students that it was not a *myth*, as some critics maintain, but rather *mythology*.

This, then, was the nature of Marx's *general* method of economic analysis, in the context of which his other tools and techniques were developed and employed. Some of these were inherited by Marx from his predecessors – the concept of equilibrium, for example, and the particular classification of social classes and class incomes which he adopted. Others were newly developed, such as the important distinctions between abstract and concrete labour, labour and labour-power, and constant and variable capital. As his analysis proceeded, certain other concepts, relations and techniques emerged – notably the concept of surplus value, the distinction between relative and absolute surplus value, the ratios representing the rate of surplus value, the rate of profit and the organic composition of capital, and the techniques associated with his famous reproduction schemes.

In so far as it is possible to distinguish *methods* and *tools* of analysis from the *results* of analysis, then, these were some of the main methods and tools which Marx employed to analyse the economic facts which he had placed at the top of his scale of relevance. The uniformities and regularities which he believed he could detect in these facts were analysed in terms of the relations of production, with the aid of these methods and tools; and causal explanations emerged which were generalized in the form of tendencies and laws, modified in the second and subsequent approximations, and eventually extrapolated into the future in the form of more or less concrete predictions.

III

The most important field of application of Marx's general economic method was of course the *theory of value* elaborated in *Capital*. Indeed, Marx's theory of value is perhaps best regarded as being in essence a kind of generalized expression, or embodiment, of his economic method.

In his analysis of value, as Engels noted, Marx "proceeds from the simple production of commodities as the historical premise, ultimately to arrive from this basis [at] capital". In other words, he begins with the "simple" commodity, and then proceeds to analyse its "logically and historically secondary form" – the "capitalistically modified commodity".[9] The first part of his analysis of value therefore consists of a set of statements concerning the way in which relations of production influence the prices of goods in that abstract pre-capitalist form of society of which I have just spoken above. The second part of his analysis consists of a further set of statements concerning the way in which this basic causal connection between prices and relations of production is modified when *capitalist* relations of production impinge upon those appropriate to "simple" commodity production – *i.e.*, when the "simple" commodity becomes "capitalistically modified". This process of capitalistic modification is conceived to take place in two logically separate stages. In the first stage, it is assumed, capital subordinates labour on the basis of the technical conditions in which it finds it, and does not immediately change the mode of production itself. In the second stage, it is assumed, the extension of capitalist competition brings about a state of affairs in which profit becomes proportional not to labour employed but to capital employed and in which a more or less uniform rate of profit on capital comes to prevail. Thus Marx's theory of value can conveniently be considered under the three headings of Pre-capitalist Society, Early Capitalism, and Developed Capitalism.[10] To each of these forms of society there may be conceived to correspond certain basic economic categories and certain basic logical problems. The task of the analysis of value as Marx understood it was to solve these basic problems in terms of the relations of production appropriate to the particular "historical" stage which was under consideration.

In Volume I of *Capital*, then, Marx proceeds "from the first and simplest relation that historically and in fact confronts us"[11] – the broad socio-economic relation between men as producers of commodities. In so far as economic life is based on the private production and exchange of goods, men are related to one another in their capacity as producers of goods intended for each other's consumption: they work

[9] *Capital*, Vol. III, p. 14.
[10] A word of caution may be appropriate here, in order to forestall possible criticisms involving the fallacy of misplaced concreteness. The three forms of society mentioned here do not necessarily represent actual historically identifiable forms: they are merely the "historical" counterparts of the three main stages in Marx's logical analysis of the value problem. In Marx's view, it will be remembered, the course of logical analysis is a *corrected* mirror-image of the actual historical course.
[11] Engels, *Ludwig Feuerbach*, p. 99.

for one another by embodying their separate labours in commodities which are destined to be exchanged on some sort of market. Historically, this "commodity relation" reached its apogee under capitalism, but it was also in existence to a greater or lesser extent in almost all previous forms of society. If we want to penetrate to the essence of a society in which the commodity relation has become "capitalistically modified", then, one possible method of procedure is to begin by postulating an abstract pre-capitalist society in which the commodity relation is assumed to be paramount but in which there are as yet no separate classes of capital-owners and land-owners. Having analysed the commodity relation as such in the context of this generalized pre-capitalist society, one can then proceed to examine what happens when capitalist relations of production impinge upon it.

Marx's *logical* starting-point in *Capital*, then, is the commodity relation as such, and his *historical* starting-point is an abstract pre-capitalist society of the type just described. In such a society, great importance clearly attaches to the fact that commodities acquire the capacity to attract others in exchange – *i.e.*, that they come to possess *exchange values*, or *prices*. The basic logical problem to be solved here is simply that of the determination of these prices. For Marx, no solution of this problem could be regarded as adequate which was not framed in terms of the appropriate set of relations of production. And for Marx, too, no solution could be regarded as adequate which did not possess as it were two dimensions – a qualitative one and a quantitative one. The qualitative aspect of the solution was directed to the question: Why do commodities possess prices at all? The quantitative aspect was directed to the question: Why do commodities possess the particular prices which they do? This distinction between the qualitative and quantitative aspects of Marx's analysis of value is of considerable importance, if only because it crops up again in the second and third stages of his enquiry.

In the context of the postulated pre-capitalist society, the answers to both the qualitative and the quantitative questions are fairly simple. The quality of exchange value is conferred upon commodities precisely because they are commodities – *i.e.*, because a commodity relation exists between their producers. The price relations between commodities which manifest themselves in the sphere of exchange are essentially reflections of the socio-economic relations between men as producers of commodities which exist in the sphere of production. And just as it is the fact that men work for one another in this particular way which is responsible for the *existence* of commodity prices, so in Marx's view it is the amount of work which they do for one another which is responsible for the *relative levels* of commodity prices. The amount of labour laid out on each commodity, Marx argued, will determine (in the postulated society) the *amount* of exchange value which each comes to possess relatively to the others. In other words, in a society based on simple commodity production the equilibrium prices of commodities will tend to be proportional to the quantities of labour normally used to produce them. This is a familiar proposition which Marx of course took over from Smith and Ricardo, and *given the particular set of assumptions upon which it is based* it is almost self-evidently true. It is this proposition which is usually abstracted from Marx's analysis and labelled "the labour theory of value" – a procedure which is of course quite illegitimate and which has had most unfortunate consequences.

Having thus proclaimed right at the beginning the general way in which he intends to unite economic history, sociology and economics in a kind of *ménage à trois*, Marx now proceeds to the second logical stage of his analysis. The "historical" counterpart of this second stage is a society based on commodity production which has just been taken over by capitalists. The formerly "independent" labourers now have to share the produce of their labour with a new social class – the owners of capital.[12] But nothing else is at this stage assumed to happen: in particular, it is supposed that capital subordinates labour on the basis of the technical conditions in which it finds it, without immediately changing the mode of production.[13] It is also assumed that commodities for the time being continue to sell "at their values" in the Marxian sense – *i.e.*, at equilibrium prices which are proportionate to quantities of embodied labour. In such a society, the crucial differentia is the emergence of a new form of class income, profit on capital, and the basic logical problem as Marx conceived it was to explain the origin and persistence of this new form of income under conditions in which free competition was predominant and both the finished commodity and the labour which produced it were bought and sold on the market at prices which reflected their Marxian "values". The conditions of the problem were carefully posed by Marx in such a way as to rule out explanations in terms of anything other than the relations of production appropriate to the new stage.

Qualitatively speaking, the Marxian answer to the problem is obvi-

[12] At this stage, the existence of a separate class of land-owners is abstracted from – a fact which throws further light on Marx's conception of the relation between the logical and the historical in analysis. The land-labour relation was historically prior to the capital-labour relation. But *under capitalism* it is the capital-labour relation which is primary, and the land-labour relation which is secondary. Since the analysis as a whole is oriented towards capitalism, the logical analysis must in Marx's view proceed from the capital-labour relation to the land-labour relation, and not vice versa.

[13] Cf. *Capital*, Vol. I, pp. 184 and 310.

ous enough. The basic feature of the new situation is that a new social class has arisen and obtained a kind of class monopoly of the factor of production capital, the other side of this medal being that labour has itself become a commodity which is bought and sold on the market like any other commodity. The existence of this class monopoly of capital means that the capitalists are able to "compel the working-class to do more work than the narrow round of its own life-wants prescribes".[14] The produce of this extra or surplus labour of the workers constitutes in effect the profit of the capitalists – or, as Marx calls it at this stage, the surplus value. But once again Marx was not content with an explanation couched solely in qualitative terms: he considered it necessary to derive in addition a *quantitative* explanation from the basic socio-economic relation between capitalists and wage-earners.[15] The "law of value" is therefore applied by Marx to the commodity labour – or rather labour-power – itself, the value of labour-power being in effect defined as the amount of labour required to produce wage-goods for the labourers at subsistence level. The surplus value received by any individual capitalist can then be regarded as determined and measured by the difference between the number of hours of work which his labourers perform and the number of hours of other men's work which are embodied in the wage-goods which he is in effect obliged to pay his labourers. This "law", as Marx noted in Volume I, implies that profits are proportional to quantities of labour employed rather than to quantities of capital employed, and thus "clearly contradicts all experience based on appearance";[16] but the solution of this "apparent contradiction" is reserved for a later logical-historical stage in the analysis.

This later stage occurs in Volume III, where Marx deals with commodity and value relations which have become "capitalistically modified" in the fullest sense. His "historical" starting-point here is a fairly well developed capitalist system in which the extension of competition between capitalists has made profit proportional not to labour employed but to capital employed, and in which a more or less uniform rate of profit on capital prevails. In this new situation, which Marx speaks of as one in which "surplus value has been transformed into profit", it is easy to see that the equilibrium prices at which commodities normally tend to sell must diverge appreciably from their Volume I "values": clearly commodities can continue to sell at these "values" only so long as the profit constituent in the price remains

[14] *Capital*, Vol. I, p. 309.
[15] Or, rather, from the broad relation between men as producers of commodities *as modified by* the impingement upon it of the class relation between capitalists and wage-earners.
[16] *Capital*, Vol. I, p. 307.

proportional to the quantity of labour employed.[17] Once commodities come to sell not at their Volume I "values" but at their Marshallian "costs of production" (or "prices of production", as Marx called them) a new logical problem arises for solution – that of the determination of prices of this new type. In particular, the question arises as to whether these Volume III "prices of production" can be explained in terms of the relations of production postulated as determinants in Volume I (suitably modified, of course, to reflect the transition to the new historical stage), or whether Adam Smith was correct in thinking that an entirely new type of explanation of prices was necessary in the stage of developed capitalism.

Qualitatively speaking, Marx's answer was that the "capitalistically modified" commodity relation was still of primary importance in determining prices even in this final stage, when actual equilibrium prices obviously diverged appreciably from Volume I "values". In a commodity-producing society of the modern capitalist type, the labour-capital production relationship still determined the distribution of the national income between wages and profits – *i.e.*, it determined the total amount of profit available over the economy as a whole for allocation among the individual capitalists. As capitalism developed, changes certainly occurred in the *mode* of allocation of this profit between industries and enterprises, but these changes were logically and historically secondary. The socio-economic production relation between workers and capitalists, determining as it did the proportion of the national income available for allocation in the form of profit, was still in a meaningful sense the primary and determining relation. Given the total amount of profit, and given the amount of capital employed in producing each commodity, the profit constituent in the price of each commodity, and therefore its "price of production", were automatically determined.

Once again, however, Marx was not content with a mere qualitative statement of this kind: he felt it necessary to translate the socio-economic relations involved in this analysis into quantitative terms. The result was his famous and much-criticized statement to the effect that under developed capitalism "the sum of the prices of production of all commodities produced in society . . . is equal to the sum of their values",[18] together with the equally famous arithmetical illustrations of this proposition. What these statements and illustrations really amounted to was an assertion that under developed capitalism there was still

---

[17] Given, of course, that what Marx called the "organic composition of capital" varies from industry to industry – which it does in fact do under developed capitalism.
[18] *Capital*, Vol. III, p. 157. Cf. below, pp. 146 ff.

an important functional relationship between embodied labour and individual equilibrium prices, which may be expressed in the following symbolic form:

$$\text{Price of commodity} = c + v + \frac{c + v}{\Sigma(c + v)} \, (\Sigma s)$$

Here c is the value of used-up machinery and raw materials; v is the value of labour-power; s is surplus value; $\Sigma(c + v)$ is the aggregate amount of capital employed over the economy as a whole; and Σs is the aggregate amount of surplus value produced over the economy as a whole. The formula expresses the idea that the profit constituent in the price of an individual commodity represents a proportionate share of the total surplus value produced over the economy as a whole, the proportion being determined by the ratio of the total capital employed in the enterprise concerned to the aggregate amount of capital employed over the economy as a whole. Since all the items on the right-hand side of the formula are expressible in terms of quantities of embodied labour, it can plausibly be maintained that there is still a causal connection, however indirect and circuitous, between Volume I "values" and Volume III "prices of production" – *i.e.*, between socio-economic production relations and the prices at which commodities actually tend to sell under developed capitalism.

This causal connection is clearly a rather complex one, particularly when it is borne in mind that for the sake of simplicity I have deliberately abstracted from the complications caused by the existence of different turnover periods for the two elements of capital, and also from the very difficult issues associated with the so-called "transformation problem".[19] It is understandable that the above formula should not have appeared very often in popular Marxist writing: clearly no revolution would ever have been achieved if this formula had been inscribed on the red banners. Much more suitable for this purpose was the familiar proposition put forward in the first stage of the development of Marx's theory of value in Volume I of *Capital*. But it must be strongly emphasized that neither the Volume I analysis nor the Volume III analysis, taken by itself, can properly be said to constitute the Marxian theory of value. The theory of value as Marx developed it was a subtle and complex compound of the Volume I and Volume III analyses, and we cut ourselves off from all hope of understanding it if we consider it as anything less.

If this interpretation of Marx's theory of value is correct, it follows that any criticism of the theory based on the assumption that it is a

[19] See below, pp. 143 ff.

crude and primitive over-simplification is entirely misconceived. The only really valid criticism of it which can be made, I would suggest, is one of precisely the opposite type – that for our present purposes today it is unnecessarily complex and refined. I am thinking here of two aspects of the theory in particular. First, there is the quite extraordinary way in which it draws upon and unites certain basic ideas of sociology, economic history, economics, and (up to a point) philosophy. In Marx's hands, the theory of value is not simply a theory which sets out to explain how prices are determined: it is also a kind of methodological manifesto, embodying Marx's view of the general way in which economics ought to be studied and calling for a restoration of the essential unity between the different social sciences. In Marx's time there was much to be said for the adoption of this line of approach, given certain points of view which were then current in the field of economics. It was indeed vitally important at that time to reassert the essential unity between economics and the other social sciences (particularly sociology) which Adam Smith had established but which the "vulgar" economists who followed Ricardo had gone far to destroy; and the theory of value had traditionally been regarded as an appropriate vehicle for the promulgation of methodological recommendations of this type. Today, of course, it remains as important as it ever was to call for inter-disciplinary co-operation in the social sciences. But I am not convinced that it would any longer be practicable to achieve that very high degree of integration which Smith and Marx still found possible. Nor am I convinced that the theory of value would any longer be the proper medium for the embodiment of an integrationist methodology. The role of the theory of value (in the traditional sense of a theory of price determination) in the general body of economic analysis is much more modest today than it was in Marx's time, and there is no longer any very compelling reason why a theorist wishing to bring sociology or economic history into his economics should feel obliged to start by reforming the theory of value.

If he *did* decide to start in this way, however, and set out to bring sociology into the picture by demonstrating the existence of a qualitative and quantitative relationship of a causal character between relations of production and relative prices, should he make the quantitative link-up in the particular way that Marx did? This is the second aspect of Marx's theory which I had in mind when stating that it seemed too complex and refined for present-day use. Joan Robinson has recently suggested[20] that it was an "aberration" for Marx to tie up the problem of relative prices with the problem of exploitation in the way that he did. I am not myself convinced that it was in fact an "aberration": as I

---

[20] J. Robinson, *Collected Economic Papers* (Oxford, 1965), Vol. III, p. 176.

have just stated, there were very good reasons, given the particular views against which Marx had to fight, for the adoption of this particular method of tying them up. Today, however, it does seem to me that Marx's method of making the quantitative tie-up between economics and sociology tends to obscure the importance of the infusion of sociology rather than to reveal it. Certainly, at any rate, generations of Marx-scholars have felt that they have proved something important about the real world when they have shown that in some moderately meaningful mathematical sense the "sum of the prices" *is* equal to the "sum of the values".[21] I am now persuaded that this was in some measure an illusion. In my more heretical moods, I sometimes wonder whether much of real importance would be lost from the Marxian system if the quantitative side of the analysis of relative prices were conducted in terms of something like the traditional supply and demand apparatus – *provided* that the socio-economic relationships emphasized by Marx were fully recognized as the basic cause of the existence of the prices whose level was shown to vary with variations in supply and demand, and *provided* that these Marxian sociological factors, where relevant, were also clearly postulated as lying behind the supply and demand schedules themselves.[22]

IV

Marx's theory of value, as we have seen, was a complex piece of analysis, replete with profound methodological implications, which depicted in a general way the process whereby the causal relationship between relations of production and relative prices was gradually modified as "simple" commodity production was transformed into capitalist commodity production. For the purposes of this theory, the only change *within capitalism* which it was necessary for Marx to take into account was the emergence of an average or normal rate of profit as a result of the extension of competition between capitalists. When Marx turned to the task of elucidating the "laws of motion" of capitalism, however, it was of course precisely the changes taking place within capitalism as the system developed which assumed paramount importance. And here Marx laid considerable emphasis on the *technological* changes associated with the development of capitalism, particularly in its so-called

---

[21] My own exercise in this *genre* is reprinted below, pp. 143 ff.

[22] In many cases, of course, Marxian postulates would have to *replace* those commonly employed today. A Marxist, for example, in analysing the forces lying behind the demand curve, could hardly base his analysis on the assumption that the consumer acted (in some more or less sophisticated way) so as to maximize the net income or utility he received from his purchases.

"Modern Industry" phase. "Modern Industry", wrote Marx, "never looks upon and treats the existing form of a process as final. The technical basis of that industry is therefore revolutionary, while all earlier modes of production were essentially conservative."[23] The really significant difference between the "laws of motion" put forward by Smith and Ricardo and those put forward by Marx is that in the case of the latter technological change appears as a crucial determining factor. It was indeed in terms of the mutual interaction of technological change and changes in the relations of production that Marx endeavoured to explain the main "innate tendencies" of the capitalist system. In the short period, Marx argued, the "constant revolution in production" associated with technological change, taking place as it did within a social framework which continually limited and restricted it, would be accompanied by "sudden stoppages and crises in the production process".[24] And in the long period, the mutual interaction of technological change and relations of production would produce certain other equally unpleasant consequences. In order to illustrate the general method of analysis used by Marx in this part of his enquiry, let us consider, first, the law of the falling tendency of the rate of profit, and, second, the so-called "law of increasing misery".

The basic assumptions lying behind both these laws can best be explained with the aid of Marx's three basic ratios, viz.:

$$\frac{c}{v} = \text{organic composition of capital}$$

$$\frac{s}{v} = \text{rate of surplus value}$$

$$\frac{s}{c+v} = \text{rate of profit}$$

As capitalism develops, according to Marx's account, c/v tends to rise as a result of technological changes, which Marx assumed would normally take a predominantly labour-saving form. This rise in c/v is associated with an increase in productivity in (*inter alia*) the wage-goods industries, which in its turn induces a tendency for s/v to rise. The mutual interaction of technological change and relations of production, in terms of

[23] *Capital*, Vol. I, p. 486. In a footnote to this passage, Marx quotes a well-known passage from the *Communist Manifesto*: "The bourgeoisie cannot exist without continually revolutionizing the instruments of production, and thereby the relations of production and all the social relations. Conservation, in an unaltered form, of the old modes of production was on the contrary the first condition of existence for all earlier industrial classes. Constant revolution in production, uninterrupted disturbance of all social conditions, everlasting uncertainty and agitation, distinguish the bourgeois epoch from all earlier ones . . ."

[24] *Capital*, Vol. III, p. 244.

which Marx explained the developmental process, operates primarily
through the changes which it brings about in these two key ratios and in
their relation to one another.

According to Marx, these changes in the ratios will lead to a long-
term tendency for the rate of profit on capital to decline. As we see from
the simple identity[25]

$$\frac{s}{c+v} = \frac{\dfrac{s}{v}}{1 + \dfrac{c}{v}}$$

the rate of profit will tend to rise if s/v rises and to fall if c/v rises. Now
both these ratios, on Marx's assumptions, will in fact rise as capitalism
develops, so that the net effect upon the rate of profit would seem at
first sight to be indeterminate. For reasons which are explained in
another essay in this volume,[26] however, Marx believed that the effect
upon the rate of profit of the rise in c/v would eventually win out over
that of the rise in s/v, so that the rate of profit would in fact tend to fall
over time. In other words, the advance of capitalism would itself tend
to weaken the very spring and stimulus of capitalism – as Smith and
Ricardo, although for very different reasons, had already maintained.

The changes in the two key ratios would also, Marx argued, contribute to an important historical process which has been variously called
"increasing misery", "impoverishment", and "social polarization".
The rise in c/v means the displacement of labour by machinery, which
swells the pool of unemployed and exercises a substantial downward
pressure on the level of real wages. The effect of this pressure, together
with that exercised by the formerly independent artisans and peasants
whom capitalism throws on to the labour market, is such that real
wages per head rise, if indeed they rise at all, only very slowly and
inconsiderably. The rise in s/v means, by definition, an increase in the
share of the national income going to the capitalists and a decrease in
the share going to the workers, so that even if the workers' real wages
rise absolutely they still suffer *relatively* to the capitalists. The social
polarization which results from these processes is accentuated by the
growth of monopoly in the ownership of capital; and the misery-
increasing effects of all this are enhanced by the growing degradation of
the labourers in manufacture to the level of the appendage of a machine.

Naturally Marx's analysis of these "laws of motion" was much more
sophisticated and much less schematic than I may have suggested in this
very brief account.[27] But Marx did, I think, really believe that these

[25] Cf. below, p. 129.   [26] See below, pp. 133–4.
[27] A fuller account is given in the two essays which follow.

"laws" and "tendencies" (as well as certain others, such as the "law" of the increasing severity of cyclical crises), would, in spite of the various qualifications and modifications and "counteracting influences" which he was usually careful to insert, in fact reveal themselves on the surface of economic reality in the course of time as capitalism developed. If they never did so, why should the expropriators ever be expropriated?

Now it is a simple fact that most of Marx's "laws of motion of capitalism" have *not* revealed themselves on the surface of economic reality, at any rate during the last quarter of a century and at any rate in the advanced capitalist countries. The rate of profit in the Marxian sense, so far as one can gather from the rather inadequate data which is available, has not tended to fall; only some of the predictions embodied in the "increasing misery" doctrine – and those probably not the most important ones – have been fulfilled; and economic crises of the classical type, so far from increasing in severity as they indeed appeared to be doing in the 30's, seem to have virtually disappeared. Clearly we should not "blame" Marx for this, any more than we should "blame" Ricardo for the even worse failure of most of his predictions. In Marx's time the tendencies which he described and analysed had in fact been revealing themselves on the surface of economic reality – or at any rate were commonly believed to have been doing so – for some considerable time. All Marx really did was to extrapolate these tendencies into the future, on the implied assumption that the relevant economic facts would remain substantially the same and retain the same relative positions on the scale of relevance, and he cannot be blamed if the tendencies he analysed have in fact been offset by the emergence of various new factors which he could not possibly have foreseen. But to say this is not of course to dispose of the problem of what now remains of Marxian economics, as a result of the emergence of these new factors.

It is obvious that the particular "laws of motion" developed by Marx can no longer be used today as a guide to what is actually going to happen as capitalism develops further. This does not mean, however, that they may not still be useful, even as they stand, for other and more modest purposes. They may still be useful, for example, as aids to the understanding of the development of capitalism up to Marx's time. They may still be useful in some of the less advanced countries as a guide to the actual situation there. And even in the more advanced capitalist countries, as I suggest in the next essay,[28] they may still be useful as a sort of awful warning of what might happen if the tempo of social legislation and trade union activity were allowed to slacken. But these are extremely limited uses compared with those which Marx himself

[28] Below, p. 125.

had in mind when he designed his model. Broadly speaking, and subject to a number of qualifications which will be made below, it can properly be said that all that really remains of Marxian economics today is the body of general methods and tools of analysis which Marx employed to analyse the facts of his time.

V

The most effective way of demonstrating the validity and utility of these methods and tools, of course, would be to use them to construct a completely new model of capitalist development in which the postulated "laws of motion" reflected tendencies which were actually manifesting themselves on the surface of reality.[29] Pending the construction and testing of a new Marxian model of this type, however, all we can really do is to attempt to introduce certain basic Marxian ideas into orthodox economic theory, particularly those parts of it where there appear to be deficiencies due to a neglect of the sociological factors which Marx emphasized. In recent years, it is true, something of this kind has in fact been occurring on quite a large scale: we have indeed been witnessing, as Mrs Robinson has pointed out, "the same sort of infiltration of Marxian ideas into economic theory as had already occurred in history".[30] Sometimes this infiltration has been conscious, as in the case of Kalecki, Lange, Sraffa, and Mrs Robinson herself. More often it has been unconscious, as in the case of Harrod's growth model and Richardson's *Information and Investment*. It is only natural that the recent rediscovery of the importance of certain typically Marxian problems should have been accompanied by the rediscovery of certain typically Marxian methods and techniques. But there still remains a great deal of room for further useful infiltration.

Take, for example, the theory of monopoly. Marx's general analysis of value and distribution, it is true, was worked out primarily with reference to a world of more or less free competition. But his discussion of the interrelations between the growth of monopoly on the one hand and the growth of economic instability on the other was far-reaching and acute, and he foresaw with remarkable accuracy some of the basic features of our contemporary world of monopolies. Thus, starting from what we know of his vision and general method of analysis, it is fairly easy to reconstruct the line of approach which he would probably have adopted in an examination of the contemporary trends. In the first place, he would certainly have emphasized that individual monopolies

---

[29] Cf. below, pp. 127–8.
[30] *Collected Economic Papers*, Vol. III, p. 149.

in different industries should be looked at not in isolation but in the context of a new monopolistic *stage* in the development of capitalism – a stage in which monopoly had become intimately connected with imperialism and the new functions of the state, and in which the inter-relations between monopoly, accumulation and instability had to some extent taken on new forms. In the second place, he would probably have insisted that monopolistic price-phenomena should be studied in close connection with the main characteristics of this new stage of development; that attention might more profitably be directed to analysing the effects of monopoly on the prices of broad *groups* of goods and services (wage goods and labour-power, for example) than to analysing its effects on the prices of individual goods and services in isolated markets; and that priority should be given to the analysis of the *leading* forms of monopoly, notably oligopoly. He would almost certainly have criticized the tendency of many monopoly theorists to lay their main emphasis on the qualitative *resemblance* between the "monopoly position" of the small tobacconist at the corner and the monopoly position of a firm like I.C.I. Such an approach, he might have said, which starts off by saying in effect that all men are monopolists, is likely to discourage economists from going on to make the vitally necessary distinction between weak monopolists and strong ones. The infiltration of this kind of attitude into orthodox monopoly theory would, I think, be likely to effect an appreciable improvement in the realism and relevance of the theory.

The same can be said of the infiltration of a Marxian attitude into the theory of wages. Here it is true that the orthodox theory has certain important achievements to its credit, particularly in the field of the analysis of short-run wage levels in individual industries under monopolistic conditions of various kinds; and it is also true that the general laws which Marx himself formulated concerning long-run trends in wages have been largely invalidated by the unexpected con-currence and increase in intensity of certain "counteracting influences". But this does not mean that some of the key factors upon which Marx's theory of wages depended are not still operative in the modern world. In particular, any new theory of long-run trends in wages which neg-lected to lay emphasis on the accumulation of capital, and the techno-logical changes and market problems which it brings about, would be likely to possess little interest or relevance.[31] In an important sense, it is still true to say in our modern world that "relative surplus-population is . . . the pivot upon which the law of demand and supply of labour

[31] Cf. Rogin, *The Meaning and Validity of Economic Theory* (New York, 1956), pp. 407–8. See also *ibid.*, p. 405.

works".[32] And it should also be borne in mind that the above-mentioned "counteracting influences" have as yet been unable to eliminate economic instability or to prevent the growth of monopoly, both of which in themselves may have significant effects on wage levels. Once again there would seem to be a decided advantage in bringing the relations of production in, as Marx always did, on the ground floor.

Finally, a brief mention may be made of one of the most important areas of all – the theory of profit. Surely in this field nothing would be lost, and much might be gained, by an attempt to explain the origin and persistence of net profit in terms of, rather than in abstraction from, the existence under capitalism of a class monopoly of capital. And surely Marx's theory of the falling rate of profit, in spite of the failure of the prediction which Marx based on it, may have something to offer those modern theorists who are concerned with the problem of secular changes in the rate of profit. Whatever else may be said about it, at least it puts before us the interesting suggestion that changes in the rate of profit may depend not on technological factors alone but rather on the interaction of these with sociological factors.[33]

What I am trying to say here, putting it in general terms, is simply that many modern Western economists have still to learn one fundamental lesson from Marx – that the analysis of economic categories ought so far as possible to be conducted in terms of, rather than in abstraction from, "relations of production" in Marx's sense. The really original and essential aspects of Marx's economic model are the vision and general method of analysis which Marx employed in building it. Everyone pays lip-service nowadays to the aim of bringing sociology back into economics, but somehow no one ever manages actually to achieve this aim, particularly in sensitive spheres like that of the theory of distribution where we most need to achieve it. Whatever one may think about Marx, at least he *did* achieve it – and by no means least in the sphere of distribution theory. We cannot simply reproduce his achievements today: "official" textbooks of Marxian political economy are coming to look more and more antediluvian with every year that passes. But we *can* experiment with the use of Marx's general economic method. A vision and method which produced such interesting results when applied to the capitalism of Marx's day are surely capable of producing at least *some* useful results when applied to the not so very different capitalism of our own day.

---

[32] *Capital*, Vol. I, p. 639.   [33] Cf. below, p. 142.

MARX'S "DOCTRINE
OF INCREASING MISERY"[1]

I

Marx's economic writings, particularly Chapters 25 and 32 of Volume I of *Capital*, contain a number of general statements about the lot of the labourer under capitalism which have come to be known as the "doctrine of increasing misery". What exactly did Marx mean by these statements? Was he making a concrete prediction about what would in fact happen in the future in capitalist countries? Were the statements meant to imply that the material standard of living of the workers would grow worse as capitalism developed? If so, did Marx envisage that it would grow worse in an absolute sense, in a relative sense, or in both these senses?

The main reason why so many nonsensical and misleading answers to these questions have been given in the past, and are still being given today, is simply that the motives of most of the interpreters of Marx's "doctrine of increasing misery" have been and continue to be interested. This is true of the friends of Marx as well as of his foes. Starting out with a knowledge of the facts concerning contemporary working-class conditions in the advanced capitalist countries, many friends have sought for an interpretation of Marx's "doctrine of increasing misery" which will make it square with these facts; and many foes, starting with the same knowledge, have sought for an interpretation which will make it conflict with these facts. "Seek, and ye shall find", we are told on good authority, and both friends and foes have duly found. In a world divided as it is this could hardly have been otherwise, and few of us are in a position to throw stones. But the questions at issue here are today of such importance that we ought to make strenuous efforts to throw off our preconceptions, to renounce for a moment the benefit of hindsight, and to examine as dispassionately as we can *what Marx actually said* on this subject. Only if we disentangle what Marx actually said about the future of capitalism from the glosses of his interested interpreters can we determine the nature and extent of the discrepancies which have emerged between his predictions and the facts; and only then can we

[1] This essay is an amended version of an article which was published in *Science and Society*, Fall 1962.

hope to solve the problem of the validity of Marx's basic methods and techniques of analysis which was raised in the previous essay.[2]

II

Chapter 25 of Volume I of *Capital*, entitled "The General Law of Capitalist Accumulation", sets out to consider "the influence of the growth of capital on the lot of the labouring class". In this enquiry, Marx starts off by telling us, the most important factor is "the composition of capital and the changes it undergoes in the course of the process of of accumulation".[3]

Marx assumes that, as capital accumulates, technological innovations will take a predominantly labour-saving form, and that this will be reflected in a change in what he calls the "value-composition" of capital. "There may be, e.g., originally 50 per cent. of a capital laid out in means of production, and 50 per cent. in labour-power; later on, with the development of the productivity of labour, 30 per cent. in means of production, 20 per cent. in labour-power, and so on."[4] This process, which goes hand in hand with and is hastened by the familiar processes of "concentration" and "centralization" of capitals, means that "the additional capital formed in the course of accumulation attracts fewer and fewer labourers in proportion to its magnitude", and that "the old capital periodically reproduced with change of composition, repels more and more of the labourers formerly employed by it".[5] Thus "capitalistic accumulation itself . . . constantly produces . . . a relatively redundant population of labourers, *i.e.*, a population of greater extent than suffices for the average needs of the self-expansion of capital, and therefore a surplus-population".[6]

This "surplus-population" comes to form what Marx called "a disposable industrial reserve army",[7] whose size varies with (*inter alia*) the phases of the trade cycle, and whose expansion and contraction exclusively regulate the "general movements of wages".[8] It comprises those who are only partially or irregularly employed, those whose unemployment is (as we would say today) "disguised", those who are wholly unemployed for long periods, and those who in Marx's time were classified as "paupers".[9] It is to this "relative surplus-population" that Marx's first formulation of the "general law of capitalist accumulation" primarily applies. This formulation is in the following words:

The greater the social wealth, the functioning capital, the extent and energy

2 Cf. above, pp. 110–12.   3 *Capital*, Vol. I, p. 612.   4 *Ibid.*, Vol. I, p. 622.
5 *Ibid.*, Vol. I, p. 628.   6 *Ibid.*, Vol. I, p. 630.   7 *Ibid.*, Vol. I, p. 632.
8 *Ibid.*, Vol. I, p. 637.   9 *Ibid.*, Vol. I, pp. 640–44.

of its growth, and, therefore, also the absolute mass of the proletariat and the productiveness of its labour, the greater is the industrial reserve army. The same causes which develop the expansive power of capital, develop also the labour-power at its disposal. The relative mass of the industrial reserve army increases therefore with the potential energy of wealth. But the greater this reserve army in proportion to the active labour-army, the greater is the mass of a consolidated surplus-population, whose misery is in inverse ratio to its torment of labour. The more extensive, finally, the lazarus-layers of the working-class, and the industrial reserve army, the greater is official pauperism. *This is the absolute general law of capitalist accumulation.* Like all other laws it is modified in its working by many circumstances, the analysis of which does not concern us here.[10]

The main emphasis in Marx's discussion in the chapter so far has been on the way in which, as capital accumulates, the mass of unemployed and semi-employed workers among whom distress is rampant grows in extent. Relatively little has been said directly about the effect of accumulation upon the general wage level.[11] And in the celebrated passage about the two "poles" of society which follows shortly after that just quoted, Marx deliberately abstracts from the question of the general wage level by arguing that there are certain important senses in which the lot of the labourer must grow worse as capitalism develops, "be his payment high or low". In this passage, which deserves complete quotation, Marx restates a number of conclusions already reached in Part IV of the book concerning the social and moral effects of capital accumulation upon the labourer; and (at the end of the passage) he links these up with the conclusion about the growth of the pool of unemployed which he has just reached. "We saw in Part IV," he writes,

when analysing the production of relative surplus-value: within the capitalist system all methods for raising the social productiveness of labour are brought about at the cost of the individual labourer; all means for the development of production transform themselves into means of domination over, and exploitation of, the producers; they mutilate the labourer into a fragment of a man, degrade him to the level of an appendage of a machine, destroy every remnant of charm in his work and turn it into a hated toil; they estrange him from the intellectual potentialities of the labour-process in the same proportion as science is incorporated in it as an independent power; they distort the conditions under

[10] *Ibid.*, Vol. I, p. 644.

[11] Marx has, however, as we have seen, emphasized that the expansion and contraction of the reserve army regulate the "general movements of wages". "The industrial reserve army," he writes, "during the periods of stagnation and average prosperity, weighs down the active labour-army; during the periods of over-production and paroxysm, it holds its pretensions in check. Relative surplus-population is therefore the pivot upon which the law of demand and supply of labour works. It confines the field of action of this law within the limits absolutely convenient to the activity and to the domination of capital" (*ibid.*, Vol. I, p. 639).

which he works, subject him during the labour-process to a despotism the more hateful for its meanness; they transform his life-time into working-time, and drag his wife and child beneath the wheels of the Juggernaut of capital. But all methods for the production of surplus-value are at the same time methods of accumulation; and every extension of accumulation becomes again a means for the development of those methods. It follows therefore that in proportion as capital accumulates, the lot of the labourer, be his payment high or low, must grow worse. The law, finally, that always equilibrates the relative surplus-population, or industrial reserve army, to the extent and energy of accumulation, this law rivets the labourer to capital more firmly than the wedges of Vulcan did Prometheus to the rock. It establishes an accumulation of misery, corresponding with accumulation of capital. Accumulation of wealth at one pole is, therefore, at the same time accumulation of misery, agony of toil, slavery, ignorance, brutality, mental degradation, at the opposite pole, *i.e.*, on the side of the class that produces its own product in the form of capital.[12]

Finally, in Chapter 32, entitled "Historical Tendency of Capitalist Accumulation", Marx repeats in very similar words the conclusion at which he arrives in the last sentence of this passage, and predicts that it will lead eventually to the "expropriation of the expropriators":

Along with the constantly diminishing number of the magnates of capital, who usurp and monopolize all advantages of this process of transformation, grows the mass of misery, oppression, slavery, degradation, exploitation; but with this too grows the revolt of the working-class, a class always increasing in numbers, and disciplined, united, organized by the very mechanism of the process of capitalist production itself. The monopoly of capital becomes a fetter upon the mode of production, which has sprung up and flourished along with, and under it. Centralization of the means of production and socialization of labour at last reach a point where they become incompatible with their capitalist integument. This integument is burst asunder. The knell of capitalist private property sounds. The expropriators are expropriated.[13]

So much, then, for what Marx actually said in his mature economic work on the question of the effect of the accumulation of capital upon the lot of the labourer. Although Marx himself never used the words "doctrine of increasing misery" to refer to this set of statements, the expression does not seem to be unduly misleading.

III

A number of commentators, observing that Marx in these statements made little direct reference to the question of the behaviour of the general wage level – and, indeed, in one place (as we have seen) deliberately abstracted from this question – have suggested that no prediction

[12] *Ibid.*, Vol. I, p. 645.   [13] *Ibid.*, Vol. I, p. 763.

whatsoever about the general wage level was implied. And it is certainly true that Marx's main emphasis in the quoted passages was explicitly or implicitly laid upon such factors as the increasing size of the reserve army, the growth of job-insecurity, the increase in the area covered by the capitalist mode of production, the extinction of formerly independent social groups such as peasants and self-employed artisans, and the fragmentation of the human personality associated with capitalist industrialization. At any rate in theory, it would be quite possible for most of these tendencies to operate while at the same time a substantial rise in overall real wages was taking place.

The question at issue, however, is whether Marx in fact *expected* that a substantial rise in overall real wages would take place. It is true that his theory of wages was much more flexible than the old "iron law"; it is also true that there is absolutely no evidence in his economic writings – at any rate in those of his maturity – of a belief that real wages per head would show a long-run tendency to decline.[14] But it seems fairly clear that he did *not* expect that a substantial rise in real wages – of anything like the order, say, of that which has actually occurred since his time in the advanced capitalist countries – would take place. The evidence surely suggests (i) that he expected that if any rise in real wages per head took place at all, it would be very slow and inconsiderable; (ii) that he expected "relative" wages (*i.e.*, labour's share in the national income) to fall; and (iii) that these views of his about the behaviour of wages should properly be regarded as constituent parts of, or at any rate as assumptions underlying, his "doctrine of increasing misery". Let me deal with these three points in order.

(*i*) The main emphasis in almost all Marx's discussions of wages is laid on the fact that in the bargaining process between capital and labour the dice are in the long run very heavily loaded against the workers. If the composition of capital remained the same as development proceeded, and if accumulation were rapid, then the demand for labour would

[14] John Strachey, in his *Contemporary Capitalism* (London, 1956), argues that when Marx said that the wage-earners would sink into ever-increasing misery "he undoubtedly envisaged that the actual concrete heap of commodities which the wage earners received each week would get even smaller than it was in the hungry 'forties' " (*op. cit.*, p. 129). But neither of the two passages Strachey quotes (on p. 101) can properly be interpreted to mean this. The first, from the *Communist Manifesto*, clearly refers to the growth of the reserve army of labour and thus of "pauperism"; the second consists of the opening part of the passage quoted on p. 116 of the present essay, and makes no direct reference to wages (let alone to falling wages) at all. To find any statement in Marx's writing which could reasonably be interpreted as implying a prediction of declining real wages, Mr Strachey would have had to go right back to Marx's *Economic and Philosophic Manuscripts of 1844* (see, e.g., *ibid.*, (Moscow, 1959), pp. 66 and 69). And the significant point here, surely, is not that Marx wrote down such statements as this in 1844, but that he did not repeat them in 1867, when Vol. I of *Capital* appeared.

increase *pari passu* with accumulation, and wages would indeed be likely to rise. But even under these exceptionally favourable conditions a time would probably come when the rise in wages began to blunt the stimulus of gain. The rate of accumulation would then slacken, and wages would fall again.[15] And, of course, the important point is that in Marx's view the composition of capital does *not* remain the same as development proceeds: as we have seen, labour-saving innovations are claimed to bring about a secular rise in the composition of capital, thus generating a reserve army of labour which exerts a very powerful downward pressure on wages. Marx's emphasis on this latter factor was strong and consistent, and it seems most unlikely that he expected trade union activity to be successful in appreciably and permanently countering its effects. Thus in *Value, Price and Profit* (which is usually quoted by those taking a different view from that which I am expressing here) Marx certainly advocates that the workers should not "renounce their resistance against the encroachments of capital and abandon their attempts at making the best of the *occasional* chances for their *temporary* improvement";[16] but he is careful to add that "they ought not to forget that they are fighting with effects, but not with the causes of those effects; that they are retarding the downward movement, but not changing its direction".[17] The workers, in other words, in Marx's view, would (and should) try to maintain or increase their share of the rising national product, but it was very unlikely that they would succeed in making permanent gains which were anything like proportionate to the rising productivity.

But was there really, in Marx's opinion, no possible means of permanent escape from the inexorable pressure of these economic forces? Some commentators, Mr Sowell, for example,[18] have seen a ray of hope in Marx's definition of "subsistence" as consisting not only of "natural wants" but also of "so-called necessary wants", which are "the product of historical development".[19] This means, says Mr Sowell, that in Marx's view "once a new higher standard of living becomes established, it too becomes subsistence, and represents the new value of labor-power".[20] Whether real wages will be set at this "subsistence" level or

---

[15] *Capital*, Vol. I, p. 619.

[16] *Selected Works*, Vol. I (London, 1942), p. 336. (My italics.)

[17] *Ibid.*, p. 337. The passage in which this statement occurs does not, I think, imply a prediction of declining real wages. All that Marx really says is that if real wages happen to rise above what he calls the "minimum limit" there will be a strong tendency for them to be pulled down again.

[18] T. Sowell, "Marx's 'Increasing Misery' Doctrine", *American Economic Review*, March 1960.

[19] *Capital*, Vol. I, p. 171. Cf. *Selected Works*, Vol. I, pp. 332–3.

[20] Sowell, *op. cit.*, pp. 115–16.

at some point above it depends, according to Mr Sowell's interpretation of Marx's teaching, upon the relative bargaining power of labour and capital. The picture we are presented with, then, is one of a more or less steadily-rising "customary" floor under wages, above which the wage battles take place.

It is true that Marx defined "subsistence" in the way that Mr Sowell describes; that he laid more stress than most of his predecessors on the importance of relative bargaining power;[21] and that he probably believed that if the workers succeeded in holding the wage level above the "minimum limit" for a sufficiently long period of time they might succeed in altering society's idea as to what constituted the "minimum limit", *i.e.*, in Marx's terminology, they might be able to raise the *value* of their labour-power. But does the textual evidence really warrant the elevation of these attitudes to the status of what virtually amounts to a "Marxian" law of increasing real wages, *i.e.*, of *decreasing* absolute misery in the purely economic sense? Do not Marx's writings on this subject, taken as a whole and read in their context, suggest that in his view the possibilities of escape by this route were very limited? Certainly, at any rate, there is no textual justification for the notion that in Marx's view "subsistence" (*i.e.*, the value of labour-power) must be regarded as equivalent to the currently-established standard of living among the workers, *however high this may happen to be*. No doubt it is highly convenient for modern Marxists to postulate this equivalence, since it enables them to reconcile the Marxian view that the prices of all commodities (including labour-power) depend upon the labour necessary to produce them, with the fact that the average real wage in the advanced capitalist countries today is appreciably higher than "subsistence" in the ordinary sense of that word. But this convenience is purchased only at the cost of violating customary English usage, and, what is worse from the point of view of Marxism, only at the cost of implying that the position of the vital boundary between "cost" and "surplus" depends largely upon market conditions. If the value of labour-power at any given time is taken to be simply what the workers happen to have been getting for their labour-power during the previous few years, Marx's theory of wages becomes so general as to be virtually meaningless. Marx, I think, would have recognized quite frankly that the average worker in the advanced capitalist countries today was getting a real wage substantially higher than the value of his labour-power, and would have tried to explain why.

Taking the evidence of Marx's work as a whole, then, I think there is

[21] Cf., e.g., *Selected Works*, Vol. I, p. 334: "The question resolves itself into a question of the respective powers of the combatants."

little doubt that he would have endorsed the view which Engels expressed in 1891 to the effect that "the part [of the whole mass of products produced] falling to the working class (reckoned per head) either increases only very slowly and inconsiderably or not at all, and under certain circumstances may even fall".[22]

(*ii*) What about "relative" wages? Mr Sowell, in the article just referred to, argues that Marx's prediction of "increasing misery" for the workers under capitalism, in so far as it was concerned with the purely economic aspect of the workers' condition, referred essentially to *relative* misery, *i.e.*, to a decline in labour's relative share.[23] In this connection Mr Sowell lays considerable stress on Marx's adoption of Ricardo's notion that it was proper to speak of a "fall in wages" when labour's relative share fell, even if at the same time real wages rose.

Three things at any rate are certainly true:

(*a*) That Marx laid considerable emphasis on the importance of changes in "relative wages" (*i.e.*, roughly, in the ratio of wage incomes to property incomes); that he insisted that "relative wages" should be evaluated on the basis of the quantity of labour expended to produce the real goods which wage-earners and property-owners respectively consumed; and that he applauded Ricardo's treatment of "relative wages" as an implied recognition of the fact that the worker ought properly to be considered in his social relationship.

(*b*) That Marx believed that as capitalism developed, and improvements in productivity gradually affected the wage-goods industries, "relative surplus value" would be created.[24] Given that the length of the working day was not reduced, and given the basic Marxian assumptions regarding the correspondence of prices and "values", it followed that "relative wages" would tend to fall as capitalism developed, and with them the "relative social position" of the worker as compared with that of the capitalist.[25]

(*c*) That Marx, in a passage in one of his early economic works, emphasized that even if real wages and therefore the "enjoyments of the

---

[22] Marx, *Selected Works*, Vol. I, p. 250.   [23] Sowell, *op. cit.*, p. 111.

[24] Marx defined "relative surplus value" as "the surplus-value arising from the curtailment of the necessary labour-time, and from the corresponding alteration in the respective lengths of the two components of the working-day" (*Capital*, Vol. I, p. 315). Mr Sowell, curiously enough, does not specifically refer in his article to Marx's analysis of relative surplus value.

[25] Cf. the case considered by Marx in *Value, Price and Profit* (*Selected Works*, Vol. I, p. 326), where it is assumed that the increased productivity of labour lowers the amount of labour required to produce wage-goods, but that real wages remain the same. In this case, writes Marx, "although the labourer's absolute standard of life would have remained the same, his *relative* wages, and therewith his *relative social position*, as compared with that of the capitalist, would have been lowered".

worker" rose, this rise would necessarily presuppose a "rapid growth of productive capital", which would bring about "an equally rapid growth of wealth, luxury, social needs, social enjoyments". Thus "although the enjoyments of the worker have risen, the social satisfaction that they give has fallen in comparison with the state of development of society in general".[26]

If we put (*a*), (*b*) and (*c*) together – which, incidentally, Marx himself never did and which even Mr Sowell does rather unsatisfactorily – we may, I think, quite fairly impute to Marx something like a doctrine of "increasing relative misery" in the purely economic sphere. I think there is little doubt that Marx did anticipate that as capitalism developed *relative* wages would decline, whatever happened to *absolute* wages.

(*iii*) What is the connection, if any, between these views of Marx's about the behaviour of wages and the "doctrine of increasing misery" outlined above? It is true, as we have already seen, that the key statements of this doctrine which I have quoted, and even the supporting theoretical argumentation, contain relatively little that can reasonably be construed as a prediction about the behaviour of wages, whether "absolute" or "relative". But it is important to note that when Marx leaves the theoretical sphere and proceeds to give what he calls "illustrations of the general law of capitalist accumulation",[27] the question of the behaviour of wages is by no means abstracted from. In these "illustrations", Marx does not devote a great deal of time to "pauperism" and the condition of the reserve army of labour, and he makes relatively few references to the social and moral effects of capital accumulation upon the labourer.[28] Instead he concentrates, as he himself puts it, upon the worker's "condition outside the workshop", *i.e.*, upon his "condition as to food and dwelling", with particular reference to "the worst paid part of the industrial proletariat, and [to] the agricultural labourers, who together form the majority of the working-class". A consideration of these aspects of the worker's condition, he tells us specifically, is necessary "for a full elucidation of the law of accumulation".[29]

The implication of this method of treatment is fairly obvious. The "general law of capitalist accumulation", as Marx envisaged it, manifested itself not only in the formation of a growing number of poverty-stricken unemployed, not only in increasing exploitation, increasing fragmentation of the human personality, etc., but also in *a very low material*

[26] *Selected Works*, Vol. I, pp. 268–9.
[27] *Capital*, Vol. I, pp. 648 ff.
[28] In relation to the latter, he refers the reader once again to "the chapters on the 'working-day' and 'machinery' ", *i.e.*, to Part IV of *Capital*. See *ibid.*, Vol. I, p. 653.
[29] *Ibid.*, Vol. I, p. 653.

*standard of living, i.e., roughly, in very low real wages for the great majority of
the employed workers.* No one, surely, could rise from Marx's vivid descrip-
tions in this part of the chapter of the appalling material conditions
endured by the majority of workers in the Britain of his time with any
other notion of what he meant.

It seems wrong, then, to place too much emphasis on the words "be
his payment high or low" in the passage quoted on p. 116. Marx
admittedly believed that there were certain important "non-economic"
respects in which the lot of the labourer would grow worse even if his
real wages rose; but he also believed that any rise in real wages which in
fact took place would be too slow and inconsiderable to provide an
appreciable offset to the misery-increasing effects of these "non-
economic" factors. In addition, he believed that the misery-decreasing
effect of any rise in real wages would be offset or more than offset by the
misery-increasing effect of the fall in "relative wages" which would
normally accompany it.[30]

IV

There is no doubt that *some* of the things which Marx had in mind when
he spoke of an "accumulation of misery" have in fact happened, even
in the more advanced capitalist countries. At least up to the time of the
Second World War, a good case could be made out in support of Marx's
notion that the reserve army of labour would increase. Few economists
today would seriously deny that "centralization of capitals" in Marx's
sense has increased since his time, or that capitalism, by and large, has
diminished the numbers of certain of the formerly "independent" social
groups. And the effect of some of the "non-economic" misery-increasing
factors noted by Marx is still extremely important, even if sometimes in
ways which he himself did not anticipate. But some of the other things
which Marx had in mind have *not* happened, and unfortunately these
tend to be by far the most important from a political viewpoint. In
particular, Marx's predictions about the behaviour of wages have not
been borne out by the facts, at any rate in the more advanced capitalist
countries. It is in this respect that the discrepancy between the theory
and the facts which I have mentioned above[31] is most apparent and
significant.

I do not propose to argue about the facts here. I shall simply take it as
more or less axiomatic that (a) the rise in real wages which has actually

---

[30] See, e.g., the interesting and little-noticed reference to this point in *ibid.*, Vol. I,
p. 652.
[31] P. 109.

taken place in the advanced capitalist countries since Marx's time is much greater than that which Marx anticipated;[32] and that (b) the appreciable fall in "relative wages" which Marx anticipated has not in fact taken place. The most effective answer I have ever heard to those who deny these facts was given by Mr J. R. Campbell at a meeting held a few years ago to discuss Marx's "doctrine of increasing misery". "I live in a typical London working-class suburb", said Mr Campbell, "and my neighbours are typical London working-class people. If these neighbours of mine are the end-product of a long historical process of 'impoverishment', then all I can say is that their grandfathers and great-grandfathers must have been bloody rich men."

To those who do not deny the facts, but who at the same time wish to proclaim the utility of Marx's analysis *as it stands*, only one line of approach is really at all defensible. It has to be argued that the "tendencies" and "laws" enunciated in Volume I of *Capital* – including the "tendency" towards "increasing misery" – were derived on a high level of abstraction, and that therefore "their validity is relative to the level of abstraction on which they are derived and to the extent of the modifications which they must undergo when the analysis is brought to a more concrete level".[33] If one begins by emphasizing this point, one can then go on to argue that the "tendencies" ought not to be interpreted as direct and concrete predictions about the future; and that a failure of the "tendencies" to manifest themselves on the actual surface of events indicates merely that they are being "offset" or "counteracted", and not that they do not exist.

It is true, of course, that in Volume I of *Capital* Marx did usually operate at a high level of abstraction, and that (up to a point) the "tendencies" and "laws" which he there enunciated were those appro-

---

[32] The great improvement in the material standard of living of the British workers between the 1840's (when Engels wrote his *Condition of the Working Class*) and the 1890's, and the similar improvement in the position of the French workers between the end of the eighteenth and the end of the nineteenth centuries, were noted by Lenin in an extraordinarily perceptive and little-noticed paragraph in his early essay *On the So-called Market Question* (1893). Lenin did not attempt here to minimize this improvement, or to treat it as exceptional or temporary. On the contrary, he emphasized "the indubitable fact that the development of capitalism inevitably entails a rising level of requirements for the entire population, including the industrial population", and went so far as to speak of a "law of increasing requirements", which the French and British examples showed had "manifested itself with full force in the history of Europe". Nor did Lenin beat about the bush in his explanation of this tendency. One of the main causes, in his opinion, was "the crowding together, the concentration of the industrial proletariat, which enhances their class-consciousness and sense of human dignity and enables them to wage a successful struggle against the predatory tendencies of the capitalist system" (Lenin, *Collected Works*, Vol. I (Moscow, 1960), p. 106).

[33] Paul M. Sweezy, *The Theory of Capitalist Development* (New York, 1942), p. 18.

priate to a sort of "ideal" or "purified" capitalism from which all "inessential" features had been deliberately removed. But was the level of abstraction on which the "doctrine of increasing misery" was derived really as high as that on which, say, the theory of value of Volume I was derived? I do not think this can plausibly be maintained. This is shown not only by the highly realistic way in which Marx expounds and illustrates the "doctrine of increasing misery" in Volume I, but also – and perhaps more cogently – by the fact that in Volumes II and III, where the analysis is conducted on "progressively lower levels of abstraction"[34] and many of the conclusions of Volume I are as a result seriously qualified, there is no real qualification at all of the "doctrine of increasing misery". It is also true that Marx was usually careful to express his "tendencies" in a provisional form, and that he would not have felt that a failure of these "tendencies" to manifest themselves on the surface of reality *in this or that country, at this or that time, or in the short run*, would be at all fatal. But so far at least as the "doctrine of increasing misery" is concerned, I do not think we can safely go much further than this. Is there really very much doubt that Marx *did* expect the tendency towards "increasing misery" to manifest itself on the surface of reality, even if only in the sort of general way which we usually describe by the use of such terms as "in the long run", "by and large", "on the average", etc.? If he did *not* expect at least this, what was his reason for postulating a tendency towards "increasing misery" at all? What justification would there have been for drawing conclusions from it regarding the inevitability of the socialist revolution?

The line of argument I am now considering, then, although it does contain an element of truth, does not enable us to get rid of the discrepancy between what has actually happened and what Marx expected to happen. It does, however, point to a way of *explaining* the discrepancy which may be useful. There does indeed exist, we may plausibly argue, at any rate in a kind of "pure" capitalist system, an "innate tendency" towards "increasing misery" in Marx's sense, but for various reasons this "innate tendency" has been "offset" or "counteracted" in our own times by various factors which Marx abstracted from in his model. We may then go on to cite the main "counteracting causes" which have prevented the "innate tendency" from manifesting itself on the surface of reality, in so far as it has not in fact done so. If we adopt the Leninist line, we may put the blame on imperialism. Or we may point, alternatively or in addition, to the great waves of technical innovation and consequent increases in productivity which have occurred since Marx's time; to the immense growth in the extent and power of

[34] *Ibid.*, p. 19.

trade unionism which has increased the power of the workers to press for a higher share of the growing national product; to the change in the aims of the trade union movement which has made it more interested in getting what it can out of the capitalist system than in putting an end to it; and to the growth of the socialist sector of the world which has made the capitalists more willing to grant the workers the wage increases they demand.[35] Such factors as these, we may claim, have in our own time "counteracted" to quite a large extent the "innate tendency" towards "increasing misery".

I think myself that this is a perfectly proper method of approach which has definite, if limited, utility. It points a very valuable moral: that if we allow the tempo of social legislation, trade union activity, State intervention, etc., to slacken, and give the "innate tendencies" of capitalism their head, the long-run result may well be "increasing misery" in something very like Marx's sense. But in so far as contemporary Marxists adopt this line *and say nothing more*, they are using Marx's model for much less spectacular purposes than those for which it was originally designed. They are using it not to explain what actually *is* happening but to explain what *would* happen if certain things were otherwise than they in fact are. It may be useful on occasion to do this, but it is clearly not enough.

V

At this point some readers may object that a mountain is being made out of a molehill. "We agree", they may say, "that this particular prediction of Marx's has indeed been falsified by the facts, at least in part, for reasons such as those you describe. Certain new factors have emerged – factors which Marx could hardly have been expected to foresee – which have counteracted, and which may well continue to counteract, the innate tendency towards 'increasing misery' postulated in Marx's original model. But so much of Marx's basic analysis remains valid and useful, and so many of his other predictions have been confirmed by the facts, that it is surely absurd to make such a fuss about this one failure."

I would be the last to deny that a great deal of Marx's basic theory remains valid and useful today. His "vision" and general method of analysis, his broad approach to the problem of value and distribution, and the general conceptual framework within which he developed his

---

[35] We may also, perhaps, point to the increased importance of capital-saving innovations in our own time, which may have had some effect in diminishing the size of the reserve army of labour and thus in easing the downward pressure on the general wage level which this army undoubtedly exerted in Marx's time.

main "laws of motion", still constitute, in my opinion, an indispensable starting-point for the understanding of contemporary capitalism, just as they did for the understanding of the capitalism of Marx's own time.[36] I would also not wish to deny that a number of Marx's other predictions have in fact been confirmed. Socialism has, after all, arrived on the historical scene (even if in a rather different way from that which Marx anticipated); a process of "concentration of capitals" has taken place; and the organized working-class movement has grown in strength. But it does nòt follow from these facts that when we are faced with the particular discrepancy I am talking about we can simply deal with it in terms of the "counteraction of an innate tendency" and leave it at that.

For the prediction of "increasing misery" was no minor or incidental part of Marx's analysis. On the contrary, it formed an essential and extremely important constituent of his general theory of the transition from capitalism to socialism. The main agency in this historical transition, in Marx's view, would be the working class, and it was above all this class's "increasing misery" which would impel it to take the decisive revolutionary action required to bring about the transition. And the prediction of "increasing misery" is not the only one of Marx's predictions which has been falsified by the facts: it is merely the leading species of a genus which embraces a significant number of Marx's most famous and most crucial "laws of motion of capitalism". "The resultants of the contradictory inner forces of capitalist production", Mr Gillman writes, "Marx summarized in the form of 'laws of motion'. These may be characterized as: (i) the law of the falling rate of profit; (ii) the law of the increasing severity of cyclical crises; (iii) the law of concentration and centralization of capital, and (iv) the law of the increasing misery of the working class."[37] In Marx's opinion, it was largely through the operation of these "laws of motion", and particularly through that of the last, that capitalism would eventually reach its historical limits. Now of these four laws I think it is fair to say that during the last half-century only the third has manifested itself on the surface of reality in a reasonably unambiguous manner, at any rate in the more advanced capitalist countries. In the case of the other three

---

[36] After all, as Marx himself often pointed out, an improvement in the material conditions of the working class under capitalism does not mean that this class ceases to be subject to "exploitation" in Marx's sense of the word. The slave remains a slave even if the amount of subsistence allotted to him is increased. "A rise in the price of labour," writes Marx in Vol. I of *Capital* (p. 618), "as a consequence of accumulation of capital, only means, in fact, that the length and weight of the golden chain the wage-worker has already forged for himself, allow of a relaxation of the tension of it." We have a long way to go yet before the concepts which Marx employed in his basic analysis of exploitation lose their utility.

[37] Joseph M. Gillman, *The Falling Rate of Profit* (New York, 1958), p. 1.

laws, things have by and large turned out to be substantially different from what Marx expected.

What are Marxists to do about this? Half a century is quite a long time; and while it may be plausible enough to argue that *one* of these allegedly crucial "innate tendencies" has been "counteracted" during this period, such an argument begins to wear a little thin when it is extended at the same time to *three* of them. Critics are bound to ask how much longer Marxists really think they can go on jogging along with a theory of capitalist development which talks in terms of certain "innate tendencies" which hardly ever seem to manifest themselves on the surface of reality but are always being "counteracted". Surely, they will say, if a model of capitalist development is going to be really useful the "innate tendencies" must by and large be those which reveal themselves on the surface of reality, at any rate "in the long run", "by and large", etc.; and the "offsetting factors" which it postulates must be those which normally operate only "in the short run", "in this or that time or place", etc.

It is possible, of course, for Marxists to reply that if we think in sufficiently broad terms the really essential part of Marx's predictions about the future of capitalism has in fact been fulfilled. The crucial point for Marx, it may plausibly be argued, was that the capitalist economy would eventually begin to slow down: the particular "laws of motion" which he put forward were important only because he believed that they happened to be the belts and levers through which the basic contradictions of capitalism would operate to bring the system to its historical limits. Thus a critique of certain of Marx's "laws of motion" on the grounds that they have not in fact unambiguously manifested themselves on the surface of economic reality in recent times is not a critique of the real *essence* of Marx's theory of capitalist development. It can be successfully countered by a demonstration that in our times the basic contradictions of capitalism are working through rather different belts and levers to produce the *general* result which Marx predicted.

I have much sympathy with this argument, which seems to me to constitute quite a useful methodological starting-point for further thought on the question at issue. But it is important to add that if it is to be justified, the demonstration just mentioned must in fact be given. If the Marxian model of capitalist development is to be rehabilitated, in other words, contemporary Marxists must use Marx's general methods and tools of analysis to work out in detail the *new* "laws of motion" through which they claim that the basic contradictions are now operating to bring capitalism to its historical limits. And these new "laws of motion", as we have seen, must reflect "innate tendencies" which (subject to the appropriate qualifications) are actually manifesting themselves on the surface of reality.

If a new Marxist model along these lines is not forthcoming, or if the advanced capitalist economies manage to solve the problem of their low rate of growth,[38] it is clear that Marxists will have to settle for something less than rehabilitation. Capitalism will have proved to be more resilient, and the Marxist economic analysis of it more transitory, than we might reasonably have anticipated. But the heavens will not fall, surely, if this turns out to be the case. We have learned an incredible amount from Marx, and we may still have a great deal to learn from him – particularly, as I have suggested in the last essay, in the sphere of methodology. Of what other economist whose system of analysis was worked out over a century ago can it be said that his work may still be seriously considered as a possible guide to the understanding and reformation of our own world today? In the long run – let us face it – none of us can really expect to go down in history as more than just another genius; and no one is exempt from the universal law of the mutability and eventual diffusion of systems of thought.

---

[38] It would be rather ill-advised of Marxists to assert that capitalist economies are in fact inherently incapable of solving this problem. My generation of Marxists was brought up to believe that mass unemployment could never be eradicated under capitalism; and it is not very long since we were told on the highest authority that the industries of the major capitalist countries would operate more and more below capacity in the post-war world.

THE FALLING RATE OF PROFIT[1]

I

The purpose of this essay is to clear up a point of some importance which for many years now has bedevilled arguments about Marx's "law of the falling tendency of the rate of profit".

The way in which Marx's theory is usually described, by both friends and foes alike, is something like this:[2] Take c (*constant capital*) to represent the value of used-up machinery, raw materials, etc., calculated in terms of units of embodied labour. Take v (*variable capital*) to represent the value of labour-power, also calculated in terms of units of embodied labour. And take s (*surplus value*) to represent the excess of value which the labour-power employed by v produces over and above its own value. Then the *total value* of an individual commodity, or of the output of an individual enterprise over a given period of time, or of the output of the economy as a whole over a given period of time, can be expressed in the familiar general formula:

$$\text{Total value} = c + v + s$$

Now define the ratio c/v as the *organic composition of capital*; s/v as the *rate of surplus value* (or, alternatively, the *rate of exploitation*); and $s/(c + v)$ as the *rate of profit*.[3] It can then easily be shown, by simple manipulation of these ratios,[4] that the rate of profit is connected with the rate of surplus value and the organic composition of capital in the following way:

$$\text{Rate of profit} = \frac{\text{Rate of surplus value}}{1 + \text{Organic composition of capital}}$$

It follows logically from these definitions that *if the rate of surplus value remains constant* a rise in the organic composition of capital will bring

[1] This essay is an amended version of an article which was published in *Science and Society*, Winter 1960.

[2] Cf. above, pp. 107–8.

[3] If we take the rate of profit to be $s/(c+v)$, we are of course assuming that the elements of both c and v are turned over once during the period in question, so that $c+v$ also represents the *stock* of capital. This assumption is highly unrealistic, but since the complications which result from its removal do not affect the substance of the following argument we may ignore them.

[4] Rate of profit $= s \div (c + v) = \dfrac{s}{v} \div \left(\dfrac{c + v}{v}\right) = \dfrac{s}{v} \div \left(1 + \dfrac{c}{v}\right)$

about a fall in the rate of profit. And this, it is claimed, is what Marx said would actually happen with the development of capitalism over time. As capitalism developed, machinery would be more and more substituted for labour; the organic composition of capital would therefore tend to rise; and the rate of profit would therefore tend to fall. There were of course certain "counteracting influences" (e.g., rises in the "intensity of exploitation" and falls in the value of "elements of constant capital") which would retard the fall in the rate of profit, but the effect of these would not be sufficient to offset the effect of the rising organic composition of capital. At any rate in the long run, the rate of profit would fall.

It is around this version of Marx's theory that most of the recent controversy has centred. Two points of criticism in particular have been raised.

(*i*) The rate of profit will fall when organic composition rises *only if the rate of surplus value remains constant*. But in actual fact, it is argued, the postulated rise in organic composition will normally bring about a rise in productivity, which will affect (*inter alia*) the industries producing wage goods. As organic composition rises, the value of the elements of variable capital will tend to fall. Therefore, unless real wages rise in proportion to the rise in productivity (which Marx generally assumes will not in fact happen), the rate of surplus value is likely to rise when organic composition rises. And this rise in the rate of surplus value cannot legitimately be treated merely as a "counteracting influence", since it is in fact an integral part of the general process of rising productivity which the postulated rise in organic composition will bring about. Thus, not only is Marx's procedure methodologically unsound, but it also turns out to be very doubtful whether one can in fact lay down any definite "tendency" for the rate of profit to fall.

(*ii*) The substitution of machinery for labour as capitalism develops, it is argued, does not necessarily lead to an increase in organic composition *measured in terms of value* (*i.e.*, in terms of units of embodied labour). The increase in productivity which the substitution of machinery for labour brings about will reduce the value not only of wage goods but also of capital goods, with the result that organic composition in terms of value may not fall at all, or may fall only very slowly. Once again, it is claimed, it is methodologically illegitimate to treat this "cheapening of elements of constant capital" as a mere "counteracting influence", since it is in fact an integral part of the general process of rising productivity. And when this "cheapening of elements of constant capital" is put together with the cheapening of elements of variable capital, it becomes quite impossible to make any generalizations at all concerning the direction in which the rate of profit will tend to move.

In the remainder of this essay, I shall try to sort out the elements of truth and the elements of falsity in these two criticisms.

II

Let us begin by considering the charge that Marx relegated the rise in the rate of surplus value, which the postulated rise in organic composition would bring about, to the status of a mere "counteracting influence".[5] If one looks carefully at the items which Marx considers under the heading "Increasing Intensity of Exploitation" in his chapter on *Counteracting Influences*, in Volume III of *Capital*, one sees that they are in fact confined to certain means of the intensification of labour, the lengthening of the working day, etc., which are not essentially connected with the rise in organic composition and the consequent rise in productivity which it brings about.[6] And the reason why Marx here excludes the type of rise in the rate of surplus value which *is* essentially connected with the rise in organic composition is very simple: *he has already taken this type of rise into account* in his earlier chapter on *The Law as Such*. Since this fact has been strenuously denied by many critics, detailed citations must be given.

It is true that in the illustration given at the beginning of the chapter on *The Law as Such* Marx specifically assumes that the rate of surplus value remains constant as organic composition increases. But even in the paragraph which immediately follows and generalizes from this illustration, we find Marx saying that the rise in organic composition will cause a fall in the rate of profit "at the same, *or even a rising*, degree of labour exploitation"[7] – a form of words which is repeated several times in his subsequent exposition.[8] Two pages further on, having pointed out that "what is true of different successive stages of development in one country, is also true of different coexisting stages of

[5] In this section, I shall be leaning heavily on an important and unduly neglected article by Mr Roman Rosdolsky, "Zur neuren Kritik des Marxschen Gesetzes der fallenden Profitrate", which appeared in *Kyklos*, Vol. IX, No. 2, 1956.

[6] There are certain aspects of intensification, Marx explains, which do not affect the relation of the value of constant capital to the price of the labour which sets it in motion. "Notably, it is prolongation of the working-day, this invention of modern industry, which increases the mass of appropriated surplus-labour without essentially altering the proportion of the employed labour-power to the constant capital set in motion by it" (*Capital*, Vol. III, p. 228).

[7] *Ibid.*, Vol. III, p. 209. (My italics.) By a fateful mischance, the vital words which I have italicized were omitted from the well-known Kerr edn. of Vol. III (Chicago, 1909, p. 249).

[8] E.g., on pp. 211, 216 and 282 of *ibid.*, Vol. III.

development in different countries", he proceeds to show how "the difference between . . . two national rates of profit might disappear, or even be reversed, if labour were less productive in the less developed country", so that the value of labour-power was higher and the rate of surplus value accordingly lower.[9] And this section of the chapter concludes with an illustration in which the rate of profit is shown to fall even though "the unpaid part of the labour applied may at the same time grow in relation to the paid part" – *i.e.*, even though the rate of surplus value rises owing to "the greater productivity of labour".[10]

In the next section of the chapter, where Marx deals with the increase in the *mass* of surplus value which accompanies the accumulation of capital and the fall in the rate of profit, the question of the fundamental relation between organic composition and the rate of surplus value is not discussed, for the simple reason that it is not relevant. But even here Marx goes out of his way to point out that the mass of surplus value will grow if there is "a drop in the value of wages due to an increase in the productiveness of labour".[11]

In the short section which follows, dealing with the question of the mass of profit contained in each individual commodity, we once again come face to face with the problem of the effect of a rising rate of surplus value. In spite of the rise in organic composition, says Marx, "the mass of profits contained in the individual commodities may nevertheless increase if the rate of the absolute or relative surplus-value grows". But this, he suggests, can be the case "only within certain limits". For a reason which I shall discuss below, he argues that "the mass of profit on each individual commodity will shrink considerably with the development of the productiveness of labour, in spite of a growth in the rate of surplus-value".[12] And four pages further on, after Engels's interpolation on the question of the effect of differences in turnover periods on the rate of profit, Marx again returns to the same problem. He admits that "considered abstractly" the rate of profit may remain the same or even rise, if the increase in the productivity of labour exercises its effects in certain ways upon the value of elements of constant and variable capital, but he argues, for the same reason as before, that "in reality . . . the rate of profit will fall in the long run".[13]

It is quite clear, then, on the evidence of the chapter on *The Law as Such* alone, that Marx was well aware of the fact that a rise in organic composition was likely to bring about a rise in the rate of surplus value, and that this fact was very relevant to the question of the behaviour of the rate of profit. And in subsequent chapters the point is made even

[9] *Ibid.*, Vol. III, p. 210.   [10] *Ibid.*, Vol. III, p. 212.   [11] *Ibid.*, Vol. III, p. 215.
[12] *Ibid.*, Vol. III, p. 221.   [13] *Ibid.*, Vol. III, p. 225.

more explicitly. In the chapter on *Counteracting Influences*, for example, Marx says that "the tendency of the rate of profit to fall is bound up with a tendency of the rate of surplus-value to rise", because the rise in productivity associated with the rise in organic composition will lower the value of labour-power. "The rate of profit", he argues, "does not fall because labour becomes less productive, but because it becomes more productive. Both the rise in the rate of surplus-value and the fall in the rate of profit are but specific forms through which growing productivity of labour is expressed under capitalism."[14] In the chapter on *Exposition of the Internal Contradictions of the Law*, again, in a passage which most of the critics have either missed or misinterpreted, Marx repeats the point that the development of the productivity of labour shows itself not only in an increase in organic composition but also in a rise in the rate of surplus value. And once again, for the same reason as before, he argues that "the compensation of the reduced number of labourers by intensifying the degree of exploitation has certain insurmountable limits".[15]

What, then, was Marx's reason for believing that it had these "insurmountable limits"? Why, in other words, did he believe that the downward pull on the rate of profit exercised by the rising organic composition of capital would be greater, at any rate "in the long run", than the upward push exercised by the rising rate of surplus value? This problem is first raised in Volume I of *Capital*, a few pages before Marx embarks upon his study of relative surplus value. The key passage here is as follows:

The compensation of a decrease in the number of labourers employed, or of the amount of variable capital advanced, by a rise in the rate of surplus-value, or by the lengthening of the working-day, has impassable limits. Whatever the value of labour-power may be, whether the working-time necessary for the maintenance of the labourer is 2 or 10 hours, the total value that a labourer can produce, day in, day out, is always less than the value in which 24 hours are embodied . . . The absolute limit of the average working-day – this being by nature always less than 24 hours – sets an absolute limit to the compensation of a reduction of variable capital by a higher rate of surplus-value, or of the decrease of the number of labourers exploited by a higher degree of exploitation of labour-power.

This "palpable law", says Marx, "is of importance for the clearing up of many phenomena, arising from a tendency (to be worked out later

---

[14] *Ibid.*, Vol. III, p. 234.
[15] *Ibid.*, Vol. III, p. 242. Mr Rosdolsky, in the article referred to above, has unearthed a number of passages in Marx's *Theories of Surplus Value* in which the point is made even more clearly.

on) of capital to reduce as much as possible the number of labourers employed by it . . ."[16]

It is this point which is emphasized in Marx's discussion of the law of the falling rate of profit in Volume III. "Even a larger unpaid portion of the smaller total amount of newly added labour", he writes in the chapter on *The Law as Such*, "is smaller than a smaller aliquot unpaid portion of the former larger amount."[17] A further example is given in the chapter on *Exposition of the Internal Contradictions of the Law*: "Two labourers, each working 12 hours daily, cannot produce the same mass of surplus-value as 24 who work only 2 hours, even if they could live on air and hence did not have to work for themselves at all."[18] As organic composition rises, less labourers than before will be employed with a given capital, and even if the rate of surplus value rises considerably the total mass of surplus value which that capital yields must necessarily (at any rate after a certain point) fall below its original level. This means that the rise in the rate of surplus value can compensate the effect of the rise in organic composition upon the rate of profit only within "certain insurmountable limits".

It is clear, then, that the first of the two criticisms described above is somewhat wide of the mark. In arguing that the tendency of the rate of profit was to fall as organic composition increased, Marx definitely did *not* assume that the rate of surplus value would remain constant. On the contrary, he fully recognized that a rise in organic composition would normally be accompanied by a rise in the rate of surplus value. He argued, however, that this rise in the rate of surplus value would not prevent the rate of profit from falling "in the long run", and he adduced in support of this argument the reason just outlined.[19]

Marx can, however, be justly criticized for a certain lack of rigour in his argument. In some contexts he speaks of the falling tendency of the rate of profit in terms which suggest that he believed that it would tend to fall more or less continuously as organic composition increased.[20] In actual fact, however, all that his own argument as it stands really

---

16 *Capital*, Vol. I, p. 305.

17 *Ibid.*, Vol. III, p. 222. Cf. pp. 211–12 and 224–5, where the same point is clearly implied.

18 *Ibid.*, Vol. III, p. 242.

19 In his *Theories of Surplus Value*, as Mr Rosdolsky points out (*loc. cit.*), Marx adduces certain additional reasons for his belief that the rise in the rate of surplus value will not be sufficient to prevent the rate of profit from falling. For one thing, the increase of productivity in agriculture will probably be less than its overall increase; and for another, the workers will probably enforce a rise in real wages as productivity increases. It has to be emphasized, however, that in the sections of *Capital* dealing with the falling rate of profit the reason outlined in the text is the only one which is mentioned.

20 See, e.g., *Capital*, Vol. III, p. 209.

allows us to say is that as organic composition increases and the number of men employed with a given capital diminishes, there will eventually come a point beyond which no conceivable rise in the rate of surplus value – not even a rise to infinity – could possibly prevent the mass of surplus value produced by the given capital (and thus the rate of profit) from falling below its original level.[21] It is true, of course, that in the real world the rate of profit will probably begin to fall before this point is reached, since the rate of surplus value obviously cannot in fact rise to infinity.[22] But it is clear that under certain conditions (e.g., if we start from a situation in which the rate of surplus value is low), the rate of profit may not in fact begin to fall below its original level until the number of men employed with a given capital has been very substantially reduced. Marx's "long run", in other words, may be very long indeed. And it is also clear that in the intervening period, under certain conditions which are by no means as exceptional as Marx seems to have believed, the rate of profit may well *rise* above its original level.[23] Marx's argument as it stands in *Capital* requires a certain amount of modification and elaboration before anything like a "law of the falling tendency of the rate of profit" can properly be based on it.

III

The second criticism described above is rather more justified than the first. It is true that Marx *mentions* the "cheapening of elements of constant capital" in his chapter on *The Law as Such*, but his references are purely incidental. For example he mentions, as an exception to the rule that the rate of profit will fall in spite of the increased rate of surplus value, the case where "the productiveness of labour uniformly

[21] If we start from a situation in which X men are employed with a given capital, the rate of surplus value being R, then the point in question will evidently be reached when the number of men employed with the given capital has fallen to $RX/(R + 1)$.

[22] The point at which the rate of profit will in fact begin to fall below its original level can be defined in various ways, none of them particularly helpful except in a formal sense. Suppose that in an initial situation 1, the organic composition of capital is O_1, the number of men employed with a given capital is X_1, and the rate of surplus value is R_1. Suppose that in a later situation 2, the organic composition of capital is O_2, the number of men employed with the given capital is X_2, and the rate of surplus value is R_2. The rate of profit in situation 2 will have fallen below its level in situation 1 if $(O_1 + 1)/(O_2 + 1) < R_1/R_2$, or alternatively, if $X_1/X_2 > [R_2(R_1 + 1)]/[R_1(R_2 + 1)]$. These formulae, like that given in the previous footnote, are only valid if the length of the working day remains unchanged.

[23] If, for example, we start from a situation in which the number of men employed with a given capital is 20 and the rate of surplus value is 1, and move to a situation in which the number of men employed is 15 and the rate of surplus value is 3, it is obvious that the rate of profit will rise.

K

cheapens all elements of the constant, and the variable, capital";[24] and in another place he admits that the rate of profit "could even rise if a rise in the rate of surplus-value were accompanied by a substantial reduction in the value of the elements of constant, and particularly of fixed capital".[25] But it does seem fair to complain that whereas the fall in the value of elements of *variable* capital is in effect taken into account by Marx in his basic chapter on *The Law as Such*, the fall in the value of elements of *constant* capital is treated merely as one of the "counteracting influences".

I am not sure, however, whether this procedure involves quite such a grave methodological sin as some of Marx's critics have suggested. What Marx in effect does, in his chapter on *The Law as Such*, is to assume that the increase in the *mass* of constant capital relative to variable which takes place as capitalism develops does in fact reflect itself in some increase (though not necessarily a proportionate increase) in the *value* of the constant capital relative to that of the variable.[26] The effect of this *given* secular increase in value composition, he argues, will eventually be to lower the rate of profit, in spite of the rise in the rate of surplus value which will normally accompany it. Then later, in his chapter on *Counteracting Influences*, he reminds us of the fact (which he has already elaborated at considerable length in the first part of Volume III) that the "cheapening of elements of constant capital" may well retard the decline in the rate of profit. This is at any rate one way of going about the job, and only a purist could really take exception to it on methodological grounds.

The main criticism which can properly be made of Marx's treatment of the problem is that nowhere does he precisely define the conditions under which the rate of profit will fall with a rising organic composition of capital, if we assume that this rising organic composition is associated with a lowering of the value of elements not only of variable but also of constant capital. As his argument stands, all he really says is (a) that there are certain "insurmountable limits" to the extent to which the cheapening of elements of variable capital can offset the effect of a rising organic composition upon the rate of profit; and (b) that cases where the cheapening of elements of constant capital causes the rate of profit to rise or remain constant, although "abstractly" possible, are very unlikely to be met with in practice. This is clearly not enough to support the general conclusions which Marx draws. In the next section of this essay, therefore, an attempt is made to provide a set of simple

[24] *Capital*, Vol. III, p. 222.   [25] *Ibid.*, Vol. III, p. 225. Cf. p. 243.
[26] Marx's reasons for making this assumption are well described by Mr Rosdolsky, *loc. cit.*

illustrations in which various different assumptions are made about, for example, the functional relation between increases in organic composition and increases in productivity, and on the basis of which a number of generalizations are made about the conditions under which the rate of profit will in fact fall.

IV

What we shall do, in effect, is to imagine the average organic composition of capital over the economy as a whole gradually increasing from a fairly low level to a fairly high one. We shall halt the process at various stages, and examine what happens to the rate of profit when we make various assumptions about the effect of the rise in organic composition upon productivity.

Case 1: As our first case, let us start with a situation in which technical conditions are such that over the economy as a whole the average 100 of capital employs 20 men. We assume that the length of the working day is 8 hours, and that the daily wage (equal to the value of labour-power) is 4, whence it follows that the rate of surplus value is 1. Taking one day's operations as our basis, the situation will be as follows:

$$
\begin{array}{cccc}
 & c & v & s \\
(1) & 20 & 80 & 80
\end{array}
$$

The 20 men will produce a total of 160 new value, of which 80 represents their wages and 80 the surplus value accruing to the capitalist. Organic composition is $\frac{1}{4}$, and the rate of profit is 80 per cent.

In this initial situation, 20 men are employed in conjunction with 20 constant capital – *i.e.*, constant capital per man employed is 1. Let us now suppose that technical innovations are introduced which raise constant capital per man from 1 to $2\frac{2}{3}$. In other words, at the current prices for wage goods and capital goods (which we assume for the moment to be unaffected by the technical innovations), for every $2\frac{2}{3}$ spent on constant capital, 4 will be spent on wages. This means that the average 100 of capital will be divided between 40 constant and 60 variable, 15 men being employed. The situation will be as follows:

$$
\begin{array}{cccc}
 & c & v & s \\
(2A) & 40 & 60 & 60
\end{array}
$$

The rate of surplus value will remain at 1, but organic composition will rise to $\frac{2}{3}$ and the rate of profit will fall to 60 per cent.

Now it is very probable that the increase in organic composition from $\frac{1}{4}$ to $\frac{2}{3}$ will raise productivity, in both the wage-goods and capital-goods industries. Let us assume that the increase in productivity is such as to reduce the value of all elements of constant and variable capital by $\frac{1}{4}$. This means that the elements of constant capital which cost 40 in situation 2A can now be bought for 30, and that the 15 men who require to be employed in conjunction with this amount of constant capital can now be obtained at a wage of 3 per day instead of 4 – *i.e.*, for a total expenditure of 45 instead of 60. The organic composition of the average 100 of capital will not change as compared with situation 2A, since the values of the elements of both constant and variable capital have been reduced equally, but both the mass of constant capital and the number of labourers employed will increase by $\frac{1}{3}$ as compared with situation 2A. 20 men will now be employed with the average 100 of capital, creating in the day's operations 160 new value, of which 60 will represent their wages and 100 the surplus value accruing to the capitalist. The situation will be as follows:

$$\begin{array}{cccc} & c & v & s \\ \text{(2B)} & 40 & 60 & 100 \end{array}$$

The rate of surplus value will rise to $1\frac{2}{3}$, and the rate of profit will rise to 100 per cent.[27]

Now suppose that further technical innovations are introduced which, at current prices, raise constant capital per man to $4\frac{1}{2}$. In other words, for every $4\frac{1}{2}$ spent on constant capital, 3 will be spent on wages, so that the average 100 of capital will be divided between 60 constant and 40 variable, $13\frac{1}{3}$ men being employed. The situation will be as follows:

$$\begin{array}{cccc} & c & v & s \\ \text{(3A)} & 60 & 40 & 67 \end{array}$$

Now assume that another increase in productivity, such that the elements of both constant and variable capital are reduced in value by a further $\frac{1}{4}$, follows the technical innovations. The wage will now fall to

----

[27] If the increase in productivity had affected only the elements of variable capital, reducing their value by $\frac{1}{4}$ but leaving the elements of constant capital unaffected, the average 100 of capital would have been divided between 47 constant and 53 variable, with a rate of profit of 88 per cent. If on the other hand the increase in productivity had affected only the elements of constant capital, reducing their value by $\frac{1}{4}$ but leaving the elements of variable capital unaffected, the average 100 of capital would have been divided between 33 constant and 67 variable, with a rate of profit of 67 per cent. Clearly the role played by the cheapening of elements of variable capital in retarding "the falling tendency of the rate of profit" is much more important than that played by the cheapening of elements of constant capital. The reason for this is fairly obvious: under given technical conditions, a cheapening of elements of variable capital not only increases the number of workers employed with a given capital, but also increases the proportion of unpaid to paid labour time. A cheapening of the elements of constant capital, on the other hand, although it also increases the number of workers employed with a given capital, has no effect at all on the proportion of unpaid to paid labour time.

$2\frac{1}{4}$, and $17\frac{2}{9}$ men (as compared with 20 in situation 2B) will be employed with the average 100 of capital. The general situation will be as follows:

$$\begin{array}{cccc} & c & v & s \\ \text{(3B)} & 60 & 40 & 102 \end{array}$$

The rate of surplus value will rise to $2\frac{11}{20}$, and the rate of profit will rise to 102 per cent.

Finally, suppose further technical innovations which raise constant capital per man to 9, and assume that the consequential increase in productivity reduces the values of the elements of constant and variable capital by a further $\frac{1}{4}$. The "A" and "B" situations, before and after the change in productivity, will be as follows:

$$\begin{array}{cccc} & c & v & s \\ \text{(4A)} & 80 & 20 & 51 \\ \text{(4B)} & 80 & 20 & 75 \end{array}$$

In the final situation $11\frac{23}{27}$ men will be employed, the rate of surplus value will rise to $3\frac{3}{4}$, and the rate of profit will fall to 75 per cent.

In relation to our problem, the relevant comparisons are of course between situations 1, 2B, 3B, and 4B. Calling these four situations simply 1, 2, 3, and 4, we may summarize our results as follows:

	Organic Composition	Assumed Reduction in Value of c and v	Rate of Surplus Value	Rate of Profit (%)
(1)	$\frac{1}{4}$	—	1	80
(2)	$\frac{2}{3}$	$\frac{1}{4}$	$1\frac{2}{3}$	100
(3)	$1\frac{1}{2}$	$\frac{1}{4}$	$2\frac{11}{20}$	102
(4)	4	$\frac{1}{4}$	$3\frac{3}{4}$	75

On the assumptions of our first case, then, the rate of profit rises during the first three stages, but falls at the last stage.

Case 2: Using the same method of procedure, and halting the process at the same stages, we now take a case where we start with a rate of surplus value of 1, as before, but where the increase in productivity associated with each move from one stage to the next is assumed to reduce the value of the elements of constant and variable capital by $\frac{1}{8}$, instead of by $\frac{1}{4}$ as before. The result is as follows:

	Organic Composition	Assumed Reduction in Value of c and v	Rate of Surplus Value	Rate of Profit (%)
(1)	$\frac{1}{4}$	—	1	80
(2)	$\frac{2}{3}$	$\frac{1}{8}$	$1\frac{17}{60}$	77
(3)	$1\frac{1}{2}$	$\frac{1}{8}$	$1\frac{3}{5}$	64
(4)	4	$\frac{1}{8}$	2	40

The increase in productivity associated with the rising organic composition of capital is in this case too small to prevent the rate of profit from falling continuously.

Case 3: We now take a case where the rate of surplus value in the initial stage is $\frac{1}{2}$, and where each move is assumed to reduce the value of the elements of constant and variable capital by $\frac{1}{4}$. The result is as follows:

	Organic Composition	Assumed Reduction in Value of c and v	Rate of Surplus Value	Rate of Profit (%)
(1)	$\frac{1}{4}$	—	$\frac{1}{2}$	40
(2)	$\frac{2}{3}$	$\frac{1}{4}$	1	60
(3)	$1\frac{1}{2}$	$\frac{1}{4}$	$1\frac{27}{40}$	67
(4)	4	$\frac{1}{4}$	$2\frac{11}{20}$	51

The rate of profit begins by rising, and falls only at the last stage; but even at the last stage it remains higher than it was in the initial stage. (Compare case 2.)

Case 4: We now take a case where the rate of surplus value in the initial stage is $1\frac{1}{2}$, and where each move is assumed to reduce the value of the elements of constant and variable capital by $\frac{1}{4}$. The result is as follows:

	Organic Composition	Assumed Reduction in Value of c and v	Rate of Surplus Value	Rate of Profit (%)
(1)	$\frac{1}{4}$	—	$1\frac{1}{2}$	120
(2)	$\frac{2}{3}$	$\frac{1}{4}$	$2\frac{1}{3}$	140
(3)	$1\frac{1}{2}$	$\frac{1}{4}$	$3\frac{9}{20}$	138
(4)	4	$\frac{1}{4}$	$4\frac{19}{20}$	99

The rate of profit begins by rising, but falls at an earlier stage than in case 3.

Case 5: We now take a case where the rate of surplus value in the initial stage is 1, and where each move is assumed to reduce the value of the elements of constant capital by $\frac{1}{8}$ and of variable capital by $\frac{1}{4}$. The result is as follows:[28]

[28] In cases 5 and 6 the actual organic composition at each stage, when the effect of the increase in productivity has been taken into account, will be rather different from that shown in the first column of the tables. In these two cases readings of organic composition are taken at the "A" stages, whereas readings of the rate of surplus value and rate of profit are taken at the "B" stages.

	Organic Composition	Assumed Reduction in Value of			Rate of Surplus Value	Rate of Profit (%)
		c	and	v		
(1)	$\frac{1}{4}$	–		–	1	80
(2)	$\frac{2}{3}$	$\frac{1}{8}$		$\frac{1}{4}$	$1\frac{37}{56}$	93
(3)	$1\frac{1}{2}$	$\frac{1}{8}$		$\frac{1}{4}$	$2\frac{5}{9}$	92
(4)	4	$\frac{1}{8}$		$\frac{1}{4}$	$3\frac{13}{18}$	67

Case 6: Finally, we take a case where the rate of surplus value in the initial stage is 1, and where each move is assumed to reduce the value of the elements of constant capital by $\frac{1}{4}$ and of variable capital by $\frac{1}{8}$. The result is as follows:

	Organic Composition	Assumed Reduction in Value of			Rate of Surplus Value	Rate of Profit (%)
		c	and	v		
(1)	$\frac{1}{4}$	–		–	1	80
(2)	$\frac{2}{3}$	$\frac{1}{4}$		$\frac{1}{8}$	$1\frac{9}{32}$	82
(3)	$1\frac{1}{2}$	$\frac{1}{4}$		$\frac{1}{8}$	$1\frac{27}{44}$	71
(4)	4	$\frac{1}{4}$		$\frac{1}{8}$	2	46

In this case the initial rise in the rate of profit is relatively small as compared with case 5, and the fall, when it occurs, is much more drastic.

This problem obviously cries out for mathematical treatment (which the present writer is not equipped to provide), and it would obviously be unsafe to come to any very firm conclusions on the basis of a mere half-dozen examples of the type given above. But the following tentative generalizations may perhaps be made.

(*i*) In all the cases considered, except number 2 (where the assumed rise in productivity is very small), the rate of profit begins by rising above its original level, and the direction of its movement does not change until the process of rising organic composition has got well under way. If we start from a fairly low level of organic composition, then, I think it can possibly be said that on Marx's premises the "tendency" of the rate of profit is first to rise, and then some time afterwards to fall.[29]

(*i.*) The initial rise in the rate of profit will be higher and the point of downturn will be later (a) the lower is the rate of surplus value in the situation from which we start; (b) the greater is the rise in overall productivity associated with the rising organic composition; and (c) the

---

[29] Cf. the conclusions reached by H. D. Dickinson, "The Falling Rate of Profit in Marxian Economics", *Review of Economic Studies*, Vol. XXIV, 1956–7, pp. 120 ff.

greater is the rise in productivity in the wage-goods industries relatively to that in the capital-goods industries.

V

In conclusion, one important point must be emphasized. The fact that the "tendency" just described appears in Marx's model does not of course mean that it will necessarily appear in the real world. It is true that Marx built his model in an endeavour to explain a *real* tendency for the rate of profit to fall which had apparently shown itself before his time[30] and which he undoubtedly believed would continue to show itself in the future. But such a model, because of the complexity of the processes actually involved, can in itself really do little more than draw attention to the main determining factors and the general manner of their interaction; and it can be used for purposes of prediction only (a) if the assumptions of the model are true of the real world, and (b) if the subsidiary determining factors abstracted from in the model do not exercise any significant influence. And these are two very big "if's" indeed. For example, it is assumed in Marx's model that real wages remain constant as productivity increases, and that the effect of increasing productivity in the capital-goods industries is merely to retard, and not actually to prevent, the secular increase of organic composition in value terms. In a world in which these assumptions are not valid, and in which, in addition, certain factors abstracted from in the model (the intensification of labour and the prevalence of monopoly, for example) have become significant, it is virtually impossible to predict how the rate of profit will in fact behave.

We should not be too disappointed, then, if the statistics we gather do not in fact show a "falling tendency of the rate of profit".[31] The main value of Marx's model in the present-day world is two-fold. In the first place, it provides us with a conceptual framework within which certain problems relating to the long-term behaviour of the rate of profit may perhaps be usefully considered. And in the second place, it keeps before our eyes the extremely important fact that changes in the rate of profit depend not on technical factors alone, but rather on the interaction of these with sociological factors.[32]

[30] It is quite possible that such a tendency had not in actual fact revealed itself in the preceding period. It is true that the rate of profit on *commercial* capital in the earlier stages of capitalist development was higher than the rate of profit on *productive* capital in the later stages. It is also true that the rate of interest on loans *for personal consumption* in the earlier stages of capitalist development was higher than the rate of interest on loans *for productive purposes* in the later stages. But it is not logical to deduce from these facts alone (as many contemporary economists did) that the tendency of the rate of profit on productive capital is to fall.

[31] Cf. Joseph M. Gillman, *The Falling Rate of Profit, passim.*

[32] Cf. above, p. 112.

SOME NOTES ON THE
"TRANSFORMATION PROBLEM"[1]

The debate initiated by Böhm-Bawerk on the alleged "great contradiction" between Volume I and Volume III of Marx's *Capital* has not yet been resolved to the satisfaction of all parties. In one form or another, and with various degrees of sophistication, a number of aspects of the question continue to be hotly disputed today. In particular, literature on the so-called "transformation problem" has multiplied considerably since Paul Sweezy drew the attention of English-speaking readers to it in 1946 in his *Theory of Capitalist Development.*[2]

The present essay sets out to do three things. First, it examines Marx's own discussion of the transformation of "values" into "prices of production", dealing in particular with the meaning which ought properly to be ascribed to his famous statement to the effect that "total values equal total prices of production". Second, it reviews two solutions of the "transformation problem", and suggests an alternative method of solution which (it is submitted) illustrates more effectively than the others the essential point which Marx was trying to make. Third, it says something about an important gap in Marx's argument which still remains after the "transformation problem" has been solved.

"Profit", wrote Marx, "is the form in which surplus-value presents itself to the view, and must initially be stripped by analysis to disclose the latter. In surplus-value, the relation between capital and labour

---

[1] This essay was originally published in *The Economic Journal*, March 1956. No amendments of substance have been made.

[2] See Sweezy, *The Theory of Capitalist Development*, pp. 109 ff.; Ladislaus von Bortkiewicz, "Value and Price in the Marxian System" (reprinted in *International Economic Papers*, No. 2, 1952); Bortkiewicz, "On the Correction of Marx's Fundamental Theoretical Construction in the Third Volume of 'Capital' " (reprinted as an appendix to Sweezy's edn. of Böhm-Bawerk's *Karl Marx and the Close of his System* and Hilferding's *Böhm-Bawerk's Criticism of Marx* (New York, 1949); J. Winternitz, "Values and Prices: A Solution of the So-called Transformation Problem" (*The Economic Journal*, June 1948, p. 276); K. May, "Value and Price of Production: A note on Winternitz's Solution" (*The Economic Journal*, December 1948, p. 596); Joan Robinson, in a review in *The Economic Journal*, June 1950, p. 358; Rudolf Schlesinger, *Marx: His Time and Ours* (London, 1950), pp. 139 ff.; and M. H. Dobb, "A Note on the Transformation Problem", in *On Economic Theory and Socialism* (London, 1955), p. 273. See also the important article by F. Seton in the *Review of Economic Studies*, Vol. XXIV, No. 3, which appeared after the original publication of the present essay.

is laid bare."[3] In Volume I of *Capital*, therefore, Marx presents us with an analysis of surplus value with its disguise removed. In this first stage of his argument the surplus value produced in each branch of industry is assumed to accrue to the capitalists *in that branch* in the form of a net gain. Now, since the only possible source of this surplus value, according to Marx's account, is the surplus labour performed by the labourers actually employed on the job, it follows that the ratio of net gain to capital must be unequal in cases where the organic composition[4] of the capitals concerned is unequal.[5] In actual fact, however, the rates of profit in the different branches tend towards equality under developed capitalism, and the organic compositions of capital tend if anything towards greater inequality. It is evidently necessary, therefore, that the Volume I assumptions should be removed at a later stage in the analysis and the effect of their removal upon the Volume I conclusions duly examined.

The assumptions are removed in Parts 1 and 2 of Volume III of *Capital*, where the question of the relation between surplus value and profit is considered. In actual fact, Marx argues, the amount of profit which the capitalists in each branch of industry receive must be sufficient to yield them the average rate of profit on the *total* quantity of capital which they employ, so that in the majority of cases the amount of profit they receive will differ from the amount of surplus value actually generated in their own branch of industry. But this does not mean that the Volume I analysis is vitiated. On the contrary, Marx believed that without this analysis political economy would be "deprived of every rational basis".[6] For, according to him, the profit which the capitalists in each branch of industry receive must be conceived as accruing to them by virtue of a sort of redivision of the aggregate surplus value produced over the economy as a whole. This aggregate surplus value is, as it were, reallocated among the different branches of industry so that the capitalists in each branch share in it not in accordance with the amount of capital they have spent on wages but in accordance with the *total* amounts of capital they have severally employed. Without the Volume I analysis to determine the magnitude of this aggregate, Marx maintained, the average rate of profit would be, as he put it in one place, "an average of *nothing*".[7]

[3] *Capital*, Vol. III, p. 47.

[4] The organic composition of capital is the ratio between the part of capital spent on equipment, raw materials, etc., which Marx calls *constant* capital (c), and the part spent on wages, which he calles *variable* capital (v). Cf. above, p. 107.

[5] Marx assumes here that the ratio of surplus value (s) to v is the same in all branches of industry.

[6] *Capital*, Vol. III, p. 147.   [7] *Theories of Surplus Value*, p. 231.

In his analysis of surplus value in Volume I, Marx had assumed that the commodities which the capitalist producers supplied were bought and sold "at their values" in the Marxian sense – *i.e.*, at equilibrium prices which were proportionate to the quantities of socially-necessary simple labour required to produce them. So long as it is taken for granted that the net gain received by the capitalists in each branch of industry consists of the surplus value generated in that branch, this is a plausible enough assumption. But the conversion of surplus value into average profit necessarily implies the transformation of values into what Marx called "prices of production".[8] It implies, in other words, that the majority of commodities do *not* tend to sell "at their values", but at "prices of production" which normally diverge to some extent from their values. The question immediately arises, therefore, whether Marx's Volume III analysis of exchange ratios in terms of prices of production can be regarded merely as a modification of his Volume I analysis in terms of values (as Marx himself argued), or whether it should be regarded as being in contradiction to it (as Böhm-Bawerk and his followers have insisted).

The basic point in Marx's answer to this question is as follows. The transformation of values into prices is brought about as a result of the conversion of surplus value into profit. Now the volume and rate of surplus value[9] are evidently determined by the ratio $\Sigma a / \Sigma v$ (where a is the total value, in the Marxist sense, of a given finished commodity); and the volume and rate of profit are determined by the ratio $\Sigma a_p / \Sigma v_p$ (where the subscript p indicates that a and v have been transformed from values into prices).[10] Marx argues, in effect, that $\Sigma a / \Sigma v = \Sigma a_p / \Sigma v_p$. (This, as we shall see, was what Marx had mainly in mind when he said that "total values equal total prices".)[11] In other words, he argues that the ratio between the value of commodities in general and the value of the commodity labour-power, upon which he had in Volume I conceived surplus value to depend,[12] remains unchanged when it is

---

[8] "The price of production", wrote Marx, "includes the average profit. We call it price of production. It is really what Adam Smith calls *natural price*, Ricardo calls *price of production*, or *cost of production*, and the physiocrats call *prix nécessaire*, because in the long run it is a prerequisite of supply, of the reproduction of commodities in every individual sphere" (*Capital*, Vol. III, p. 194).

[9] I am using the expression "rate of surplus value" here to mean the ratio of surplus value to *total* capital. Marx normally used it to mean the ratio of surplus value to *variable* capital.

[10] It is, of course, assumed here that the national income resolves itself only into wages and profits.

[11] Cf. M. H. Dobb, *Political Economy and Capitalism*, pp. 46 and 72–3.

[12] Marx starts in Vol. I with the fundamental exploitation ratio $s/v (=$ surplus labour/necessary labour). Adding unity to this ratio we get $(v + s)/v (=$ working day/ necessary labour). When the latter expression is applied to the totality of commodities,

expressed in terms of prices rather than values, so that profit can still be said to be determined in accordance with the Volume I analysis. If this is so, it can be plausibly argued that the very degree to which individual prices of production diverge from values is ultimately determined according to the Volume I analysis. Thus the disturbance introduced into the operation of the law of value as described in Volume I is a *predictable* disturbance, and "in the exact sciences it is not customary to regard a predictable disturbance as a refutation of a law".[13]

Marx's discussion of this problem is developed in two stages, the first of which has received much more attention than the second. In the first stage he takes "five different spheres of production", deliberately assuming that none of the commodities concerned enters into the production of any of the others. Thus capitals I to V in the accompanying table[14] can be considered as the component parts of one single capital of 500.

1		2	3	4	5	6	7	8
								Deviation
		Used-					*Price of*	*of Price*
		up	*Cost*	*Surplus*			*Produc-*	*from*
	Capitals	*c*	*Price*	*Value*	*Value*	*Profit*	*tion*	*Value*
(I)	$80c + 20v$	50	70	20	90	22	92	+2
(II)	$70c + 30v$	51	81	30	111	22	103	−8
(III)	$60c + 40v$	51	91	40	131	22	113	−18
(IV)	$85c + 15v$	40	55	15	70	22	77	+7
(V)	$95c + 5v$	10	15	5	20	22	37	+17
				110	422	110	422	

it becomes $\Sigma(v + s)/\Sigma v (=$ total labour force/labour required to produce wage-goods); and, given conditions of equilibrium between the different branches of the economy, this ratio (total labour force/labour required to produce wage-goods) is equal to the ratio value of finished commodities/value of wage-goods $(= \Sigma a/\Sigma v)$. For example, in the following case Department I produces means of production and Department II consumer's goods; the ratio s/v is the same for both Departments; and the equilibrium conditions appropriate to simple reproduction prevail between them (*i.e.*, $c_2 = v_1 + s_1$):

	c_1	v_1	s_1	a_1
(I)	80	60	40	180
	c_2	v_2	s_2	a_2
(II)	100	90	60	250

It will be seen that the three ratios, working day/necessary labour $(= \frac{5}{3})$, total labour force/labour required to produce wage-goods $(= \frac{250}{150})$, and value of finished commodities/value of wage-goods $(= \frac{250}{150})$, are all equal.

[13] P. Fireman, quoted by Engels in the latter's preface to Vol. III of *Capital*, p. 14.
[14] This table is an amalgamation of those on pp. 153–5 of Vol. III of *Capital*, with some of the figures rearranged.

Each of the constituent capitals shown in column 1 totals 100, but the cost price of each of the outputs is less than 100, since it is assumed that only a portion of the value of the constant capital is transferred to the commodity in the period we are considering.[15] The amount so transferred is shown in column 2, and the cost price, which is the sum of v and used-up c, is shown in column 3. It is assumed that the working day is everywhere equally divided between necessary and surplus labour, so that surplus value (shown in column 4) is equal to v. The total *value* of each of the outputs being considered (shown in column 5) represents the sum of the cost price and the surplus value. Now it is evident that the sale of these commodities at their values would result in very unequal rates of profit on each of the capitals. In actual fact, however, Marx maintains, the total pool of surplus value, amounting to 110, is allotted ("by competition")[16] to the individual capitals in accordance with the total size of each – in this case uniformly, so that each receives a profit of 22 (column 6). The "price of production" (column 7), then, at which each output actually tends to sell, is the sum of the cost price and the profit, and differs in each case from the value. But since the total profit is by definition equal to the total surplus value, it naturally follows that in the present case the sum of the prices of production is equal to the sum of the values, or, to put the same thing in another way, that the deviations of prices from values (column 8) cancel one another out.[17]

Marx's statement that the sum of the prices is equal to the sum of the values has come in for considerable criticism. From Böhm-Bawerk onwards, critics have questioned whether this statement can be held to be meaningful, whether it embodies a tautology, and so on, and have generally concluded that Marx's "argument" is quite untenable. Some of the difficulty no doubt arises from the fact that Marx, having illustrated this equality arithmetically in the particular case just described (the case where mutual interdependence is abstracted from), immediately went on, rather rashly perhaps, to say that "in the same way the sum of the prices of production of all commodities produced in society – the totality of all branches of production – is equal to the sum of their values".[18] The implication of this statement, read in its context, might seem to be that when the assumption that none of the commodities concerned enters into the production of any of the others is dropped, so

---

[15] The turnover periods of v are assumed to be the same in each case.

[16] *Capital*, Vol. III, p. 156.

[17] It is evident that the only case in which price and value would coincide would be one in which the composition of the capital concerned coincided with the "social average".

[18] *Capital*, Vol. III, p. 157.

that the values of input as well as those of output have to be transformed into prices of production, a transformation carried out on the basis of a redistribution of the pool of surplus value will bring out total prices equal to total values in the arithmetical sense. This is in fact not so. On any plausible set of assumptions regarding the manner in which the different branches of the economy are interrelated, it will soon be found upon experimenting with various sets of figures that if the values of input as well as those of output are to be transformed into prices of production, it is normally impossible to effect a simultaneous transformation which will make total profit equal to total surplus value and at the same time make total prices of production equal to total values. In all but very exceptional cases we may preserve one of these equalities but not both.[19] If Marx's attention had been drawn to this fact, he might well have reformulated some of his statements regarding the equality of total prices and total values, while still insisting on the essential point they were designed to express – viz., that after the transformation of values into prices of production the fundamental ratio upon which profit depended[20] could still be said to be determined in accordance with the Volume I analysis. In the special case where

[19] For an example of one of the exceptional cases, see the transformation exhibited in Tables II and IIIb on pp. 111 and 120 of Sweezy's *Theory of Capitalist Development*.

[20] There is a slight technical difficulty here. When Marx said that "total values equal total prices" it is fairly clear that what he had in mind was the equality of the ratios $\Sigma a/\Sigma v$ and $\Sigma a_p/\Sigma v_p$, each calculated over the economy as a whole. (Cf. Dobb, *loc. cit.*) Given conditions of equilibrium between the different Departments, these ratios will be equal to the basic exploitation ratio $\Sigma(v + s)/\Sigma v$. In the case we have just considered, however, where the information which we are given covers only a part of the economy, it is obvious that the numerical value of the ratio $\Sigma a/\Sigma v$ derived from this information alone (assuming that we are able to derive it at all) is likely to differ from the numerical value of $\Sigma a/\Sigma v$ which we could derive from complete information regarding the economy as a whole. (For example, if we assume that the table gives us complete information regarding the output of finished goods, but of no other branches of production, Σa will be the same but Σv will be underestimated.) A similar sort of difficulty arises in the second stage of the argument (to be considered shortly), where we have full information concerning the economy, but where it is not desirable to postulate equilibrium conditions. In both these cases, our calculation of $\Sigma a/\Sigma v$ from the information which we are given is likely to differ from that of the basic exploitation ratio $\Sigma(v + s)/\Sigma v$. In such cases, then, if we want to illustrate by an arithmetical example what Marx had in mind when he said that "total values equal total prices", the best we can do is to start with a ratio whose numerator is the sum of the total values of all the commodities (whether finished or otherwise) about which we are given information, and whose denominator is the sum of all the v's which we are given; and then to show that the numerical value of this ratio remains the same when those values which the particular problem requires to be transformed into prices are so transformed. The numerical value of this ratio will not normally be identical with that of $\Sigma a/\Sigma v$ calculated for the economy as a whole, but it will express the same underlying idea. In what follows the symbol a will be used for the total value of any commodity, whether finished or not.

none of the commodities concerned enters into the production of any of the others, he might have said, the ratio remains the same for the simple reason that the relevant quantities remain the same – the denominator remains the same by hypothesis, and the numerator remains the same because *in this case* the sum of the prices necessarily equals the sum of the values. In the more difficult case where the various branches of production are mutually interdependent, he might have said, the sum of the prices does not necessarily come out equal to the sum of the values, but the fundamental ratio can still be said to be determined in accordance with the Volume I analysis. And it would have been possible for him to illustrate this, as I shall show below, by an arithmetical example rather similar in character to that described above.

However, it would be wrong to suggest that Marx simply ignored this more difficult case. On the contrary, his examination of it, although by no means rigorous, was sufficiently well organized to be said to constitute that second stage in his argument of which I have spoken above. He begins by dropping the assumption that none of the commodities concerned enters into the production of any of the others. In actual fact, he writes, "the elements of productive capital are, as a rule, bought on the market", so that "their prices include profit which has already been realized, hence, include the price of production of the respective branch of industry together with the profit contained in it, so that the profit of one branch of industry goes into the cost-price of another". At first sight it might seem as if this would mean that the profit accruing to each capitalist might be counted several times in a calculation such as that which has just been described, but Marx has little difficulty in disposing of this superficial objection. The dropping of the assumption, however, does indeed make one essential difference, which Marx describes as follows:

Aside from the fact that the price of a particular product, let us say that of capital B, differs from its value because the surplus-value realized in B may be greater or smaller than the profit added to the price of the products of B, the same circumstance applies also to those commodities which form the constant part of capital B, and indirectly also its variable part, as the labourers' necessities of life. So far as the constant portion is concerned, it is itself equal to the cost-price plus the surplus-value, here therefore equal to cost-price plus profit, and this profit may again be greater or smaller than the surplus-value for which it stands. As for the variable capital, the average daily wage is indeed always equal to the value produced in the number of hours the labourer must work to produce the necessities of life. But this number of hours is in its turn obscured by the deviation of the prices of production of the necessities of life from their values. However, this always resolves itself to one commodity receiving too little of the surplus-value while another receives too much, so that the deviations from the value which are embodied in the prices of production compensate one another. Under capitalist production, the general law acts as the prevailing tendency only in a very complicated and approximate manner, as a never ascertainable average of ceaseless fluctuations.[21]

Marx returns to the same point a few pages later, emphasizing that the transformation process involves a modification of the Volume I assumption that "the cost-price of a commodity equalled the *value* of the commodities consumed in its production". But for the buyer, Marx writes,

the price of production of a specific commodity is its cost-price, and may thus pass as cost-price into the prices of other commodities. Since the price of production may differ from the value of a commodity, it follows that the cost-price of a commodity containing this price of production of another commodity may also stand above or below that portion of its total value derived from the value of the means of production consumed by it. It is necessary to remember this modified significance of the cost-price, and to bear in mind that there is always the possibility of an error, if the cost-price of a commodity in any particular sphere is identified with the value of the means of production consumed by it. Our present analysis does not necessitate a closer examination of this point.[22]

And in a later passage, repeating the same point once more, Marx argues that "this possibility does not detract in the least from the correctness of the theorems demonstrated which hold for commodities of average composition".[23]

This is where the so-called "transformation problem" comes into the picture. Marx's method of transforming values into prices, it is said, meaning by this his original calculation outlined in the table above, contains an error, since it does not take account of the fact that the values of elements of input as well as those of elements of output have to be transformed into prices.[24] It is then claimed that Marx can be rescued from this error simply by showing the *formal possibility* of a consistent derivation of prices from values in the case of mutual interdependence. When values are transformed into prices, the ratio of price to value must be the same when a given commodity is considered as input as when it is considered as output; and after the transformation the rate of profit must come out equal in the case of each capital concerned. These ratios of price to value, and the rate of profit, are regarded as the main unknowns. The "transformation problem" then reduces

---

[21] Quotations from *Capital*, Vol. III, pp. 157–9. There is a similar passage at the end of Marx's comments on Bailey in the *Theories of Surplus Value* which shows that the point had occurred to Marx several years before the publication of the first volume of *Capital*.

[22] *Capital*, Vol. III, p. 162.   [23] *Ibid.*, Vol. III, p. 203.

[24] As will be clear from what has been said above, it was not intended to take account of this fact, since mutual interdependence was specifically abstracted from.

itself to this: can the relations between the various branches of production, and the various conditions which are to be fulfilled as a result of the transformation, be expressed in the form of an equational system which is "determinate" in the mathematical sense – *i.e.*, in which the number of independent equations is equal to the number of unknowns? The assumption lying behind these enquiries is that if the relations and conditions can in fact be so expressed, Marx's method of transforming values into prices will itself be transformed from an invalid to a valid one.

The best-known solution, that of Bortkiewicz, commences with the particular set of value relationships postulated by Marx as existing between the three main Departments of the economy (I = means of production; II = workers' consumption goods; III = capitalists' consumption goods) under conditions of simple reproduction. Employing the usual notation, these value relationships can be expressed in the form of three equations:

$$\text{(I)} \quad c_1 + v_1 + s_1 = c_1 + c_2 + c_3$$
$$\text{(II)} \quad c_2 + v_2 + s_2 = v_1 + v_2 + v_3$$
$$\text{(III)} \quad c_3 + v_3 + s_3 = s_1 + s_2 + s_3$$

If we take the ratio of price to value to be x in the case of means of production, y in the case of workers' consumption goods, and z in the case of capitalists' consumption goods; if we further call the average rate of profit r; and if we state as a condition of the problem that the relations appropriate to simple reproduction should continue to obtain after the transformation of values into prices as before it, then the following equalities must hold:

$$\text{(I)} \quad c_1 x + v_1 y + r(c_1 x + v_1 y) = (c_1 + c_2 + c_3)x$$
$$\text{(II)} \quad c_2 x + v_2 y + r(c_2 x + v_2 y) = (v_1 + v_2 + v_3)y$$
$$\text{(III)} \quad c_3 x + v_3 y + r(c_3 x + v_3 y) = (s_1 + s_2 + s_3)z$$

Here there are four unknowns (x, y, z and r), and only three equations. Bortkiewicz reduces the unknowns to three by assuming (a) that the value scheme was expressed in terms of money, and (b) that gold is the money commodity, and is produced in Department III, in which case z may reasonably be taken as equal to 1. The equational system thereupon becomes determinate, and solutions for x, y and r can be fairly readily derived. Upon applying these solutions to various sets of figures, it is seen that total profit comes out equal to total surplus value, but that total prices normally diverge from total values. Neither the equality nor the inequality, however, has anything more than formal significance. As Bortkiewicz says, in relation to a particular set of figures,

That the total price exceeds the total value arises from the fact that Department III, from which the good serving as value and price measure is taken, has a relatively low organic composition of capital. But the fact that total profit is numerically identical with total surplus value is a consequence of the fact that the good used as value and price measure belongs to Department III.[25]

It is only in the special case where the organic composition of the capital employed in Department III is equal to the social average that the sum of the prices will come out equal to the sum of the values.

Winternitz adopts the same general attitude towards the problem as Bortkiewicz, but clears the Bortkiewicz solution of certain redundancies and unnecessary artificialities. He commences with the usual value schema in the three Departments:

$$\text{(I)} \quad c_1 + v_1 + s_1 = a_1$$
$$\text{(II)} \quad c_2 + v_2 + s_2 = a_2$$
$$\text{(III)} \quad c_3 + v_3 + s_3 = a_3$$

But instead of assuming the equilibrium conditions appropriate to Marx's reproduction schemes, he assumes merely that when a_1 varies by x (the price-value ratio for means of production), then c_1, c_2 and c_3 also vary by x; and that when a_2 varies by y (the price-value ratio for workers' consumption goods), then v_1, v_2 and v_3 also vary by y. Thus he arrives at the following simple equational system:

$$\text{(I)} \quad c_1 x + v_1 y + S_1 = a_1 x$$
$$\text{(II)} \quad c_2 x + v_2 y + S_2 = a_2 y$$
$$\text{(III)} \quad c_3 x + v_3 y + S_3 = a_3 z$$

By putting $a_1 x/(c_1 x + v_1 y) = a_2 y/(c_2 x + v_2 y)$ (each of these expressions being equal to $1 + r$), solutions for x, y and for r are easily obtained. A further set of relationships between x, y and z must then be postulated in order to determine the price level for the system as a whole. From a purely logical point of view, it obviously does not matter what relationships are postulated, but Winternitz puts

$$a_1 x + a_2 y + a_3 z = a_1 + a_2 + a_3$$

(*i.e.*, the sum of prices = sum of values), because in his opinion this is "the obvious proposition in the spirit of the Marxian system".[26] Solutions for x, y and z are then yielded immediately without any special difficulty. When applied to various sets of figures, these solutions naturally bring out the sum of prices equal to the sum of values, but total profit normally diverges from total surplus value.

[25] Bortkiewicz, in Sweezy's edn. of Böhm-Bawerk's *Karl Marx and the Close of his System*, p. 205.
[26] *The Economic Journal*, June 1948, p. 279.

Winternitz's solution, although in essence very similar to Bortkie-wicz's, is evidently simpler and therefore more acceptable from a purely mathematical point of view. Indeed, it is the special merit of Winternitz to have exposed the triviality of the whole problem as so posed – a triviality which tended to be hidden by Bortkiewicz's over-elaborate and rather confusing method. The Winternitz solution is an effective reply to those who said that it was not formally possible to transform values into prices when elements of input as well as output were in-volved. But it seems to me that something more is required before a transformation of the Bortkiewicz-Winternitz type can properly be used to illustrate the second stage of Marx's Volume III argument. The essential point for Marx, as we have seen, was that after aggregate surplus value had been converted into profit, and values consequently transformed into prices, the ratio $\Sigma a/\Sigma v$ should be equal to the ratio $\Sigma a_p/\Sigma v_p$. Is it possible to effect a transformation which brings these ratios out equal, and if so under what conditions?

This problem can be dealt with as follows. Select three sets of quan-tities for c, v and s in Departments I, II and III, such that the rate of surplus value in the Marxist sense (s/v) is equal in each case, and that the organic composition of capital in Department II is equal to the social average[27] – for example:

$$c_1 + v_1 + s_1 = a_1$$
$$\text{(I)} \quad 3 + 4 + 4 = 11$$
$$c2 + v_2 + s_2 = a_2$$
$$\text{(II)} \quad 18 + 15 + 15 = 48$$
$$c_3 + v_3 + s_3 = a_3$$
$$\text{(III)} \quad 9 + 6 + 6 = 21$$

Proceed now to transform these expressions into the following:

$$\text{(I)} \quad c_1 x + v_1 y + S_1 = a_1 x$$
$$\text{(II)} \quad c_2 x + v_2 y + S_2 = a_2 y$$
$$\text{(III)} \quad c_3 x + v_3 y + S_3 = a_3 z$$

on the basis of the following equalities:[28]

$$\frac{S_1}{c_1 x + v_1 y} = \frac{S_2}{c_2 x + v_2 y} = \frac{S_3}{c_3 x + v_3 y}$$

and

$$S_1 + S_2 + S_3 = s_1 + s_2 + s_3$$

[27] *I.e.*, that $c_2/(c_2 + v_2) = \Sigma c/(\Sigma c + \Sigma v)$.

[28] These two equalities express, of course, the equality of profit rates, and the equality of the sum of profits with the sum of surplus values

The result of this calculation in the given case is as follows:

$$\begin{array}{cccc} c_1x & v_1y & S_1 & a_1x \\ \text{(I)} \quad 2{\cdot}592 + & 3{\cdot}710 + & 3{\cdot}202 = & 9{\cdot}504 \end{array}$$

$$\begin{array}{cccc} c_2x & v_2y & S_2 & a_2y \\ \text{(II)} \quad 15{\cdot}552 + & 13{\cdot}911 + & 15{\cdot}052 = & 44{\cdot}515 \end{array}$$

$$\begin{array}{cccc} c_3x & v_3y & S_3 & a_3z \\ \text{(III)} \quad 7{\cdot}776 + & 5{\cdot}564 + & 6{\cdot}784 = & 20{\cdot}124 \end{array}$$

This calculation, like Marx's original one in the case where mutual interdependence was abstracted from, shows the result when a fixed aggregate of surplus value is reallocated in the form of profit at the average rate among the various capitals concerned. The sum of prices diverges from the sum of values, but the real point to which Marx wished to draw attention when he emphasized the equality between total prices and total values in the original case – *i.e.*, that after the transformation of values into prices the fundamental ratio upon which profit depended[29] could still be said to be determined in accordance with the Volume I analysis – is illustrated in this case too. It is no longer true that the numerator and the denominator of the ratio remain unchanged as a result of the transformation, but under the assumed conditions *both will always change in the same proportion*, so that $(a_1x + a_2y + a_3x)/(v_1y + v_2y + v_3y)$ remains equal to $(a_1 + a_2 + a_3)/(v_1 + v_2 + v_3)$. The achievement of this result is dependent (in the great majority of cases) upon the equality initially postulated between $c_2/(c_2 + v_2)$ and $\Sigma c/(\Sigma c + \Sigma v)$ – *i.e.*, upon the assumption that the organic composition of capital in the wage-goods industries is equal to the social average.[30,31]

Such an illustration, however, would fill only part of the gap in Marx's analysis. To fill the rest of it, we must turn to economic history and methodology rather than to mathematics. The derivation of prices

---

[29] See above, pp. 145–6.

[30] I am indebted to Dr G. A. P. Wyllie, of Glasgow University, for a mathematical proof both of this general result and of its dependence in normal cases upon the condition $c_2/(c_2 + v_2) = \Sigma c/(\Sigma c + \Sigma v)$. While the result will always be reached when this condition is satisfied, there may be a few special cases in which it could be reached without the condition being satisfied.

[31] In Marx's arithmetical illustration to the first stage of his argument, the conditions laid down do not require that the values of the elements of input should be transformed into prices. It is possible to reinterpret his figures, however, so that they illustrate a situation in which the values of v (but not of c), as well as those of a, have to be transformed into prices, and in which the organic composition of capital in the wage-goods industries is equal to the social average, so that v is the same whether expressed in price or in value terms (*i.e.*, that $y = 1$). In the present case, where c, v and a have all to be transformed into prices, the fact that the organic composition of capital in the wage-goods industries is equal to the social average no longer necessarily means that $y = 1$.

from values, according to Marx's general economic method,[32] must be regarded as a historical as well as a logical process. In "deriving prices from values" we are really reproducing in our minds, in logical and simplified form, a process which has actually happened in history. Marx began with the assumption that goods sold "at their values" under capitalism (so that profit rates in the various branches of production were often very different), not only because this appeared to be the proper starting-point from the logical point of view but also because he believed that it had "originally"[33] been so. He proceeded on this basis to transform values into prices, not only because this course appeared to be logically necessary but also because he believed that history itself had effected such a transformation. The exchange of commodities at their values, or approximately at their values, Marx wrote,

requires a much lower stage than their exchange at their prices of production, which requires a definite level of capitalist development . . .

Apart from the domination of prices and price movement by the law of value, it is quite appropriate to regard the values of commodities as not only theoretically but also historically *prius* to the prices of production. This applies to conditions in which the labourer owns his means of production, and this is the condition of the land-owning farmer living off his own labour and the craftsman, in the ancient as well as in the modern world. This agrees also with the view we expressed previously, that the evolution of products into commodities arises through exchange between different communities, not between the members of the same community. It holds not only for this primitive condition, but also for subsequent conditions, based on slavery and serfdom, and for the guild organization of handicrafts, so long as the means of production involved in each branch of production can be transferred from one sphere to another only with difficulty and therefore the various spheres of production are related to one another, within certain limits, as foreign countries or communist communities.[34]

But Marx did not pursue the historical aspects of the problem of the transformation of values into prices very much further than this, and his critics have taken full advantage of the fact that a number of problems still remain unsolved.[35] Böhm-Bawerk, for example, argued

---

[32] Cf. above, pp. 96–7.   [33] *Capital*, Vol. III, p. 156.

[34] *Ibid.*, Vol. III, p. 174. Cf. p. 177: "What competition, first in a single sphere, achieves is a single market-value and market-price derived from the various individual values of commodities. And it is competition of capitals in different spheres, which first brings out the price of production equalizing the rates of profit in the different spheres. *The latter process requires a higher development of capitalist production than the previous one.*" (My italics.) Cf. also pp. 172–4.

[35] Engels, referring to the passage just quoted, said that "if Marx had had an opportunity to work over the third volume once more, he would doubtless have extended this passage considerably. As it stands it gives only the sketchy outline of what is to be said on the point in question" (*Engels on "Capital"*, p. 102).

that if the derivation of prices from values had in fact proceeded in the manner which Marx's analysis suggests, "there must be traces of the actual fact that *before* the equalization of the rates of profit the branches of production with the relatively greater amounts of constant capital have won and do win the smallest rates of profit, while those branches with the smaller amounts of constant capital win the largest rates of profit"; and he went on to assert (following Sombart) that there are in fact "no traces of this to be found anywhere, either in the historical past or in the present".[36] Engels attempted to deal with this and other related problems in his important "Supplement" to Volume III of *Capital*,[37] giving a suggestive account of the manner in which, in the formative years of the development of capitalism, the prices of commodities were adjusted above or below their values in order to bring the surplus value into equality with the average rate of profit. This essay is certainly the most ambitious attempt to bridge the gap in Marx's argument which we possess. But even this is really little more than a preliminary sketch, and many details still remain to be filled in.

It is, of course, quite open to us, if we wish, to by-pass this question by characterizing the view expressed by Marx in the passage just quoted as a sort of "Robinsonade". Marx, it might be argued, was really doing little more than take over the traditional Classical idea that exchange ratios were proportional to embodied labour ratios only in that "early and rude state of society" of which Adam Smith spoke. Such a characterization would not necessarily affect the utility of the labour theory of value as a tool for the analysis of *capitalist* society – given (*inter alia*) a satisfactory solution to the logical problem of the transformation of values into prices; but on the other hand it does not seem likely that Marx himself would have been prepared to accept it. Marx and Engels always insisted very strongly that the logical method of treatment which they adopted in their work on political economy was "nothing else than the historical method, only divested of its historical form and disturbing fortuities". The chain of thought, said Engels,

must begin with the same thing that this history begins with and its further course will be nothing but the mirror-image of the historical course in abstract and theoretically consistent form, a corrected mirror-image but corrected according to laws furnished by the real course of history itself, in that each factor can be considered at its ripest point of development, in its classic form.[38]

Given this approach, it seems probable that Marx would have con-

---

[36] *Karl Marx and the Close of his System* (ed. Sweezy), p. 49. See also Hilferding's reply on pp. 169–72.

[37] Reprinted in *Engels on "Capital"*, pp. 94 ff.

[38] Engels, *Ludwig Feuerbach*, p. 99. Cf. above, pp. 96–7.

tinued to take the view that his *logical* transformation of values into prices was the "corrected mirror-image" of some actual *historical* transformation.

Engels, in the "Supplement" referred to above, tried to solve the problem by suggesting that up to the time when the capitalist form of production came upon the scene, commodity prices in actual fact normally tended to "gravitate towards the values fixed by the Marxian law and oscillate around these values".[39] This suggestion does not on the whole seem very plausible, for fairly obvious reasons connected with the prevalence of various forms of monopoly, the low degree of factor mobility, etc., in most actual pre-capitalist societies. Fortunately, however, it is not necessary to follow Engels all the way in this matter: it is quite sufficient to show that history has in fact effected a transformation of one type of *supply price* into another.[40] Broadly speaking, there are two main types of supply price to be found in the history of commodity exchange – first, that of the producer who thinks of his net receipts as a reward for his labour, and second, that of the producer who thinks of his net receipts as a profit on his capital. What Marx did, in effect, was to assume that the first type of supply price was characteristic of all pre-capitalist forms of society (abstracting here from those specific features differentiating pre-capitalist societies from one another which in other contexts he was especially concerned to emphasize), and to concentrate on the task of showing how the coming of capitalism, with its conversion of labour-power into a commodity, accomplished the transformation of the first type of supply price into the second.[41] This, I think, is the historical transformation of which the logical transformation considered above must be regarded as the counterpart.

[39] *Engels on "Capital"*, p. 106.
[40] The labour theory of value, like all cost theories, approaches the value problem *via* the supply price, and can afford a determinate explanation of actual prices only in so far as these are equal to or tend towards supply prices.
[41] See on this point *Capital*, Vol. I, pp. 169–70.

PART THREE
MODERN ECONOMICS

Mr SRAFFA'S REHABILITATION
OF CLASSICAL ECONOMICS[1]

I

Mr Sraffa's important book, *Production of Commodities by Means of Commodities*,[2] can be looked at from various points of view. It can be regarded, if one pleases, simply as an unorthodox theoretical model of a particular type of economy, designed to solve the traditional problem of value in a new way. It can be regarded as an implicit attack on modern marginal analysis: the sub-title of the book is "Prelude to a Critique of Economic Theory", and Sraffa in his preface expresses the hope that someone will eventually attempt the job of basing a critique of the marginal analysis on his foundations. Or, finally, it can be regarded as a sort of magnificent rehabilitation of the Classical (and up to a point Marxian) approach to certain crucial problems relating to value and distribution. It is upon this third aspect of the book that I wish to concentrate in the present essay. In doing so, I do not of course want to suggest that the *essence* of Sraffa's book lies in this rehabilitation of the Classical approach: Sraffa's primary aim is to build a twentieth-century model to deal with twentieth-century problems. I am approaching his book in this particular way largely because I think it affords the best method of understanding his basic argument.

Let me begin by making three general points about the relation between Sraffa's model and the old Classical models. First, both Sraffa's model and the Classical models are concerned with the investigation of one and the same set of properties of an economic system – those properties, as Sraffa puts it, which "do not depend on changes in the scale of production or in the proportions of 'factors' ".[3] The Classical

---

[1] This essay is a slightly amended version of an article which was published simultaneously in the *Scottish Journal of Political Economy*, June 1961, and *Science and Society*, Spring 1961. Since I wrote the article, a number of other reviews and articles relating to Sraffa's book have of course appeared, but since very few of them have dealt at all thoroughly with the particular points I was concerned to emphasize I have not given any specific references to them in the present version of my article. I would like to acknowledge my indebtedness, however, to an article by Joan Robinson which appeared in the *New Left Review*, June 1965, and which has now been reprinted, under the title "A Reconsideration of the Theory of Value", in Vol. III of her *Collected Economic Papers*.

[2] Cambridge, 1960.   [3] *Op. cit.*, p. v.

economists, at any rate in their basic analysis of the economy as such, were usually *in effect* concerned with these properties alone, since they often tended to assume that under given technological conditions returns to scale for the industry as a whole would be constant, and that the proportions in which the different means of production were used in an industry would be technically fixed. Sraffa, by way of distinction, makes no assumption whatever about the variability or constancy of returns. Rather, he simply selects for analysis a particular kind of economic system in which the question of whether returns are variable or constant is irrelevant. This system is one in which production goes on from day to day and from year to year in exactly the same way, without any changes in scale or factor proportions at all. By this means Sraffa is able *deliberately* to concern himself with the investigation of the same properties of an economic system which the Classical economists *objectively* concerned themselves with, while at the same time avoiding the necessity of making any (possibly objectionable) assumptions about the nature of returns.

The second point is this: the Classical economists, anxious as they were to propound generalized statements or "laws" relating to the economy in which they were interested, naturally wanted to make their systems "determinate" in some useful and meaningful sense of that word. The methods they employed to secure the requisite degree of determinacy were often ingenious and stimulating. But they did not hit on the idea that it would help greatly to secure determinacy if certain specific interrelations were postulated between elements of input and elements of output over the economy as a whole, so that the output of certain industries was assumed to constitute the input of others. They were of course aware that such interrelations did exist and were important: Quesnay, after all, framed his remarkable *Tableau Economique*; Marx worked out his famous reproduction schemes; and Ricardo (if Sraffa is right) held at one stage a "corn-ratio theory of profits".[4] The point I am making is simply that they did not, by and large, use these postulated interrelationships as an integral part of the methods which they employed to make prices and factor incomes determinate – *i.e.*, to solve the general problem of value. This is precisely what Sraffa *does* do.[5]

The third point is this: the Classical economists were primarily interested in the problem of the *development* of the capitalist system, but they believed that a necessary preliminary to the study of this problem

[4] *Op. cit.*, p. 93.
[5] There is a close and obvious intellectual affinity here between Sraffa's approach and that of the Walrasian-type analysis and modern input-output techniques.

was an analysis of the nature of the capitalist system as such. And the best method of going about this analysis, they believed, was to begin by imagining capitalism suddenly impinging upon a pre-capitalist form of economy in which, in effect, labour was the only "factor" receiving a reward. In this pre-capitalist economy, which Smith called the "early and rude state of society" and Marx called "simple commodity production", the whole produce of labour went to the labourers.[6] In such an economy, it was claimed, the relative equilibrium prices of commodities would tend to be equal to the relative quantities of labour required from first to last to produce them. What happened, then, when a class of capitalists arrived on the scene, and the net product of the economy consequently came to be shared between labourers and capitalists? In particular, what happened to relative equilibrium prices? Did they remain equal to relative quantities of embodied labour, or did they now diverge from these quantities? If they diverged, were the divergences haphazard, or could they be shown to be in some useful sense "subject to law"? Did the divergences render it necessary to throw out completely the simple "law of value" which used to operate in the pre-capitalist economy, or could they be regarded as merely *modifying* its operation? These questions were not regarded as purely academic ones, with little relevance to problems of practical policy. On the contrary, the Classical economists believed that if one could give adequate answers to them one would then have penetrated to the very essence of the capitalist system, and would be properly equipped to proceed to the major task – that of the determination of what Marx (and Mill) called the "laws of motion" of the capitalist system.[7] The general procedure which Sraffa adopts, and the questions he asks, are very similar to those I have just described.

II

Sraffa begins with a very simple model of a subsistence economy in which there are only two commodities produced – wheat and iron – and in which the total amount of each of these commodities which goes into the productive process each year is precisely the same as the total amount which comes out.[8] A conceivable set of conditions of production in such an economy is as follows:

$$280 \text{ qr. wheat} + 12 \text{ t. iron} \rightarrow 400 \text{ qr. wheat}$$
$$\underline{120 \text{ qr. wheat} + 8 \text{ t. iron}} \rightarrow 20 \text{ t. iron}$$
$$400 20$$

[6] Cf. Adam Smith, *Wealth of Nations*, Vol. I, pp. 49 and 66.
[7] Cf. above, pp. 97–8.   [8] Sraffa, *op. cit.*, pp. 3–5.

In the wheat industry (represented by the first line) 280 quarters of wheat and 12 tons of iron are used up during the year in order to produce an annual output of 400 quarters of wheat. In the iron industry (represented by the second line) 120 quarters of wheat and 8 tons of iron are used up during the year in order to produce an annual output of 20 tons of iron.[9] It will be seen that a total of 400 quarters of wheat and 20 tons of iron goes into the productive process and is used up there, and that 400 quarters of wheat and 20 tons of iron come out of the productive process at the end of the year.

Now, at the end of each year the wheat producers are going to have 400 quarters of wheat in their hands, 280 quarters of which have to be earmarked for the following year's input. If the process of production is to continue from year to year at the same level, it is clear that the proceeds from the sale of the remaining 120 quarters of wheat must be sufficient to enable the wheat producers to buy the 12 tons of iron which they will need as input in the following year. Similarly, the iron producers are going to have 20 tons of iron in their hands, 8 tons of which have to be earmarked for the following year's input. If the process of production is to continue from year to year at the same level, it is clear that the proceeds from the sale of the remaining 12 tons of iron must be sufficient to enable the iron producers to buy the 120 quarters of wheat which they will need as input in the following year. It is evident, therefore, that prices in this economy must be such that 12 tons of iron are exchangeable on the market for 120 quarters of wheat – *i.e.*, that the price of a ton of iron must be ten times the price of a quarter of wheat. This analysis can readily be generalized to cover the case of a more complex subsistence economy in which any number k of different commodities is produced. A set of k production equations in price terms can be drawn up in which the number of independent equations is equal to the number of unknowns, so that the prices of all the commodities produced become determinate.[10]

Let us now drop the assumption of a subsistence econony, and turn, as Sraffa does,[11] to the case of an economy in which a surplus over subsistence is yielded. Such an economy might be one with the following conditions of production:

---

[9] We assume for the moment that subsistence goods for the labourers are included in the wheat and iron inputs.

[10] It will be appreciated that since any one of the k equations can be inferred from the sum of the others, there are in fact only $k - 1$ *independent* equations. But it is easy to reduce the number of unknowns to $k - 1$ by taking one commodity as the standard of value and making its price equal to unity. See Sraffa, *op. cit.*, p. 5.

[11] *Op. cit.*, pp. 6 ff.

280 qr. wheat + 12 t. iron → 575 qr. wheat

<u>120 qr. wheat + 8 t. iron → 20 t. iron</u>

400   20

It will be seen that this economy is the same as the previous one except that the wheat industry is now assumed to produce 575 quarters of wheat every year instead of 400. If we assume that the rewards going to labour are fully taken care of in the wheat and iron inputs of the two industries, as we have so far been doing,[12] this means that the whole value of the surplus of 175 quarters of wheat will be available for distribution in the form of profit. Let us assume that this profit is distributed in such a way as to make the *rate* of profits equal in both industries – in other words, that the owners of each industry earn what the Classical economists called the "normal" or "average" rate of profits on their advances. The situation now is that prices must be such as to allow the elements of input in each industry to be replaced, *and* to allow profits on the value of these elements of input to be earned at the same rate in each industry. In the present example, these two conditions will be fulfilled if prices are such as to make 1 ton of iron exchangeable on the market for 15 quarters of wheat, which will bring the average rate of profits out at 25 per cent.[13] Once again this analysis can readily be generalized to cover the case of a more complex economy in which any number k of different commodities is produced. A set of k production equations in price terms can be drawn up in which the number of independent equations is equal to the number of unknowns, so that the prices of the k commodities, *and* the average rate of profits, are all determined.[14]

We must now alter the assumption we have so far been making about wages. Up to this point we have in effect assumed that wages consist of necessary means of subsistence for the workers, and thus, as Sraffa puts it, enter the system "on the same footing as the fuel for the engines or the food for the cattle".[15] But wages may in fact include not only the "ever-present element of subsistence" (which is constant), but also a

---

[12] See above, p. 164, footnote.

[13] Let the price of a quarter of wheat be 1; let the price of a ton of iron be p_i; and let the average rate of profits be r. The production equations in price terms will then read as follows:

$$(280 + 12p_i)(1 + r) = 575$$
$$(120 + 8p_i)(1 + r) = 20p_i$$

These equations yield the solutions $p_i = 15$ and $r = \frac{1}{4}$.

[14] There are k independent equations, which, if one commodity is taken as the standard of value and its price made equal to unity, are sufficient to determine the $k - 1$ prices and the rate of profits r.

[15] *Op. cit.*, p. 9.

"share of the surplus product" (which is variable).[16] What is one to do about this? The most appropriate thing to do would be to separate the wage into its two component parts, continuing to treat the goods required for the subsistence of the workers as means of production along with the fuel, fodder, etc., and treating the variable element in the wage as a part of the surplus product of the system. Sraffa, however, in order to avoid "tampering with the traditional wage concept", from now on treats the whole of the wage as variable – *i.e.*, as part of the surplus product. This means that the quantity of labour employed in each industry has from now on to be represented explicitly in our statements of the conditions of production, taking the place of the corresponding quantities of subsistence goods in our previous statements.

When the wage is recognized as containing a variable element, or when, as with Sraffa, the whole of the wage is assumed to be variable, we have another unknown to be added to our list. In a system where k commodities are produced, we now have $k + 2$ unknowns – the k prices, the rate of profits, r, and the wage, w.[17] And the best we can do, when we put the production equations in price terms, is to provide $k + 1$ equations in order to find these $k + 2$ unknowns. Thus the system is not determinate, unless one of the variables can be taken as fixed.[18] As

---

[16] This implies that Sraffa is in effect defining the "surplus product" of a system as the difference between gross output and what Ricardo called "the absolutely necessary expenses of production".

[17] "We suppose labour to be uniform in quality or, what amounts to the same thing, we assume any differences in quality to have been previously reduced to equivalent differences in quantity so that each unit of labour receives the same wage" (*op. cit.*, p. 10).

[18] Let A be the quantity annually produced of commodity "a"; let B be the quantity annually produced of commodity "b"; and so on. Let $A_a, B_a, \ldots, K_a$ be the quantities of commodities "a", "b", $\ldots$, "k" annually used as means of production by the industry which produces A; let $A_b, B_b, \ldots, K_b$ be the quantities of commodities "a", "b", $\ldots$, "k" annually used as means of production by the industry which produces B; and so on. Let $L_a, L_b, \ldots, L_k$ be the quantities of labour annually employed in the industries producing $A, B, \ldots, K$. These quantities are the "knowns" in our equational system.

Let $p_a, p_b, \ldots, p_k$ be the unit prices of commodities "a", "b", $\ldots$, "k". Let r be the average rate of profits. Let w be the wage per man. These quantities are the "unknowns" in our equational system.

In generalized form, the production equations in price terms will read as follows:
$$(A_a p_a + B_a p_b + \ldots + K_a p_k)(1 + r) + L_a w = A p_a$$
$$(A_b p_a + B_b p_b + \ldots + K_b p_k)(1 + r) + L_b w = B p_b$$
$$\cdot \quad \cdot \quad \cdot \quad \cdot \quad \cdot \quad \cdot$$
$$(A_k p_a + B_k p_b + \ldots + K_k p_k)(1 + r) + L_k w = K p_k$$

By putting the surplus product of the system equal to unity (thereby making it the standard in terms of which the wage and the k prices are expressed), we obtain an additional equation, making a total of $k + 1$ equations. But there are $k + 2$ unknowns, so that the system is not determinate unless one of the variables (e.g., the wage w) can be taken as fixed. (See Sraffa, pp. 4, 6 and 10–11.)

Sraffa puts it, "the system can move with one degree of freedom; and if one of the variables is fixed the others will be fixed too".[19] In particular, if we know what the wage is, the rate of profits and all the prices will be determined.

III

Having erected this simple model, Sraffa now proceeds to investigate what we have seen to be the basic Classical problem – what happens to prices and profits when a class of capitalists arrives on the scene to share the net product of the economy with labour? Sraffa deals with this problem by giving the wage successive values ranging from 1 to 0 – a wage of 1 representing a situation in which *all* the net product goes to labour (*i.e.*, in which there is no class of capitalists and therefore no profit), and a wage of 0 representing the other extreme in which *none* of the net product goes to labour (*i.e.*, in which there is a class of capitalists which manages to secure *all* the net product for itself in the form of profit). The main task is to show what happens to prices and to the rate of profits as the wage is reduced from 1 to 0.

When the wage is 1 – *i.e.*, when the whole of the net product goes to wages – we in effect revert to the simple set of equations with which we started, except that (as already stated) the quantities of labour employed in each industry will now be shown explicitly in our equations instead of being represented, as they were before, by quantities of subsistence goods. It is easy to show that in this situation the equilibrium prices of the different products will be proportionate to the different quantities of labour which have been directly and indirectly employed to produce them. For if the only form of income is wages, all input-costs ultimately reduce to wage-costs. This means that the value of each end-product will be equal to the sum of its inputs at wage cost, which of course implies (if wages are uniform) that price ratios will be equal to embodied labour ratios.[20] What this proposition amounts to, of course, is a reaffirmation of the truth of the Smithian, Ricardian and Marxian proposition that in the "early and rude state of society", where there is

---

[19] *Op. cit.*, p. 11.

[20] Suppose that a two-industry economy produces a gross output of 400 quarters of wheat and 25 tons of iron. Let the sum of the inputs at wage-cost in the two industries be £200 and £250 respectively. Since the value of the end-product will in each case equal the sum of its inputs at wage-cost, the price of a ton of iron will be 20 times the price of a quarter of wheat. Let the wage per man be £5. This means that 40 units of direct and indirect labour are required to produce 400 quarters of wheat, and 50 units of direct and indirect labour are required to produce 25 tons of iron. Thus 20 times as much labour is required to produce a ton of iron as is required to produce a quarter of wheat. Thus the price ratio is equal to the embodied labour ratio.

no profit, the Classical "law of value" acts, as it were, directly, so that price ratios will in equilibrium be equal to embodied labour ratios.

Now Smith, Ricardo and Marx, having established this proposition, went on to argue that in a capitalist society, where the net product was shared between wages and profits, prices no longer followed this simple rule. The "law of value" which originally operated in this direct and simple way was now subject, as Ricardo put it, to important "modifications".[21] Sraffa, like his Classical predecessors, now goes on to consider the nature and causes of these "modifications".

Sraffa's explanation of the basic reason for the emergence of the "modifications" is substantially the same as that of Ricardo and Marx. "The key to the movement of relative prices consequent upon a change in the wage", Sraffa writes, "lies in the inequality of the proportions in which labour and means of production are employed in the various industries."[22] It may be helpful, I think, to begin by explaining this crucial point in Ricardo's terms. Let us assume that we have an economy which consists of three separate industries, A, B and C, in each of which the proportions in which labour and means of production are combined together are different. The ratio of the wage-bill to the value of used-up means of production is different in each industry. Such an economy might be the following:

	Value of Used-up Means of Production		Wages		Price
(A)	800	+	200	=	1000
(B)	600	+	400	=	1000
(C)	200	+	800	=	1000

Wages, we begin by assuming, absorb the whole of the net product, profits being 0. Under these circumstances, the price of the finished product will in each case be 1000, as indicated in the table.

Suppose now that a class of capitalists arrives on the scene and shares in the net product along with labour. Wages, let us assume, go down by

[21] Smith, broadly speaking, believed that the "modifications" were so important as to render it necessary to throw out the old "law of value" and to replace it by what amounted to a "cost of production" theory of value. Ricardo agreed that the "modifications" were important, but argued that it was still possible to say that relative prices were mainly determined by relative quantities of embodied labour (and, what was for him equally significant, that *changes* in relative prices were mainly caused by *changes* in relative quantities of embodied labour). Marx also emphasized the importance of the "modifications", but maintained that the old "law of value" still *ultimately* and *indirectly* determined prices. Sraffa, as will be shown in the last part of this article, in effect follows Marx's line of approach to this problem.

[22] *Op. cit.*, p. 12.

one-half, and, as a result of this, profits rise from 0 to a level which affords an average rate of, let us say, 25 per cent. on the value of the used-up means of production. (We leave aside for the moment the important question of how far profits will *in fact* rise as a result of this particular wage-reduction: we simply assume that they will rise from 0 to an arbitrarily-chosen figure of 25 per cent.) The price of each commodity will now be made up of the value of the means of production employed (which we assume for the moment to remain at its original level), plus the wage-bill (now cut by one-half in each case), plus profit at 25 per cent. on the value of the used-up means of production. The situation will then be as follows:

	Value of Used-up Means of Production		Wages		Profits		Price
(A)	800	+	100	+	200	=	1100
(B)	600	+	200	+	150	=	950
(C)	200	+	400	+	50	=	650

It is clear that under these circumstances the prices of the three commodities would have to change from their original levels. If the price of the product of industry A remained at 1000, that industry would show a sort of "deficit": it would not be able to pay wages at the given rate and at the same time receive profits at the given rate on its means of production. Similarly, if the price of the products of industries B and C remained at 1000, these industries would show a sort of "surplus": they would secure receipts which were more than sufficient to pay wages at the given rate and to earn profits at the given rate on their means of production. Therefore prices would clearly have to alter to the levels indicated in the second table above. The relative prices of the three commodities would change in this case, when the wage changed, simply because the proportions in which labour and the means of production are combined in the three industries are different. If these proportions were the same in each industry, it can easily be seen that relative prices would not change at all from their previous level.[23]

---

[23] Take, for example, a situation in which industry A uses up 400 means of production and pays out 800 in wages; industry B uses up 300 means of production and pays out 600 in wages; and industry C uses up 200 means of production and pays out 400 in wages. The prices of the three products in the initial situation will be 1200, 900 and 600 – *i.e.*, they will stand to one another in the ratio 4:3:2. If wages fall by one-half and profits as a result rise from zero to 25 per cent., the prices of the products will become 900, 675 and 450 respectively – *i.e.*, they will still stand to one another in the ratio 4:3:2.

Now, it *looks* from this example as if we could frame a simple general rule about what happens to prices when wages fall. Could we not say that the price of the product of an industry with a relatively low proportion of labour to means of production, like industry A in our example, would rise when wages fell; and that the price of the product of an industry with a relatively high proportion of labour to means of production, like industries B and C in our example, would fall when wages fell? This is in effect what Ricardo said. But this need not in fact necessarily be so. It certainly *looks* from our example as if the price of the product of industry B, say, is bound to fall. We have so far assumed, however, as Ricardo usually did, that the value of the means of production employed in industry B remains the same as it was initially – *i.e.*, 600 – in spite of the fall in wages. But suppose that these means of production employed in industry B were themselves produced by an industry like A in our example, where the proportion of labour to means of production is relatively low. The price of the means of production employed in B would then rise when wages fell, so that the price of the *product* of industry B, instead of falling as it does in our example, might actually rise. Thus the movements in the relative prices of any two products, consequent upon a change in wages, come to depend, as Sraffa puts it, "not only on the 'proportions' of labour to means of production by which they are respectively produced, but also on the 'proportions' by which those means have themselves been produced, and also on the 'proportions' by which the means of production of those means of production have been produced, and so on".[24]

Let us imagine that an industry existed which represented a sort of borderline between the "deficit" and "surplus" industries which we have just distinguished. In such an industry, as Sraffa puts it, "the proceeds of the wage-reduction would provide exactly what was required for the payment of profits at the general rate".[25] Suppose, for example, that there was an industry which employed labour and means of production in such a proportion that on the basis of the initial prices of the means of production the proceeds of the wage-reduction provided exactly the amount that was required to pay profits at the average rate – instead of something less, as in our industry A, or something more, as in our industries B and C. Suppose further – and this is the vital point – that the means of production which this industry employed were themselves produced by labour and means of production in the same proportion, and so on right down the line. There would be nothing in the conditions of production of such an industry which would make its product rise or fall in value relative to any other commodity when wages rose or fell.

[24] *Op. cit.*, p. 15.   [25] *Op. cit.*, p. 13.

And the value of such a commodity relative to the value of its own means of production could not possibly change, since the same "proportions" would by hypothesis apply in the case of those means of production, *their* means of production, and so on right down the line. Thus one way of expressing the quality of "invariance" which the product of this borderline industry would possess is to say that the ratio of the value of the industry's net product to the value of its means of production would always remain the same whatever change took place in the wage. And it is easy to show that this ratio must be equal to the average rate of profits which would prevail over the economy as a whole if wages were zero[26] – the "maximum rate of profits", as Sraffa calls it. Sraffa uses the term R to refer both to the ratio of the value of the net product of the borderline industry to the value of its means of production, and to the "maximum rate of profits". So we have:

$$\frac{\text{Value of net product of borderline industry}}{\text{Value of its means of production}} = \frac{\text{"Maximum rate}}{\text{of profits"}} = R$$

, Having set out in a general way the basic condition of an "invariant" industry, Sraffa now proceeds to ask whether an industry fulfilling this condition could in fact be found. No actual industry in the economy is likely to fulfil the requirements; but, Sraffa argues, a mixture of industries, or of bits of industries, would do just as well. His next task, therefore, is to show that it is in fact possible to distil, from any actual economy, a sort of composite industry in which the ratio of net product to means of production will remain invariable in the face of any change in the wage. Let us take a simple example of the distillation operation which Sraffa undertakes in order to obtain a composite industry which fulfils this basic condition. Take the economy whose conditions of production in physical terms are as follows:

$$375 \text{ qr. wheat} + 6 \text{ t. iron} \rightarrow 750 \text{ qr. wheat}$$
$$\underline{300 \text{ qr. wheat} + 24 \text{ t. iron}} \rightarrow \underline{40 \text{ t. iron}}$$
$$675 \qquad\qquad 30$$

The net product of this economy consists of 10 tons of iron plus 75 quarters of wheat. Now, suppose that we separate off *two-thirds* of the wheat industry and *one-half* of the iron industry, and treat the two

---

[26] If the wage fell to zero, the ratio of the value of the net product of the borderline industry to the value of its means of production would become equivalent to the rate of profits in the borderline industry, and by hypothesis this ratio cannot change. Thus if wages are zero, prices in the rest of the economy must so change as to bring the average rate of profits into equality with the ratio of the value of the net product of the borderline industry to the value of its means of production.

resultant fractions of these industries as constituting together a sort of composite industry.[27] The conditions of production of this composite industry would be as follows:

$$250 \text{ qr. wheat} + 4 \text{ t. iron} \rightarrow 500 \text{ qr. wheat}$$
$$\underline{150 \text{ qr. wheat}} + \underline{12 \text{ t. iron}} \rightarrow 20 \text{ t. iron}$$
$$400 \qquad\qquad 16$$

Let us now identify the crucial ratio of net product to means of production in this composite industry. The net product consists of 4 tons of iron plus 100 quarters of wheat; and the means of production consist of 16 tons of iron plus 400 quarters of wheat. Thus the ratio is:

$$\frac{4 \text{ t. iron} + 100 \text{ qr. wheat}}{16 \text{ t. iron} + 400 \text{ qr. wheat}}$$

The numerator and denominator of this ratio, it will be noticed, are made up of quantities of the same commodities combined in the same proportions, which means that we can speak of a ratio between the two sets of commodities without the need to reduce them to the common measure of price. The ratio in this case is of course one-quarter. And it is clear that this ratio would remain the same whatever the *prices* of the two commodities happened to be. The ratio between the two sets of commodities in *price* terms would always be the same as it is in *physical* terms – one-quarter. In other words, even though wages altered and prices subsequently changed, the ratio of the value of the net product of this composite or "standard" industry to the value of its means of production would necessarily remain unchanged. Thus this industry would fulfil the basic condition of invariance which we have already established.

By what subtle magic has this rather startling result been obtained? We have obtained it because the fractions which we selected as our multipliers were cunningly chosen so that in the reduced-scale system the proportions in which the two commodities are produced (20:500) are the same as those in which they enter the aggregate means of production (16:400). It is only because the multiplying fractions which we chose were such as to yield us a reduced-scale system possessing this particular property that the numerator and denominator of the ratio of net product to means of production have come to consist of quantities of the same commodities combined in the same proportions, so that the ratio necessarily remains invariant to price changes. Sraffa now proceeds

---

[27] We leave aside for the moment the question of how the appropriate multiplying fractions are arrived at.

to show very elegantly that there is always a set of multipliers, and never more than one set, which when applied to the industries of any actual economy will rearrange them in the "right" proportions.

Let us now consider what happens to the rate of profits *in the composite or "standard" industry* when the wage changes. If we write R (as before) for the ratio of net product to means of production, *r* for the rate of profits, and *w* for the proportion of the net product going to wages, the relation between wages and profits in the "standard" industry can be expressed in the form of the following simple relation:

$$r = R(1 - w)$$

Take as an example the "standard" industry which we have just considered, where $R = \frac{1}{4}$. Suppose that three-quarters of the net product (*i.e.*, 3 t. iron + 75 qr. wheat) went to wages, so that the remaining one-quarter (*i.e.*, 1 t. iron + 25 qr. wheat) went to profits. The rate of profits would then be:

$$\frac{1 \text{ t. iron} + 25 \text{ qr. wheat}}{16 \text{ t. iron} + 400 \text{ qr. wheat}} \left(= \tfrac{1}{16} \right)$$

and this rate of profits of $\frac{1}{16}$, or $6\frac{1}{4}$ per cent., is clearly given by the expression $r = R(1 - w)$, where $R = \frac{1}{4}$ and $w = \frac{3}{4}$. What this expression says, in essence, is that the rate of profits *in the "standard" industry* increases in direct proportion to the total deduction made from the wage, the extent of the increase depending on the value of R.

Now comes the final stage in this ingenious and persuasive argument. Sraffa maintains that this relation between wages and profits is not limited to our imaginary "standard" system, but can also be extended to the actual economic system from which the "standard" system has been derived. For the actual system, Sraffa argues, consists of the same basic equations as the "standard" system, only in different proportions, so that "once the wage is given, the rate of profits is determined for both systems regardless of the proportions of the equations in either of them".[28] Thus, Sraffa concludes, the rate of profits *over the economy as a whole* is determined as soon as we know R (the ratio of net product to means of production in the "standard" industry, which is equal to the "maximum rate of profits"), and *w* (the proportion of the net product of the "standard" industry going to wages). Or, to put the point in another way, when the proportion of the net product of the "standard" industry going to wages is given, the average rate of profits over the economy as a whole depends upon the level of R.

[28] *Op. cit.*, p. 23.

In the remainder of his book, Sraffa makes extensive use of this simple relation between wages and profits to elucidate a number of difficult theoretical problems. In one chapter, for example, he analyses the case where commodities are produced with means of production which were themselves produced at different periods in the past (and so on down the line), so that the profit element in the prices of these means of production is different, and asks how the relative values of the commodities will vary with changes in the rate of profits.[29] In the second part of his book, again, he deals with the new problems which arise when we take account of the fact of the existence of items of fixed capital which outlast one use and gradually depreciate in value during the course of their life. What generalizations can be made, he asks, on the basis of the theoretical foundations erected in the earlier part of the book, concerning the path followed by this depreciation? Finally, carrying on with the method of successive approximations in much the same way as his Classical predecessors, he brings land into the picture, and erects a more complex system of equations in which, if wages are given, the prices of all commodities, the rate of profits, *and* the rents payable on different qualities of land are all determined. To the historian of economic thought, one of the most interesting features of these extensions of Sraffa's basic analysis is the number of old friends who are met with. For example, in the chapter on fixed capital Sraffa makes interesting use of the old Classical device, first used by Torrens, of treating what is left of fixed capital at the end of the year as a kind of joint product of the industry in which it is employed. Of special importance in these later parts of the book are the distinction which is early established between "basic" and "non-basic" products,[30] and the general analysis of joint products.

[29] In this chapter, Sraffa deals with the problem of reducing "constant capital" (to use Marx's terminology) to quantities of labour. He points out, in effect, that the reduction operation can in fact be performed, provided that the labour is *dated* labour, since the dating will affect the rate of profits and therefore the prices of the commodities concerned.

[30] A "basic" product, roughly speaking, is one which enters (no matter whether directly or indirectly) into the production of *all* commodities, and a "non-basic" product is one which does not. A "luxury" product, for example, which is not used (whether as an instrument of production or as an article of subsistence) in the production of other products, is "non-basic". (See Sraffa, *op. cit.*, pp. 7–8.) The important feature of "non-basic" products is that they "have no part in the determination of the system", their role being "purely passive". In other words, "the price of a non-basic product depends on the prices of its means of production, but these do not depend on it", whereas "in the case of a basic product the prices of its means of production depend on its own price no less than the latter depends on them" (p. 9). Specialists in Marxist theory will note the relevance of this part of Sraffa's analysis to an important question which arose in the course of the debate on the so-called "transformation problem" – the question (raised in particular by Bortkiewicz) as to whether the conditions of production of luxury goods enter into the determination of the rate of profits.

IV

One very important feature of Sraffa's analysis remains to be commented upon – his implied rehabilitation of the Classical labour theory of value in something very like the form which it assumed in the hands of Marx. The Marxian labour theory of value does *not* say, as is commonly supposed, that the equilibrium prices of commodities are always proportionate to the quantities of labour required to produce them. It affirms, certainly, that this statement is true of an economy where "the whole produce of labour belongs to the labourer"; but it agrees – indeed emphasizes – that equilibrium prices do not normally follow this simple rule in a capitalist economy where part of the net product goes to profits. In a capitalist economy, it is demonstrated, relative prices normally deviate from relative quantities of embodied labour, for reasons which have been described earlier in the present essay. Even in a capitalist economy, however, it is argued, the equilibrium prices of commodities can still be shown to be "indirectly" and "ultimately" determined by certain crucial ratios of aggregate quantities of embodied labour applicable to the economy as a whole. For the deviations of price ratios from embodied labour ratios, given the proportions in which labour and means of production are combined together in each industry, depend upon the level of the average rate of profits; and the level of the average rate of profits, it is claimed, depends in its turn upon the crucial ratios of quantities of embodied labour to which I have just referred. Thus, if it can in fact be shown that the average rate of profits is determined by these embodied labour ratios, we can reasonably conclude that the very deviations of equilibrium price ratios from embodied labour ratios are themselves determined by "quantities of embodied labour".

Marx's method of showing the dependence of the rate of profits on "quantities of embodied labour" in this sense can be illustrated with the aid of the following simple model:[31]

	Means of Production	Wages	Surplus Value
(A)	40	160	80
(B)	60	90	45
(C)	120	80	40

We here assume that the economy consists of three separate industries, A, B and C. The quantities under the three headings "Means of Production", "Wages" and "Surplus Value" are each reckoned in terms of hours of labour. Take industry A as an example. In industry A, the means of production used up during a given period of production are

[31] Cf. above, pp. 146 ff.

assumed to "contain" or "embody" a total of 40 hours of past labour. The total amount of present or direct labour expended in the industry during the period is assumed to be 240 hours – the sum of the figures 160 and 80 under the respective headings "Wages" and "Surplus Value". It is assumed that in two-thirds of this total working time – *i.e.*, 160 hours – the direct labourers are able to contribute just enough value to the product to cover their own wages. In the remaining 80 hours they contribute what Marx called "surplus value", which he assumed to be the sole source of capitalist profit. The same interpretation is given to the figures for industries B and C, where, it will be noticed, the proportions in which labour and means of production are combined together are different from those in industry A. The ratio of surplus value to wages is assumed to be the same (in this case 1:2) in each industry.

The average rate of profits in this economy, Marx argued, can be found by taking the aggregate surplus value yielded over the economy as a whole (165) and redividing it among the three industries in proportion to the means of production employed in each. Or, to put the point in a way which is perhaps easier to understand, the average rate of profits will be determined by the ratio of aggregate surplus value to aggregate means of production. In this case it will clearly be three-quarters, or 75 per cent.[32] This ratio of aggregate quantities of embodied labour, then, determines the average rate of profits, and thus the deviations of equilibrium price ratios from embodied labour ratios.

At first sight this analysis might seem to to have little in common with Sraffa's. But suppose we go on to postulate, as Marx himself did, an industry in which the ratio of used-up means of production to wages is equal to the ratio of these quantities when they are aggregated over the economy as a whole. Industry B in our illustration is clearly an industry possessing this characteristic – it is an industry in which, to use Marx's terminology, the "organic composition of capital" is equal to the "social average".[33] In such an industry, as can be seen from the illustration, the ratio of surplus value to means of production (45:60) is equal to the

[32] Marx, in common with his Classical predecessors, generally assumed that wages were "advanced" out of capital. This meant that in working out the rate of profits he normally related surplus value to means of production *plus wages*. Following Sraffa's precedent (*op. cit.*, p. 10), I am assuming here that the wage is not in fact "advanced", but "paid *post factum* as a share of the annual product", which means that the rate of profits is obtained by relating surplus value to means of production alone. To drop this particular assumption of Marx's does not affect the essence of his analysis, and greatly facilitates the comparison with Sraffa which is made below.

[33] See *Capital*, Vol. III, pp. 161–2. In the example, the "organic composition of capital" in industry B (60:90) is clearly equal to the "organic composition of capital" over the economy as a whole (220:330).

ratio of these quantities over the economy as a whole (165:220). We can thus say, as Marx did,[34] that the average rate of profits over the economy as a whole is determined by the ratio of surplus value to means of production *in this industry B*, whose conditions of production represent a sort of "social average". Or, to put the same proposition in another way, the average rate of profits over the economy as a whole is given by the following expression:[35]

$$\frac{\text{Labour embodied in net product of industry B}}{\text{Labour embodied in its means of production}} \left(1- \begin{array}{l} \text{Proportion of net} \\ \text{product of industry} \\ \text{B going to wages} \end{array} \right)$$

The similarity between this Marxian relation and that expressed in Sraffa's $r = R(1 - w)$ is surely very striking. For, in the first place, let us note that Sraffa's R, although usually expressed as the ratio of the *value* of the net product of the "standard" industry to the *value* of its means of production, is in fact equal to the ratio of the *labour embodied* in the net product of the "standard" industry to the *labour embodied* in its means of production.[36] In other words, Sraffa is postulating precisely the same relation between the average rate of profits *and the conditions of production in his "standard" industry* as Marx was postulating between the average rate of profits *and the conditions of production in his industry of "average organic composition of capital"*. What both economists are trying to show, in effect, is that (when wages are given) the average rate of profits, and therefore the deviations of price ratios from embodied labour ratios, are governed by the ratio of direct to indirect labour in the industry whose conditions of production represent a sort of "average" of those prevailing over the economy as a whole. Marx reached this result by postulating as his "average" industry one whose "organic composition of capital" was equal to the "social average". But his result could only be a provisional and approximate one, since in reaching it he had abstracted from the effect which a change in the wage would have on the prices of the means of production employed in the "average" industry.[37] Sraffa shows that the same result can be achieved, without

[34] *Capital*, Vol. III, pp. 170-1.

[35] In this expression the "net product" is taken to consist of wages plus surplus value (as, in effect, it is with Sraffa). Thus the expression is merely another way of formulating the ratio of surplus value to means of production, each of these quantities being estimated in terms of embodied labour.

[36] Cf. Sraffa, *op. cit.*, pp. 16-17. The reason for the equivalence of the value ratio and the embodied labour ratio is as follows: When profits are zero, the prices of all commodities are proportionate to the quantities of labour required to produce them (as has been shown above, p. 167). And when profits rise *above* zero, the ratio R by hypothesis does not change. Thus whatever the level of profits the value ratio remains equal to the embodied labour ratio.

[37] Marx made this abstraction quite deliberately, and was fully aware that his result was therefore provisional and approximate. See *Capital*, Vol. III, pp. 202-3.

abstracting from this effect at all, if we substitute his "standard" industry for Marx's industry of "average organic composition of capital". Sraffa's "standard" industry, seen from this point of view, is essentially an attempt to *define* "average conditions of production" in such a way as to achieve the identical result which Marx was seeking.

THE PLACE OF KEYNES
IN THE HISTORY OF
ECONOMIC THOUGHT[1]

I

Post-Keynesian macroeconomic literature today abounds with articles comparing Keynes's theoretical system with the so-called "Classical" systems which Keynes was primarily concerned to attack. Originally, the main purpose of such articles was to formulate the Keynesian and "Classical" systems in sufficiently precise (usually mathematical) terms to enable the essentially new contribution made by Keynes to be accurately pinpointed. More recently, their main purpose has become to compare and contrast the various models constructed under the general inspiration of Keynes's system with those constructed by the modern rehabilitators of the "classical" approach.

The basic arguments in these articles have from the beginning tended to revolve around rather formalistic issues, and in recent years this tendency has been accentuated. In spite of their titles – "Keynes and the 'Classicists' ", etc. – the majority of the articles are exercises in logic rather than in history, and they throw remarkably little light on the range of problems which a historian of economic thought usually has in mind when he speaks of "the place of Keynes in the history of economic thought". To illuminate this range of problems, it is important that the comparisons made should be extended backwards in time to include the *real* "Classical" economists. The present essay attempts to anticipate some of the comparisons of this type which future historians of economic thought, looking back on the period through which we are now living, may consider relevant and important.

II

The whole problem of the assessment of Keynes's relationship with other schools of economic thought is obscured by the new – and at that time rather startling – definition of "Classical" economics with which the

[1] This essay is a heavily amended and rewritten version of an article which was published in the *Modern Quarterly*, Winter 1950–51.

General Theory begins. " "The classical economists' ", Keynes writes, "was a name invented by Marx to cover Ricardo and James Mill and their *predecessors*, that is to say for the founders of the theory which culminated in the Ricardian economics."[2] If we are to do proper justice to Marx, of course, we must recognize that this statement is not sufficiently precise: Marx carefully dated the Classical school from Petty to Ricardo in England and from Boisguillebert to Sismondi in France.[3] Nor is it complete: Marx not only defined the historical boundaries of the Classical school but also delineated what he believed to be the essential characteristics which marked it off from the schools which followed it.[4] Keynes, however, was not concerned at this juncture with doing justice to Marx, but simply with attaching the label "Classical" – which had now acquired a rather more pronounced penumbra of disapprobation than was associated with it in Marx's time – to a much longer line of economists. "I have become accustomed," Keynes continued, "perhaps perpetrating a solecism, to include in 'the classical school' the *followers* of Ricardo, those, that is to say, who adopted and perfected the theory of the Ricardian economics, including (for example) J. S. Mill, Marshall, Edgeworth and Prof. Pigou."

There is no doubt that this "solecism" was a stroke of genius. No better word than "Classical" could possibly have been discovered – given Keynes's basic purposes – with which to stigmatize his predecessors and to highlight what he regarded as his own essentially new contribution. It immediately focussed attention upon Keynes's rejection of "Say's Law" – meaning by this, as Keynes did, the notion that "the whole of the costs of production must necessarily be spent in the aggregate, directly or indirectly, on purchasing the product"[5] – and upon the express or implied acceptance of it by many of his predecessors. Ricardo and Pigou – rather odd bedfellows, one might have thought – were equally branded as reactionaries (albeit worthy and well-meaning ones) because each of them, after his own fashion, had believed in the essential truth of "Say's Law".

Given that Keynes's "solecism" was suggestive, in that it laid a then rather unfamiliar emphasis on the continuity of "Say's Law" in the stream of economic thought from Ricardo's time to our own, it must immediately be added that it was also obscurantist, in that it concealed a very important discontinuity which separated "Classical" economics in Marx's sense from the systems which succeeded it. Since this discontinuity may be of importance in assessing Keynes's own place in the

---

[2] *General Theory*, p. 3, footnote. Cf. above, p. 53.
[3] *Critique of Political Economy*, p. 56.
[4] Cf. below, p. 181. [5] *General Theory*, p. 18.

history of economic thought we must say something about it. And the most useful starting-point here, I think, is Marx's statement that the Classical school "investigated the real relations of production in bourgeois society", in contradistinction to "vulgar" economics which dealt "with appearances only".[6]

The feature of Classical economics which Marx is stressing here is one which has received frequent mention in the present book.[7] The Classical economists, speaking very broadly, believed that if the phenomena of the market-place were to be properly understood, the investigator must begin by penetrating below the surface of these phenomena to *the relations between men in their capacity as producers*, which in the last analysis could be said to *determine* their market relations. The fact that commodities were exchanged for one another on the market, and acquired *values*, was in essence a reflection of the fact that the producers of these commodities in effect worked for one another by embodying their separate labours in the commodities. And this was by no means all: the relations between different socio-economic *classes* in the field of production – relations which were superimposed, as it were, on the more basic "relations of production" implicit in the very existence of commodities – altered the effects of the latter upon market phenomena in certain definite and very important ways. The Classical economists always in effect *began* with "relations of production" in this complex sense because they assumed, whether consciously or unconsciously, that these socio-economic relations were major determinants of the value relations upon which the shape and movement of the economic system as a whole primarily depended. Political economy, they believed, must *start from* these production relations, and would be doomed to superficiality and sterility if it abstracted from them. This methodological approach did not of course become really explicit until Marx, but there is no reason to doubt that most of the Classical economists in fact adopted it, even if only intuitively. The idea that the phenomenon of value is a kind of reflection of the basic relation between men as producers of commodities tended to be generalized in the labour theory of value, a peculiarly Classical product. And the notion that market phenomena (particularly in the sphere of distribution) ought to be considered in terms of the production relations between classes had become something of a commonplace by the time of Ricardo, in whose work it assumed considerable importance.

Marx inherited this attitude, made it explicit, and developed and applied it in an extraordinarily fruitful manner. But in orthodox economic thought it virtually perished with Ricardo. Post-Ricardian

---

[6] *Capital*, Vol. I, p. 81, footnote.   [7] Cf. above, pp. 15 and 49–50, and below, p. 204.

economists, quick to appreciate in the decade following Ricardo's death that it was becoming politically dangerous to start with the socio-economic relationships between men as producers, began to argue that it was permissible – and indeed necessary in the interests of scientific objectivity – to abstract from these relationships.[8] The gradual trend towards modern pre-Keynesian neo-Classical orthodoxy began. The trend was marked in particular by the emergence of a subjective theory of value based on the psychological relations between men and finished goods rather than on the social relations between men and men in production, and, eventually, by the development of a new theory of distribution which in effect claimed that the social differences between the classes which supplied land, labour and capital had nothing essentially to do with the respective rewards received by them.[9] It was largely because of the substitution of theories of this type for the older Classical theories of value and distribution, in Marx's view, that post-Ricardian economics on the whole failed to penetrate through the outward disguise into the internal essence and the inner form of the capitalist process of production.

There was another tendency in post-Ricardian economic thought – indirectly associated with the one just described – which reinforced Marx's belief that "bourgeois" economics entered into a state of decline after Ricardo's death. This was the tendency to assert (as Schumpeter put it) "that the economic process, however much given to stalling under the impact of 'disturbances', was yet free, in its pure logic, from inherent hitches".[10] This tendency had of course to some extent already manifested itself in the work of Ricardo himself, who had after all accepted "Say's Law" and explained the trend towards a stationary state in terms of the operation of exogenous factors; but it was greatly accentuated in the work of his successors. Marx put this down to political causes – to which it was indeed quite largely due – and plausibly associated it with the above-mentioned tendency to abstract from the relations of production.

Marx did not anticipate that "bourgeois" economics would eventually come round to a frank and widespread recognition of the fact that the economic process was not after all free from "inherent hitches". But had he lived to see the "Keynesian Revolution", he would, I think, have insisted that Keynes's own analysis of these "inherent hitches" was seriously inadequate, precisely because of the continuance in Keynes's thought of the old post-Ricardian tendency to abstract from the rela-

---

[8] Cf. above, pp. 15–16, and below, pp. 205–6.
[9] Cf. my *Studies in the Labour Theory of Value*, pp. 243–56.
[10] Schumpeter, *History of Economic Analysis*, p. 559, footnote.

tions of production. In other words, he would probably have explained the inadequacy of Keynes's analysis of the "inherent hitches" in similar terms to those which he used to explain the denial of the very existence of such hitches by the orthodox economists of his own time. This point will be referred to again below. In the meantime, let us simply note that Keynes's own definition of "Classical" economics, by emphasizing the continuity of "Say's Law" and glossing over a number of vital differences between Classical and post-Ricardian thought, is seriously misleading in that it diverts attention away from certain factors which may be very important in determining the place of Keynes himself in the history of economic thought.

III

So far we have accepted without question Keynes's assertion that a more or less undifferentiated "Say's Law" continued to constitute a basic part of orthodox economics from Ricardo's time right down to Keynes's own. "The idea that we can safely neglect the aggregate demand function", Keynes wrote, "is fundamental to the Ricardian economics, which underlie what we have been taught for more than a century."[11] If we accept this view, Keynes's place in the history of thought is at once fairly accurately defined: he becomes simply the man who rescued orthodox economics from its long thraldom to "Say's Law." In actual fact, however, the notion of the long historical continuity of an undifferentiated "Say's Law" requires certain important qualifications which destroy the sweet simplicity of this interpretation. Two points are especially important here.

In the first place, there was a crucial difference between the role which "Say's Law" played in Ricardo's system and the role which it gradually came to play in the systems of his successors. In Ricardo's system, broadly speaking, "Say's Law" played a progressive role. It provided an effective answer to men like Spence, Chalmers and Malthus who were arguing (objectively at any rate in the interests of the landlords and other "unproductive consumers" of the time) that capital accumulation was likely to proceed too fast and cause a "general glut" of commodities. Such an argument, in the first two decades of the nineteenth century, clearly had reactionary connotations. Not only this, but "Say's Law" was hardly "fundamental to the Ricardian economics", as Keynes assumed it to have been. At any rate so far as Ricardo's own system was concerned, it was rather something superimposed upon the basic theoretical framework than an essential element of the framework itself.[12]

[11] *General Theory*, p. 32.　　[12] Cf. above, pp. 55–66.

N

In post-Ricardian economics, on the other hand, "Say's Law" gradually began to assume a new and much less progressive role. In Ricardo's system, it had been used as a weapon against the forces which were trying to hold back the advance of the capitalist method of industrial organization. In the post-Ricardian systems, it came to be used as a weapon against a new set of more radical critics of the capitalist order, particularly those associated with the growing working-class movement. A doctrine which could be used to show that there was no inherent tendency towards general overproduction in a capitalist economy – or, still better, that such overproduction was simply impossible – was obviously a useful theoretical weapon to have at hand in the period after the repeal of the Combination Laws. It enabled orthodox economists to explain the periodical crises of capitalism (which began to manifest themselves soon after Ricardo's death) in terms of the operation of exogenous factors or the presence of irremovable rigidities, rather than in terms of what Marx was later to call the "basic contradictions of capitalism". Keynes himself realized fairly clearly the nature of the appeal which "Say's Law" possessed for a capitalist class which found itself on the defensive against the radical challenge:

> The completeness of the Ricardian victory is something of a curiosity and a mystery. It must have been due to a complex of suitabilities in the doctrine to the environment into which it was projected . . . That it could explain much social injustice and apparent cruelty as an inevitable incident in the scheme of progress, and the attempt to change such things as likely on the whole to do more harm than good, commended it to authority. That it afforded a measure of justification to the free activities of the individual capitalist, attracted to it the support of the dominant social force behind authority.[13]

In the second place, so far as Keynes's immediate predecessors are concerned the notion that their work was invalidated by the presence of an all-pervasive "Say's Law", which it was Keynes's historical mission to exorcize, is so misleading as to be almost laughable. Nothing is easier than to show that Keynes's characterization of neo-Classical economics was an Aunt Sally, and that in relation to "Say's Law" his immediate predecessors were not quite such fools as he had sometimes made them out to be.[14] They had, after all, occasionally discussed

[13] Keynes, *General Theory*, pp. 32–3. The omitted sentences include one in which Keynes refers to the "vast and consistent logical superstructure" which "Say's Law" was adapted to carry. This seems to me to be misleading: even in the post-Ricardian systems, where "Say's Law" was indeed welded rather more firmly into the basic theoretical structure, it is an absurd exaggeration to speak of it as carrying a "vast logical superstructure".

[14] Cf. G. Haberler, "*The General Theory* after Ten Years", reprinted in *Keynes' General Theory: Reports of Three Decades*, pp. 281–4.

money and the trade cycle! The really essential point – which is so simple that it can easily be overlooked – is that Keynes's immediate predecessors were mainly interested in a particular range of problems to which the question of the truth or falsity of "Say's Law" was not really relevant. "The difficulty with Keynes's characterization of orthodox theory", as Dr Blaug has said, "is not simply that no single economist ever held all the ideas Keynes attributed to the 'Classics' but that almost no economist after 1870 considered the type of macroeconomic problems with which Keynes was concerned."[15] When they *did* turn their attention to the latter type of problem, they generally recognized – often explicitly – the very limited practical significance of "Say's Law", at any rate in the short period.[16]

To sum up, then, it would be a mistake to assess Keynes's place in the history of economic thought primarily in terms of his reaction against "Say's Law", which had in fact been "fundamental to the Ricardian economics" for only a relatively short historical period. What he was really reacting against, at bottom, was the continued preoccupation of the majority of economists with microeconomic analysis at a time when the practical problems on the agenda for solution were crying out for macroeconomic analysis.

IV

One implication of what has just been said is that the *General Theory* represented something of a swing backwards from neo-Classicism to Classicism, at any rate to the extent that Keynes, like Smith and Ricardo, was interested above all in the question of *movements* in aggregate income. The typical neo-Classical problem was how to allocate a *given* income in the most "rational" or "economic" manner – *i.e.*, how to make the best of scarcity. Keynes's rejection of the assumption of a given income, and his concern with the factors determining the volume of aggregate output, did indeed mean that something like the old Classical problem of securing "an abundance of commodities" was placed on the agenda again.

Not only did Keynes's work revive interest in this Classical problem, but it also contributed to the rehabilitation of one essentially Classical concept which had tended to fall into disuse after Ricardo's death. In Ricardo's system it was generally assumed that accumulation could most usefully be considered as a function of the social surplus, and in particular of that part of the surplus which consisted of profits. The

---

[15] *Economic Theory in Retrospect* (Homewood, Illinois, 1962), p. 601.
[16] See, e.g., Marshall, *Principles of Economics* (8th edn., London, 1946), pp. 710–12.

notion that the volume of accumulation was determined by the ability to accumulate, in other words, tended to predominate over the notion that it was determined by the rate of reward for accumulation. In the post-Ricardian period, for reasons which I have analysed above,[17] the second notion gradually tended to predominate over the first, so that the volume of saving eventually came to be conceived as a function more or less exclusively of the rate of profit or interest. From here it was only a short step to the theory that saving and investment were automatically kept equal to one another by means of changes in the rate of interest.

It was Keynes's critique of this theory which constituted the crucial step in the transition from neo-Classical microstatics to Keynesian macrostatics; and in this critique the "new" notion that saving ought to be regarded as a function of income rather than of the rate of interest played an all-important role. Paul Samuelson, in an interesting passage dealing with the "thought process" leading to the *General Theory*, speaks of

the vitally important consumption function: giving the propensity to consume in terms of income; or looked at from the opposite side, specifying the propensity to save. With investment given, as a constant or in the schedule sense, we are in a position to set up the simplest determinate system of underemployment equilibrium – by a "Keynesian savings-investment-income cross" not formally different from the "Marshallian supply-demand-price cross".

Immediately everything falls into place: the recognition that the *attempt* to save may lower income and actually *realized* saving; the fact that a net autonomous increase in investment, foreign balance, government expenditure, consumption will result in increased income *greater* than itself, etc., etc.[18]

It is thus true, in a sense, to say that Keynes not only brought the Classical economic problem back again to the forefront, but also adopted as a very important tool one of the concepts which the Classical economists themselves had used to deal with that problem.

But *only* "in a sense". Keynes's interest certainly lay in investigating the causes of movements in income, but they were movements of a type very different from those with which Ricardo had been concerned. Ricardo examined the forces which produced a secular increase in income (and changes in its distribution) over the long period; Keynes examined the forces which produced fluctuations in income in the short period. Their basic aims were different, and, notwithstanding certain rather superficial resemblances, their techniques were different. It is

---

[17] Pp. 87–8.

[18] *Keynes' General Theory: Reports of Three Decades*, p. 330. Cf. Keynes's own remarks on the role of the consumption function in his system, reprinted in *The New Economics* (ed. Harris, London, 1947), p. 190.

true that Keynes, like Ricardo (although much more strongly), emphasized that saving should be considered as a function of income. But *whose* income? Ricardo always regarded accumulation as being the more or less exclusive province of a particular social class – the class which lived by profit. The labourers did not usually have the power to accumulate, and the landowners, although they had the power, did not usually have the will. In Keynes's system, on the other hand, saving appears as a function of the *aggregate* income of the community as a whole, and the differences between social classes which Ricardo in effect took as his starting-point are almost completely abstracted from.

Finally, it should be noted in the present connection that Keynes's *General Theory*, although certainly in one sense more "general" than the neo-Classical systems, was in fact in another sense less "general" than the Classical systems. Keynes used the word "general" in the title of his book in order to focus attention on his view that the full-employment equilibrium situation allegedly assumed by the neo-Classical writers was actually only "a limiting point of the possible positions of equilibrium".[19] His use of the word "general", it is clear, did *not* imply that he wanted his theory to be regarded as replacing the whole body of orthodox neo-Classical theory. His complaint against the latter was simply that it could not "solve the economic problems of the actual world" – most notably, the problem of mass unemployment. If that problem could in fact be solved, *i.e.*, "if our central controls succeed in establishing an aggregate volume of output corresponding to full employment as nearly as is practicable", then, said Keynes,

the classical theory comes into its own again from this point onwards. If we suppose the volume of output to be given, *i.e.*, to be determined by forces outside the classical scheme of thought, then there is no objection to be raised against the classical analysis of the manner in which private self-interest will determine what in particular is produced, in what proportions the factors of production will be combined to produce it, and how the value of the final product will be distributed between them.[20]

This statement reveals very clearly the sense in which Keynes's system was less "general" than the Classical systems (properly so-called). For the latter systems never made this kind of distinction between microeconomic and macroeconomic analysis. To Smith and Ricardo, the macroeconomic problem of the "laws of motion" of capitalism appeared as the primary problem on the agenda, and it seemed necessary that the *whole* of economic analysis – including the basic theories of value and distribution – should be deliberately oriented towards its solution. To

---

[19] *General Theory*, p. 3.   [20] *Ibid.*, pp. 378–9.

Keynes, on the other hand, it did not appear that a "general" theory in this Classical sense was necessary for the solution of the particular set of macroeconomic problems in which he was interested. Orthodox micro-economics could be left in peace so long as it stuck to its last: all that was necessary was a kind of macroeconomic supplement to it.

V

Marx inherited a great deal of the Classical outlook and theoretical structure, and there is no doubt an important element of truth in the now commonplace description of him as "the last of the Classical economists". But his own contribution was much more significant, and much more idiosyncratic, than this description might be taken to imply. His aim was to liberate Classical economics from its "bourgeois" prison, an aim which he pursued with special vigour in two fields. The first of these was the theory of profit: the problem of the origin and persistence of profit under conditions of competition, Marx believed, could not be adequately solved unless one *started from* the relations of production between wage-earners and capital-owners characteristic of a capitalist economy. The second was the theory of the trade cycle: the problem of cyclical fluctuations, he claimed, could not be solved in terms of the operation of exogenous factors, but only by seeing the fluctuations as the reflection of certain deep-rooted social and economic contradictions inherent in the capitalist mode of production itself.

Here there is an obvious parallel between Marx and Keynes, and it was only to be expected that the publication of the *General Theory* would give rise to a number of speculations about the relationship between the Marxian and Keynesian systems. It did not prove too difficult to reveal a number of other parallels, of varying degrees of significance, between *Capital* and the *General Theory*. There are certain fairly obvious similarities, for example, between the respective explanations given by Marx and Keynes of the forces determining the periodicity of the cycle, and between their respective accounts of the role of speculation. There is another obvious parallel – which I myself have never been able to see as anything other than purely formal – between Marx's labour theory of value and Keynes's "wage-unit" concept. Much more relevant to the question at issue are Marx's famous reproduction schemes, which have quite rightly attracted considerable attention from those who are interested in the relations between Keynes and Marx. Mrs Robinson tells us that Kahn, in the famous "circus" at which Keynes's *Treatise* was discussed in 1931, "explained the problem of saving and investment by imagining a cordon round the capital-good industries and then studying the trade between them and the consumption-good industries; he was struggling to rediscover Marx's schema".[21] Mrs Robinson adds that starting from Marx – as Kalecki did – would have saved Keynes a lot of trouble.

If a study of Marx's reproduction schemes can reveal certain important similarities with Keynes, it can also serve to bring out a number of dissimilarities which are of at least equal importance. The Marxian aggregates, as Professor Tsuru has emphasized in a stimulating article, "appear midway in Marx's theoretical journey from the most abstract discussion of value to the more concrete elucidation of crises and other typically capitalistic phenomena".[22] This means that Marx's discussion of his reproduction schemes in Volume II of *Capital* is conducted on the basis of a number of important simplifying assumptions – most notably the assumption that all the commodities concerned are bought and sold throughout at their Marxian *values*. (Similarly, in the Volume III analysis of the long-run tendency of the rate of profit to fall, all commodities are assumed to sell at "prices of production" which are derived from *values*.) This implies, of course, that Marx's aggregates are not "operational" in the sense that Keynes's are – a fact which is often held to demonstrate the superiority of the Keynesian system over the Marxian. It is indeed true, as Tsuru points out,[23] that the Marxian system would have to be further extended by the incorporation of a theory of parametric adjustments if one wished to use it to tackle the particular problems in which Keynes was interested. But Marx's method of approach was not arbitrary; and the fact that he conducted these parts of his analysis in terms of *values* and "prices of production" rather than in terms of market prices cannot be taken to indicate that he was unconcerned with the short period. Rather, it reflected his view that short-period phenomena – including most notably the phenomena of the trade cycle – could not be adequately analysed in isolation from long-period trends, and that the basic causes of both the long-period and the short-period tendencies should be sought primarily in the fundamental social relations between men and men in the sphere of production which were reflected in the first instance in the *values* and "prices of production" of commodities. For example, one could not properly put forward one set of factors as the cause of the long-period tendency of the rate of profit to fall (in terms of *values*), and another entirely separate set of factors as the cause of that short-period

[21] Robinson, *Collected Economic Papers*, Vol. III, p. 96.

[22] Shigeto Tsuru, "Keynes versus Marx: The Methodology of Aggregates", in *Post-Keynesian Economics* (ed. Kurihara, London, 1955), p. 340. I am greatly indebted to this article for a number of the ideas which follow in the present section.

[23] *Op. cit.*, pp. 335–6.

fall in profit or the expectation of profit (in terms of prices) which precipitated the crisis through its effect on the inducement to invest. The factors whose ceaseless conflict and interaction produced these two sets of phenomena were in Marx's view intimately linked together, and arose from certain contradictions implicit in the relations of production which characterized the capitalist economy.

The *basic* contradiction of the capitalist mode of production – which in a sense gave birth to all the other contradictions – was in Marx's view essentially a contradiction between *tendency* and *aim*. The *tendency* of the capitalist mode of production, Marx writes, is "towards absolute development of the productive forces, regardless of the value and surplus-value it contains, and regardless of the social conditions under which capitalist production takes place". The immediate *aim* of the system, on the other hand, is "to preserve the value of the existing capital and promote its self-expansion to the highest limit". The aim and the tendency are in continuous conflict. The capitalists endeavour to step up accumulation and productivity, in order to increase their profit and the value of their capital. But the technological changes associated with accumulation increase the organic composition of capital, and therefore, unless their effect is offset, cause a long-term fall in the rate of profit. Continued accumulation, again, increases the mass of capital goods, but at the same time brings about a periodical depreciation of the value of the existing capital, which "disturbs the given conditions, within which the process of circulation and reproduction of capital takes place, and is therefore accompanied by sudden stoppages and crises in the production process". And the struggle of the capitalist to increase his rate of profit and his rate of accumulation implies a restriction of immediate consumption, both on his own part and on the part of the workers whom he employs. "These different influences", Marx claims,

may at one time operate predominantly side by side in space, and at another succeed each other in time. From time to time the conflict of antagonistic agencies finds vent in crises. The crises are always but momentary and forcible solutions of the existing contradictions. They are violent eruptions which for a time restore the disturbed equilibrium.[24]

Thus, although in "extended reproduction" there exists the theoretical possibility of a "balance" between the different sectors of the economy, the conditions of which can be accurately defined, such a "balance" can in actual fact be achieved only by an accident, or by the kind of forcible restoration of equilibrium just described.[25]

[24] Quotations in this paragraph from *Capital*, Vol. III, p. 244.
[25] Cf. *ibid.*, Vol. II, pp. 494–5.

While it is true, then, that both Marx and Keynes rejected "Say's Law" and looked to endogenous factors for an explanation of cyclical fluctuations, the resemblance does not really go a great deal further than this. The first and most obvious dissimilarity is that whereas Marx's analysis of the trade cycle was an integral part of a macrodynamic analysis of a very broad kind, rather similar in scope to that of his Classical predecessors, Keynes's analysis of underemployment equilibrium was more or less exclusively macrostatic in character. Keynes, emphasizing that "in the long run we are all dead", deliberately assumed that techniques of production, size of plant, etc., remained unchanged. As Schumpeter put it, in Keynes's basic model (though by no means always in his supporting argument) *"all the phenomena incident to the creation and change in [the industrial] apparatus, that is to say, the phenomena that dominate the capitalist processes, are thus excluded from consideration"*.[26] The second dissimilarity follows from what was said at the end of the previous section about the comparative degrees of "generality" of the Classical and Keynesian systems. Marx, like Smith and Ricardo, made no distinction between microeconomic and macroeconomic analysis, and deliberately oriented his theories of value and distribution towards the solution of the problem of the "laws of motion" of capitalism. The third dissimilarity, which is closely related to the first two, is simply that whereas Marx's theory was couched *in terms of* the relations of production peculiar to capitalism, Keynes very largely abstracted from these relations, treating them merely as a part of the "given" environment within which the particular variables which he regarded as significant interacted with one another.

This last point deserves a little elaboration. The Keynesian aggregates, as Professor Tsuru has said, unlike the Marxian aggregates, "do not necessarily concern themselves with the specificity of capitalism . . . To any type of society, be it primitive-tribal or socialistic, we may apply them and refer to the ratios between them by means of such terms as 'the propensity to consume', 'the propensity to invest', etc."[27] In Keynes's system, a vitally important role is played by three "independent variables" which are deliberately defined in a-social terms, namely "the psychological propensity to consume, the psychological attitude to liquidity and the psychological expectation of future yield from capital-assets".[28] If the "social structure", the "existing tehnique", the "degree of competition", etc. are taken as given, Keynes argues, then the "independent variables" will determine the "dependent variables" (the volume of employment and the national income). Keynes recog-

[26] Schumpeter, in *The New Economics*, p. 93. (Schumpeter's italics.)
[27] Tsuru, *op. cit.*, p. 336.   [28] *General Theory*, p. 247.

nizes, of course, that the factors "taken as given" do in fact influence the
"independent variables". But he claims that they "do not completely
determine them", and proceeds on the assumption that the *nature* of
their influence, except in special cases, does not need to be investigated.[29] To Marx, by way of contrast, it seemed obvious that it was
precisely this field of enquiry which was the really crucial one.

VI

Those of us who prophesied in the years following the publication of the
General Theory that the framework of orthodox economics would soon
show itself sufficiently flexible to accommodate Keynes's analysis, and
that talk of a "Keynesian Revolution" was therefore ill-judged, have
simply been proved wrong. Today, thirty years after the *General Theory*,
the spate of articles and books summarizing, interpreting, developing
and attacking Keynes's work shows no sign of diminishing. So great is
the volume of this "post-Keynesian" literature, indeed, that it is very
hard to identify even those trends which are important today, let alone
those which historians of the future will recognize as important in connection with the question of the place of Keynes in the history of economic thought. Not much more can usefully be done at this juncture, I
think, than to classify a number of the current tendencies under two
very broad heads.

The first of these heads encompasses certain tendencies which in total
amount to a retrogression from Keynes's fundamental vision of capitalism as an inherently inharmonious system in which there is no
Invisible Hand automatically equilibrating investment levels with full-
employment saving levels. For Keynes himself, concerned as he was
with the analysis of short-term fluctuations in output, the assumption of
the absence of any such Invisible Hand was much more important than
the various particular *reasons* which might be postulated for its absence
in any given case.[30] After Keynes, however, when the economist's
psychological propensity to formalize had been given time to operate,
the question of these reasons began to appear much more important.
Which of the reasons did Keynes himself rely upon? Which of them were
in actual fact important? Under what circumstances might *none* of them
be operative, so that the Invisible Hand could come back into its own
again? The way was now open for the blooming of a hundred models
based on different sets of assumptions – including, of course, refurbished
"neo-Classical" models in which growth was assumed to be possible

---

[29] *Ibid.*, pp. 245–7.
[30] Cf. Samuelson, in *Keynes' General Theory: Reports of Three Decades*, p. 321.

without any serious departures from full employment. Keynes's caricature of neo-Classical economics began to provoke the inevitable retaliation, and the resurrection of the Pigou Effect served "to save face and honour for the believers in the harmony of equilibrium"[31] by making it appear less likely that liquidity traps and interest-inelastic investment schedules would prevent the achievement of full employment.

This retrogression from the original Keynesian vision – to a large extent made possible, paradoxically enough, by the use of tools and techniques provided by Keynes himself[32] – is of course something more than a mere by-product of the rash of model-building stimulated by the *General Theory*, and something more than a mere reflection of the notorious theoretical difficulty of reconciling competition with unemployment.[33] It is not easy to live without the comfortable assumption of the presence of an Invisible Hand, and to many economists, after due reflection, Keynes's approach to the problem of cyclical fluctuations – which emphasized the significance of endogenous rather than exogenous factors – began to appear perhaps a little near the bone. But the retrogression has been stimulated above all by the simple fact that, contrary to everybody's expectations, there has been no major slump in the capitalist world for more than a quarter of a century. This has provoked in the minds of many modern economists the same kind of reaction which a not too dissimilar state of affairs provoked in the minds of some of their predecessors after the death of Ricardo: if things have in fact turned out so much better than Keynes (or Ricardo) anticipated, must there not be something radically wrong with the basic theory of Keynes (or Ricardo)? It is not easy to decide what one ought to do in the face of this apparent contradiction between theory and reality. Does one begin talking in terms of "innate" Keynesian tendencies which are now being offset by government action? Or does one perhaps begin postulating the existence of tendencies towards full employment – e.g., through equilibrating shifts in income distribution? The course of action actually selected will depend upon personal predilections, and it may also, of course, depend upon the particular side of the Atlantic on which the economist concerned happens to live.

The second head encompasses the tendencies which have led to the transformation of Keynes's essentially macrostatic theory into a more realistic and far-reaching macrodynamic theory. Whether "transformation" is the correct word here is of course a matter of current

[31] Samuelson, *op. cit.*, p. 333.

[32] Cf. Samuelson, *op. cit.*, p. 334: "If only Say, James Mill and Ricardo had lived after 1936, think of what sense they might have made of Say's Law!"

[33] Cf. G. Haberler, in *Keynes' General Theory: Reports of Three Decades*, p. 284.

controversy: the extent to which the seeds of modern macrodynamics were in fact sown in the *General Theory* is not easy to measure. Nor is it easy to judge whether and in what sense Keynesian macrostatic theory was in fact an "indispensable foundation"[34] for the modern macrodynamic systems. But it can at any rate be said that Keynes's system provided the main stimulus for the emergence of the modern macrodynamic systems, in which greater attention can be and is being paid to "relations of production" than Keynes himself was prepared to do. Once the use of the appropriate aggregates has become respectable, disaggregation becomes possible: for example, the savings of profit-receivers can be separated from those of other social groups. Once the concept of a net flow of income has been incorporated into our theory, we can begin to enquire into the characteristics of the economic organism into and out of which this income flows.[35] Once the income-creating effect of investment has been given its proper emphasis, we can proceed to enquire into its effect in adding to productive capacity. And once we have analysed the problem of the determination of output under competitive conditions, we can proceed to bring monopoly into the picture. The net result of this second set of tendencies has been the emergence of a number of macrodynamic theories which are much closer to the Classical and Marxian theories, in spirit and often in actual content, than anyone could reasonably have anticipated. In the long run, it may well be the "mighty impulse"[36] given by Keynes – perhaps unintentionally – to macrodynamic analysis which is seen as the central factor determining his place in the history of economic thought.

But to say no more than this would be to ignore what might well turn out to be the most important consideration of all. We are living in an age in which the whole nature and function of economics is undergoing a profound revolution. There are various ways of describing this revolution: I myself like to think of it in terms of the transformation of economics into a science – or perhaps an art – of economic management, or social engineering, and to link this up with the decline in our own day of the concept of the economic machine.[37] The point is not simply that economic analysis is today being brought to bear on public policy to a much greater extent than ever before, but that the whole nature of economic analysis is being radically changed in order to deal effectively with the *new* policy problems which are emerging in a world in which the domain of the economic machine is steadily diminishing. Now the

[34] Harrod, in *Keynes' General Theory: Reports of Three Decades*, p. 140.
[35] Cf. Tsuru, *op. cit.*, p. 341.
[36] Schumpeter, *History of Economic Analysis*, p. 1184.
[37] See my Inaugural Lecture, *The Rise and Fall of the Concept of the Economic Machine* (Leicester, 1965).

Keynesian theoretical system was of course one of the most machine-like of them all. But by concentrating as it did on the tendency of the machine to generate unemployment and idle capacity, and by focusing attention upon aggregates which were not only crucial from a policy point of view but also statistically measurable, it gave a tremendous impetus to the development of the new type of economic thinking which our age requires. By making interference with the operation of the machine respectable, and putting it on something like a scientific basis, Keynes helped to pave the way for a new type of economic thinking which may well transcend all previous economic systems, including his own.

ECONOMICS AND IDEOLOGY[1]

I

Economics, as Joan Robinson has said, "has always been partly a vehicle for the ruling ideology of each period as well as partly a method of scientific investigation",[2] and our task is "to sort out as best we may this mixture of ideology and science".[3] The main purpose of the present essay is to discuss some of the major difficulties which arise in this sorting-out process.

I have chosen to consider these difficulties within the framework of a critique of three notable books – Schumpeter's *History of Economic Analysis*,[4] Joan Robinson's *Economic Philosophy*, and Oscar Lange's *Political Economy*.[5] Each of these books deals, in an idiosyncratic but highly illuminating way, with a particular aspect of the general problem of economics and ideology. Since the three books taken together seem to me to form a whole which is much greater than the sum of its parts, there may be a place for this running commentary upon them, even if it does little more than interpret and juxtapose the main arguments of the three authors. In this sphere of doubt and danger, where caution must necessarily be the keynote, there may well be no better way of making progress.

II

The problem of the extent to which economics is invalidated by ideological bias, and must therefore be regarded as in some sense historically relative, was one of the great questions which absorbed Schumpeter during the last decade of his life, when he was engaged in expanding his *Epochen* into the monumental *History of Economic Analysis*. One of the most basic contributions of the *History*, at least as Schumpeter himself saw it, was its demonstration that the historical development of "economic analysis", as distinct from that of "political economy" and

---

[1] Sections II–IV of this essay are an amended version of an article which was published in the *Scottish Journal of Political Economy*, February 1957.

[2] *Economic Philosophy* (London, 1962), p. 1.

[3] *Ibid.*, p. 25.   [4] London, 1954.

[5] Pergamon Press, Oxford, and Polish Scientific Publishers, Warsaw, 1963. This is the first volume (subtitled "General Problems") of a projected triology, which Lange unhappily did not live to complete.

"economic thought",[6] displays a relatively high degree of autonomy with respect to socio-historical facts. "It is . . . our main purpose", wrote Schumpeter near the beginning of the *History*, "to describe what may be called the process of the Filiation of Scientific Ideas – the process by which men's efforts to understand economic phenomena produce, improve, and pull down analytic structures in an unending sequence. And it is one of the main theses to be established in this book that *fundamentally* this process does not differ from the analogous processes in other fields of knowledge."[7]

This thesis pervades the whole book and determines its general pattern to such a large extent that it is surprising that it should have provoked so little comment from critics. For example, in none of the six major review articles which immediately followed the publication of the *History* is there anything like a proper recognition of the importance which the thesis tended to assume in Schumpeter's mind. In most of them, in fact, it is hardly even mentioned.[8] The chief reason for this apparent failure to appreciate the full force of Schumpeter's argument is, I suppose, that the thesis in question is both a very familiar and a very comfortable one, and it is difficult for those of us who have been brought up on it to imagine that anyone should think it worth while to take the great pains which Schumpeter in fact did to establish and defend it. Yet to Schumpeter it was far from being self-evident. It appeared to him to be vitally necessary to defend it against attack – and in particular against the Marxian attack. Schumpeter's attitude towards Marx, indeed, affords the main key to the proper understanding of the *History*. In this case, as in so many others (including that of Marx himself), the significance of the thesis being advanced can be properly appreciated only when it is considered in relation to the thesis being opposed.

"What a pity, but at the same time, what a lesson and what a challenge!"[9] This revealing comment by Schumpeter on Marx sums up extremely well his basic attitude towards him. It would be too simple to

[6] On the distinction made by Schumpeter between "economic analysis", "political economy" and "economic thought", see Part I of the *History*, *passim*, and particularly pp. 38 ff.

[7] *History*, p. 6.

[8] The review articles to which I am referring are those by L. Robbins (*Quarterly Journal of Economics*, February 1955), O. H. Taylor (*Review of Economics and Statistics*, February 1955), J. Viner (*American Economic Review*, December 1954), G. B. Richardson (*Oxford Economic Papers*, June 1955), I. M. D. Little (*Economic History Review*, August 1955), and F. H. Knight (*Southern Economic Journal*, January 1955). Comparison should be made with the brief but fundamentally correct assessment by A. Smithies in *Schumpeter, Social Scientist* (ed. S. E. Harris, 1951), p. 21.

[9] *History*, p. 433.

say that Schumpeter believed that Marx had asked the right questions but given the wrong answers to them, and that it was his own duty to supply alternative answers. One could hardly sum up the life-work of a thinker of Schumpeter's calibre in terms of a single generalization such as this, although there is undoubtedly an important element of truth in it. It would be more accurate to say of him, with Haberler, that "all his life he was attracted by the grandeur of the Marxian system"[10] – in particular by Marx's "vision" of a capitalist economy inexorably developing, always by virtue of its own internal laws, towards its dissolution; but that at the same time he was repelled by certain other aspects of Marx's analysis – in particular by the suggestion that a net surplus taking the form of profit was normally yielded to a capitalist employer even in the absence of monopoly and innovation, and by the associated idea that the capitalist economic system *as such* was based upon exploitation and racked by inherent contradictions. The great force of this attraction and repulsion is clearly discernible in all Schumpeter's major works. In his *Theory of Economic Development*, for example, as he himself stated, his general aim – to construct a theory of capitalist development which relied on forces internal to the system – was exactly the same as that of Marx;[11] but the actual theory of development which he constructed, and in particular the theory of profit which it involved, are probably best regarded as alternatives to those of Marx. Schumpeter liked to call Böhm-Bawerk "the bourgeois Marx",[12] and he himself, I think, might have been rather flattered by a similar title.

Where, then, does the *History* stand in this connection? Here too the familiar pattern of attraction and repulsion in relation to Marx is very evident. The attraction is towards the general principles put forward by Marx on the subject of ideological bias;[13] the repulsion is from the Marxian suggestion that the bulk of the so-called "scientific" economics of modern times is ideologically biased. It is quite true, Schumpeter admits, that we have to surrender a great deal to the Marxists on the ground that it is ideologically conditioned. "Political economy" and

[10] *Schumpeter, Social Scientist*, p. 41.
[11] Schumpeter's statement occurs in his preface to the Japanese edition of the *Theory of Economic Development*. Schumpeter added, however, that this similarity of viewpoint was *not* clear to him "at the outset".
[12] *History*, p. 846.
[13] Schumpeter uses the term "ideology", as Marx and Engels themselves often did, to refer to a theory or outlook which consists wholly of illusory elements. Today, however, the term is often used in a wider sense to include any typical theory or outlook of a particular period or class, into which scientific as well as illusory elements may enter. For accounts of the history of the term and its various uses, see A. L. Macfie, *Scottish Journal of Political Economy*, June 1963, pp. 212–17, and O. Lange, *Political Economy*, pp. 327–32.

"economic thought" must undoubtedly go. But happily there are certain important senses in which "economic analysis" can be shown to remain relatively unscathed. In particular, the *history* of "economic analysis" can be shown to display throughout the phenomenon of real scientific progress. Thus, in spite of Schumpeter's concessions to the Marxian view, the general argument of the *History* turns out to be very different indeed from that put forward in Marx's own history of analysis, *Theorien über den Mehrwert*. Marx, broadly speaking, argued that the development of the truly scientific elements in political economy continued only up to about 1830, and that thereafter superficiality and apologetics began to predominate. Schumpeter, on the other hand, argues that, in spite of numerous disturbances and detours, we can discern a more or less continuous development of scientific analysis right up to the present day, this development being particularly rapid and striking precisely in the period *after* 1830.

Schumpeter does not of course deny that ideological bias may, and often does, affect the validity of the analyst's results. Ideology in fact enters "on the very ground floor", for analytic work "begins with material provided by our vision of things, and this vision is ideological almost by definition".[14] Fortunately, however, according to Schumpeter, "the rules of procedure that we apply in our analytic work are almost as much exempt from ideological influence as vision is subject to it", and these rules tend, given time, "to crush out ideologically conditioned error from the visions from which we start".[15] Shortly after this statement, unfortunately, Schumpeter's manuscript breaks off, and the account which he might possibly have given of the various other ways in which ideology may enter into analysis is missing. But the general tenor of his views on the subject is clear enough. He is particularly concerned to combat any "sterile pessimism concerning the 'objective validity' of our methods and results".[16] Not only are there many items in our box of tools that are, and are known to be, ideologically neutral, or that can be shown to be so in spite of popular belief to the contrary;[17] not only can a judicious use of the rules mentioned above safeguard us individually, at least up to a point, against ideological bias; but also – and here is the thesis I wish to examine – these rules are in actual fact automatically applied in the historical development of economic analysis, so that over time, notwithstanding all the inhibitions, detours and setbacks to which this development is manifestly subject, it is possible to speak of real scientific progress in the analytical field. Historically speaking at any rate – in its temporal flow, as it were – economic analysis does not show any serious signs of ideological infection. The

[14] *History*, p. 42.   [15] *Ibid.*, p. 43.   [16] *Ibid.*, p. 43.   [17] *Ibid.*, p. 44.

o

clear implication of all this for present-day analysis is that "if complacency can ever be justified, there is much more reason for being
complacent today than there was [a century] or even a quarter of a
century ago".[18]

No one will be prepared to deny that there are indeed certain parts
of "economic analysis" as Schumpeter defines it – statistics, for example
– of which this thesis can be held to be essentially true. Doubts begin to
creep in, however, as soon as we turn to "pure theory" in Schumpeter's
sense, and in particular to the central propositions of the theory of
value. Now the problem of value, as Schumpeter himself emphasized,
"must always hold the pivotal position, as the chief tool of analysis in
any pure theory that works with a rational schema".[19] Thus it was
vitally necessary for Schumpeter, if he wished to establish his thesis, to
do so with special reference to the history of value theory. It is no
accident, then, that the majority of Schumpeter's illustrations of the
thesis in the body of the *History* relate to value theory, and it is around
this aspect of the problem that my own criticisms of Schumpeter will
largely turn.

III

It is in the first of Schumpeter's main historical sections, dealing with
the period from the beginnings up to about 1790, that the real ground-
work of his thesis is laid. Let me begin, therefore, by contrasting my own
view of what happened during this period with that of Schumpeter.

It is useful, I think, to begin by dividing the period into three stages.
First, there was the Aristotelian-Scholastic stage, in which the "value"
of a commodity was usually identified with the price at which it *ought*
to sell, this being in turn frequently equated with the costs (notably
labour costs) normally involved in its production. Second, there was the
Neo-Scholastic-Mercantilist stage, in which "value" came to be widely
identified with the price at which a commodity *actually did* sell, and was
conceived to be determined by the interplay of supply and demand,
with the main emphasis often being laid on the demand side. Third,
there was the Classical stage, in which "value" gradually came to be
identified with the competitive equilibrium price (which was taken to
be equal to the cost of production, including "normal" profits), and was
conceived – at least towards the close of the stage – to be ultimately
determined by the quantity of labour embodied in the commodity. This
scheme obviously suffers from all the defects which are necessarily involved in any such attempt at stadial analysis, but it does at any rate

[18] Schumpeter, *American Economic Review*, March 1949, p. 345.
[19] *History*, p. 588.

provide a conceptual framework within which the developments concerned can be seen in what I believe to be their correct perspective.

Schumpeter's approach, however, is quite different. Speaking very broadly, he tends to write as if the characteristics of the work of the second stage which I have just distinguished were more or less typical of those of the period as a whole, at least up to the time of Adam Smith. He argues that the scholastic doctors, working from Aristotelian roots, had developed an analysis of value and price in terms of "utility and scarcity" which "lacked nothing but the marginal apparatus";[20] that this analysis "went on developing quite normally right into the times of A. Smith";[21] that "it was the 'subjective' or 'utility' theory of price that had the wind until the influence of the *Wealth of Nations* – and especially of Ricardo's *Principles* – asserted itself";[22] and, in fact, that the salient feature of the analytical work of the whole period up to 1790 was actually the development of the elements of "a full-fledged theory of demand and supply".[23] In relation to the first stage, Schumpeter seems to me to overestimate the extent to which Aristotle and Aquinas actually *identified* the "just price" with the competitive equilibrium price.[24] And in relation to the third stage, he underestimates the importance of the typically "Classical" developments, in respect of both their quantity and their quality.

On the quantity side, this is perhaps best shown by his attitude towards the more or less primitive expressions of the labour theory of value (and associated ideas) which are frequently to be found in the pre-Ricardian literature. Apparently taking "all or nothing" as his slogan, he virtually rejects the idea that a "labour theory of value" is to

---

[20] *Ibid.*, p. 1054, and cf. also p. 98.   [21] *Ibid.*, p. 1054.

[22] *Ibid.*, p. 302. Even in the case of Smith, according to Schumpeter, the best piece of economic theory which he turned out ("the rudimentary equilibrium theory of Chapter 7") actually "points towards Say, and, through the latter's work, to Walras" (*ibid.*, p. 189).

[23] *Ibid.*, p. 98.

[24] There was indeed a connection between the "just price" and the competitive equilibrium price, but it was much less direct and conscious than Schumpeter's argument implies. Schumpeter suggests (*History*, p. 61) that Aristotle took competitive equilibrium prices as "standards of commutative justice", and that Aquinas similarly identified the "just price" with the competitive equilibrium price (*ibid.*, p. 93). It would be more correct to say that Aristotle and Aquinas took prices proportionate to producers' costs (notably labour costs) as standards of commutative justice, and that these standards were *ultimately* (but not necessarily consciously) derived from their observation of the fact that in the real world exchange ratios tended (in the absence of monopoly) towards equality with ratios of producers' costs. Thus when Aristotle and Aquinas spoke of the "just price" of a commodity they were not actually *thinking* of its competitive equilibrium price, which is what Schumpeter suggests. Our ideas about justice certainly come to us from earth and not from heaven, but we are not always aware of this fact.

be found either in Petty or in Smith; he omits to consider Franklin and the author of *Some Thoughts on the Interest of Money in General* in this connection; and he seriously underestimates the extent to which a large number of other writers – Boisguillebert, Mandeville, Locke, Hume, Gervaise and Tucker, for example – popularized certain concepts which helped substantially to form the climate of opinion in which the mature labour theory of value was later to flourish. But more important than this is Schumpeter's underestimation of the scientific *quality* of the "Classical" developments in value theory. In so far as he recognizes their existence, he obviously regards these developments as having inhibited scientific advance rather than promoted it. One of the chief villains of the piece, according to Schumpeter, was the idea that the "normal" or equilibrium price is determined by cost and the market price by supply and demand. This is described as a "superficial, and, as the later development of the theory of value was to show, misleading formula".[25] And the idea that relative equilibrium prices are ultimately determined by relative quantities of embodied labour, which Ricardo was to develop into the very basis of his system, seems to be regarded by Schumpeter as little more than a simple analytical error.

Why, then, were these new "Classical" ideas seized upon with such eagerness and developed by men of undoubted intellectual ability?[26] They were seized upon and developed, I would suggest, precisely because they were regarded as *scientifically* superior to the ideas current in the second stage. At the time when men first began to think seriously about the prices at which commodities actually sold (as distinct from the prices at which they ought to sell), the only useful proposition that it was really possible to put forward about these prices was that they were determined by the interplay of supply and demand. So long as there was no very marked tendency for the amount of "profit" earned by a producer to bear a reasonably regular relationship to the amount of "capital" which he employed, it was difficult to make any general statement about the price of his commodity other than that it would usually exceed prime cost by an increment ("profit" or "gain") which would vary in each individual case according to the state of supply and demand in the market. To the merchant of the sixteenth and seventeenth centuries, interested mainly in the day-to-day prices of a very limited range of goods, such a "theory of value" would appear more or less adequate for his purposes, since supply and demand could reasonably be regarded, in the context of this particular problem, as "inde-

---

[25] *History*, p. 220.
[26] A number of sentences in this paragraph are reproduced more or less verbatim from my *Studies in the Labour Theory of Value* (London, 1956).

pendent" determining factors. But it was scarcely capable of serving as the basis for forecasts of any great degree of generality. Once the phenomenon of a "normal" or "natural" rate of profit had begun to manifest itself on a sufficiently wide scale, however, it became possible to put forward a much more useful general proposition concerning commodity prices. Commodities, it could now be said, tended under competitive conditions to sell at prices equal to prime cost *plus profit at the "natural" rate*. A situation in which this "natural" rate of profit was being earned, so that there was no tendency for firms either to enter or to leave the industry, could then be defined as a situation of equilibrium, in which supply could be said to "balance" or "equal" demand. This principle, however, obviously applied only to equilibrium prices under competitive conditions: so far as prices formed under other conditions were concerned, no scientific advance was possible over the old supply-and-demand explanation.[27] To the economists of (roughly) the first half of the eighteenth century, interested mainly in the average prices of the relatively small group of goods produced on a capitalist basis and sold under competitive conditions, a cost-of-production theory of value founded on this principle would appear more or less adequate, since the level of the various distributive rewards into which the cost of production ultimately reduced itself – rent, wages and profit – could plausibly be conceived as "independent" determining factors. But as the sphere of operation of capitalist production extended, and the notion of the general interdependence of the various elements of the economic system as a whole took firmer hold of men's minds, it became evident that these ultimate constituents of the cost of production could no longer be treated as "independent" determinants of the prices of commodities, since they would themselves be partly dependent upon these prices. Thus economists who were interested in dealing with broad fundamental problems concerning "the nature and causes of the wealth of nations" began to look for some "unifying quantitative principle" (to use Mr Dobb's phrase)[28] which would serve as a "constant" capable of determining not only the equilibrium prices of commodities but also

---

[27] Those who accepted this principle naturally tended to look upon any reversion in discussion to the terms of the old supply-and-demand explanation as more or less obscurantist. But this definitely did not imply that they were blind to the fairly obvious fact that it was "supply and demand" which actually *fixed* the equilibrium price at the level defined in the principle. Schumpeter's suggestion (*History*, pp. 600–601) that Ricardo and Marx did not observe that their theories of value presupposed that "supply and demand do their work" can readily be refuted by reference to a dozen passages in the work of both of these economists – and has in fact already been so refuted, at least in the case of Ricardo, by several commentators. (See, e.g., Robbins, *op. cit.*, pp. 13–14, and Viner, *op. cit.*, pp. 904–5. In the case of Marx, see, e.g., *Capital*, Vol. III, chapter 10.)

[28] M. H. Dobb, *Political Economy and Capitalism*, p. 5.

the equilibrium prices of land, labour and capital.[29] The Classical economists gradually came to believe – or at any rate to recognize instinctively – that a value theory of this type was required before political economy could be transformed into a real science. And I do not think they can really be said to have been misled here. The pattern of intellectual development which I have just been describing is quite a familiar one in the history of science; and whatever may be thought of the actual value-principle which finally emerged in the Classical period, it must surely be conceded that it emerged as the result of enquiries which, at least when disentangled from their popular background, were in the best traditions of scientific advance.

But why was value anchored to the quantity of embodied labour rather than to some other "constant"? Partly, no doubt, for the negative reason that there did not appear to be anything else to anchor it to, which would fulfil the requirements of a theory of value as the Classical economists were coming to understand them. ("Utility" was of course available by then, but the fact that the long-term equilibrium prices of commodities normally remained unaffected when purchasers' estimates of their utility altered seemed to the Classical economists to weigh conclusively against its use.) There is, however, a much more important reason than this. The emergence of the labour theory of value was closely associated with the emergence of the idea that the "chief cement", as Harris put it, that connected men together in modern society was the simple fact that they lived by "betaking themselves to particular arts and employments"[30] and mutually exchanging the products of their separate labours. By engaging independently in the production of commodities for the market, men in effect *worked for one another*; and it was in terms of this basic socio-economic relation between men as separate but mutually interdependent producers of commodities that their relationships in the field of exchange ought properly to be explained. The value relationship between *commodities* which manifested itself on the market, in other words, was conceived as reflecting a more fundamental socio-economic relationship between *men* in the field of production. Thus the exchange of commodities was regarded as consisting in essence of the exchange of the respective quantities of labour which their producers had employed in producing them; and the relative "values" of different commodities – their respective "social weights", to use Marx's expression – were regarded as being ultimately determined by the relative quantities of labour which society found it necessary from time to time to allocate to their production. The

[29] Cf. Dobb's discussion of this whole point, *ibid.*, pp. 8–10.
[30] J. Harris, *An Essay upon Money and Coins* (1757), p. 15, footnote.

postulation of embodied labour as the value-constant was in effect a generalized expression of the view (whether consciously formulated or not) that political economy, if it was to be truly scientific, must start from, and on no account abstract from, the real relations between men in the sphere of production.[31] This view is of course debatable, and Schumpeter himself strongly dissented from it, but that is no excuse for his apparent failure to appreciate its relevance to the question of the development and scientific quality of value theory in the Classical period.

If we leave such facts as these out of consideration, it is easy enough to proceed as Schumpeter does – to minimize the importance of most of the typically "Classical" developments in the history of economic science, to undervalue Smith's contributions to analysis, and to leave Ricardo, as it were, out on a limb. The post-Ricardian developments, which Schumpeter correctly sees as constituting in essence, almost from the beginning, a *rejection* of the really basic Ricardian postulates, can then be quite plausibly described as a return to the historical line of economists' endeavours after a relatively brief Ricardian "detour".

IV

Present-day Marxists, in their interpretations of the post-Ricardian developments, have often commented critically upon that general tendency towards abstraction from the real relations between men in the sphere of production which was characteristic of the period as a whole, and of which the rejection of the labour theory of value was one of the most striking expressions. In addition, and associated with this, they have often suggested that certain specific theories which emerged during the period – notably the new theories of value and distribution – embodied significant elements of ideological illusion. In order to consolidate his thesis, therefore, Schumpeter felt obliged in the first place to argue that the abstraction which took place from the relations between men in production was scientifically justified, and in the second place to defend the new theories specifically against the charge that they were ideologically tainted.

The general tendency towards abstraction from the relations between men in production manifested itself in a number of different ways. One of its most noticeable manifestations was the retreat from the idea that a scientific analysis of the distribution of income must start from the relations between the social classes in production. There was a "prevailing tendency", as Schumpeter notes, "to get away from . . . the

[31] Cf. above, p. 181.

class connotation of the categories of economic types".[32] It is upon this tendency that Schumpeter concentrates in his consideration of the problem. Non-Marxist economics, he argues, was bound increasingly to regard this "class connotation" as "a blemish due to the survival of prescientific patterns of thought". This new view, he says,

was the inevitable consequence of analytic advance that made more and more for a clear distinction of the purely economic relations from others with which they are associated in reality. In analyzing economic phenomena, categories other than those suggested by the class structure of society have proved more useful, as well as more satisfactory, logically. This does not involve overlooking any relevant class-struggle aspects, or simply class aspects, of the relations investigated. All it does involve is greater freedom for all the various aspects of reality to assert their rights.[33]

But surely the emphases here are unduly emotive. What could be more useful and "scientific", it might at first sight be thought, than to make "a clear distinction of the purely economic relations from others with which they are associated in reality"? But there is no fixed boundary line between "purely economic" relations and others: if an analyst distinguishes one set of relations which he labels "purely economic" from another set which he describes as merely "associated in reality" with the first, all he is really doing is to say that in his opinion an analysis of basic economic phenomena couched in terms of the first set of relations is quite adequate, and that no account, or relatively little account, need be taken of the second set. And this, of course, is a proposition which requires to be proved on every occasion that such a distinction is made. Then again, who would not want to adopt an approach which did no more than allow "greater freedom for all the various aspects of reality to assert their rights"? But surely what was involved in the particular historical development which we are considering was not simply a sort of extension of democracy, but rather the dethronement of certain "aspects of reality" which had formerly been regarded as exercising a fundamental determining influence, and their supersession in this position by others. The old idea that the problem of distribution ought properly to be considered in terms of the relations of production gave way to the idea that it could be adequately considered in terms of the simple fact that a firm needs certain "scarce factors" in order to produce.[34] And naturally it cannot be assumed without proof that this constituted a scientific advance. Schumpeter would not, I think, really have wished to dissent from this view: certainly his agreement to it would seem to be implied in his statement in a footnote to the

[32] *History*, p. 552.　　[33] *Ibid.*, p. 551.　　[34] Cf. *ibid.*, pp. 558–9.

passage just quoted that "the proof of this pudding is, of course, in the eating". But both here and elsewhere in the *History* there are statements which suggest that he tended to underestimate its importance.

The fulfilment of the second task mentioned above – the defence of the new theories against the charge of ideological infection – is one of Schumpeter's major preoccupations throughout the latter part of the *History*. On many occasions he pauses to comment upon the absurdity of regarding certain theories developed in the post-Ricardian period as ideologically conditioned. For example, consider his treatment of "the victory of the marginal utility theory". Here he is quite uncompromising: the marginal utility theory is claimed to be a piece of purely scientific analysis with no political connotations whatsoever. "Economic theory", he writes, "is a technique of reasoning; . . . such a technique is neutral by nature and . . . it is a mistake to believe that something is to be gained for socialism by fighting for the Marxist or against the marginal utility theory of value."[35] Political liberalism, in so far as the theorists concerned actually espoused it,

had nothing to do with their marginal utility theories. Marxists no doubt believed that these had been excogitated for purposes of social apologetics. But the "new" theories emerged as a purely analytic affair without reference to practical questions. And there was nothing in them to serve apologetics any better than had the older theories. In fact, the contrary would be easier to maintain (compare, e.g., the equalitarian implications of the "law" of decreasing marginal utility); and it was "bourgeois" economists who developed, during that period, the rational theory of the socialist economy . . .; it was Marshall, Edgeworth, and Wicksell who reduced the doctrine that free and perfect competition maximizes satisfaction for all to the level of an innocuous tautology.[36]

Consider, too, Schumpeter's view that "the transition from the marginal utility theory of value to a theory of value based upon the concept of marginal rate of substitution was ideologically neutral in the sense that either can be shown to be equally compatible with any ideology whatsoever". Those who accepted the latter theory in preference to the former, says Schumpeter, "have done so for purely technical reasons that are completely irrelevant to any ideology of economic life".[37] So far as ideologically relevant issues are concerned, the replacement of the labour theory by the marginal utility theory, the replacement of the latter by the indifference curve approach, and the replacement of the indifference curves by a simple consistency postulate are all on a par.[38] This is a proposition which Schumpeter apparently regarded as self-evident and did not feel himself obliged to prove.

[35] *Ibid.*, p. 884.   [36] *Ibid.*, p. 888.   [37] *Ibid.*, p. 44.
[38] *American Economic Review*, March 1949, p. 352.

There are of course important elements of truth in all this, which I imagine most present-day Marxists would not be unwilling to recognize. They would no doubt be quite happy to concede, for example, that Professor Hicks, when writing *Value and Capital*, was not motivated by a sinister desire to come to the defence of monopoly capitalism. They would also probably agree that the marginal utility theory and the indifference curve approach are "equally compatible with any ideology whatsoever" *in the particular sense emphasized by Schumpeter* – namely, that one cannot *in good logic* draw any political or ethical conclusions from them. But these two concessions would by no means imply agreement with the thesis that the transition in question was "ideologically neutral" *in Marx's sense*. For the fact that the theories concerned are "non-political" in the very limited sense just described does not necessarily mean that considerations of "politics" in a wider sense did not influence their emergence and development.

The essential point here, I would suggest, is that the popularization of the marginal utility theory set the seal upon that process of abstraction from the socio-economic relations between men in production which began after Ricardo's death. Looking at the history of economics as a whole, we find that the theory of value with which an economist begins usually embodies some sort of *general principle of causation* which he believes will be useful in the explanation of economic reality. The general principle of causation embodied in the marginal utility theory is radically different from that embodied in the labour theory. What we must start with, the marginal utility theory says in effect, is not the socio-economic relations between men in the sphere of production, as the labour theory implies, but rather the psychological relation between individuals and finished goods. And the transition from the one principle of causation to the other can hardly be said to have been "ideologically neutral" in anything except the most rarefied sense. It is true, of course, that equalitarian morals could be drawn (whether legitimately or not is another matter) from the law of diminishing marginal utility. These could fairly readily be countered, however by the argument that inequality promotes the accumulation of capital, and there is surely little doubt that by and large the apologetic overtones of the marginal utility theory were much more important than the equalitarian ones.[39] Not only did the theory help to draw attention away from the sensitive area of the relations of production; not only was it able to serve as the foundation for a new theory of distribution in which the distinction between income from work and income from property became more or less irrelevant;[40] but it could also be used to support

[39] See below, pp. 212–13.   [40] Cf. Joan Robinson, *Economic Philosophy*, pp. 58–9.

the notion that a system of free competition and exchange maximized satisfaction all round. Given that consumers were free to spend their incomes in the way they wished, and given that they were imbued with the same spirit of "profit maximization" as the capitalists, they could (and in fact would) obtain the maximum possible satisfaction from their purchases. There is no doubt that the marginal utility theory gave a big fillip to the idea of the innate "rationality" of a competitive capitalist system.

The transition from the marginal utility theory to the indifference curve approach, and from the latter to the consistency postulate, can certainly be more plausibly explained in terms of "purely technical reasons" than the transition from the labour theory to the marginal utility theory. But to explain it *exclusively* in terms of internal development, as Schumpeter tends to do, is to explain very little. Two points are of significance here. First, the developments in question have succeeded in getting over certain logical difficulties in the original marginal utility theory while at the same time retaining the key assumption that consumers engage in some sort of "maximizing" behaviour, thereby in effect strengthening the old argument in favour of the innate rationality of a competitive capitalist system. Second, the successive refinements of the conceptual apparatus did not proceed haphazardly, but in fairly close association with a tendency to transform economics into a kind of formal and universal "logic of choice" – a tendency which was greatly encouraged by the substitution of what Lange calls "the praxiological interpretation of utility"[41] for the original hedonistic interpretation, and which has sometimes led (as with von Mises) to certain specific features of the capitalist system being put forward as the universal requisites of rational economic activity.[42]

V

So far, the only moral we can legitimately draw from our discussion is that at any rate in the case of some of the central propositions of the theory of *value* (as distinct from the theory of price)[43] we cannot safely leave it to history to purge our economics of ideological distortions: somehow we have to learn to do the job ourselves. Let us now proceed from Schumpeter, who sees economic analysis as more or less free from ideology, to Joan Robinson, who sees it (up to a certain point) as chock-full of it.

[41] *Political Economy*, p. 235.
[42] Cf. *ibid.*, p. 298, and see below, p. 218.
[43] Cf. my *Economics of Physiocracy*, pp. 365–6.

Mrs Robinson's main theme has already been stated at the beginning of this essay. Economics, she claims, "has always been partly a vehicle for the ruling ideology of each period as well as partly a method of scientific investigation",[44] and our task is to separate out as best we can the science from the ideology. One of the difficulties here, of course, is that in a certain sense we cannot do without ideology: "A society cannot exist unless its members have common feelings about what is the proper way of conducting its affairs, and these common feelings are expressed in ideology." Every economic system "requires a set of rules, an ideology to justify them, and a conscience in the individual which makes him strive to carry them out".[45] And the economist, willy-nilly, tends to be drawn into the job of creating and maintaining the justificatory ideology and moulding the individual conscience in the appropriate way. In the case of an economy based on the money-motive, the task of the economist is to "justify the ways of Mammon to man . . . It is the business of the economists, not to tell us what to do, but show why what we are doing anyway is in accord with proper principles."[46] In Mrs Robinson's book, as she puts it,

this theme is illustrated by reference to one or two of the leading ideas of the economists from Adam Smith onwards, not in a learned manner, tracing the development of thought, nor historically, to show how ideas arose out of the problems of each age, but rather in an attempt to puzzle out the mysterious way that metaphysical propositions, without any logical content, can yet be a powerful influence on thought and action.[47]

Let us note in passing Mrs Robinson's identification, in the passage just quoted, of "metaphysical" with "ideological" – an identification which is made rather more specifically in other places[48] but never really explained. The idea presumably is that a "ruling ideology", in the broad sense, can be taken to consist of a mixture of "scientific" and "unscientific" propositions – that is, if we accept Popper's well-known criterion, of propositions which are capable of being falsified by evidence and propositions which are not. Mrs Robinson begins in effect by labelling the latter group of propositions as "metaphysical". Now one of the great mysteries in the history of the social sciences is the way in which certain propositions which are "metaphysical" in this sense have nevertheless been "a powerful influence on thought and action". The main solution to the mystery is to be sought, Mrs Robinson suggests, in the fact that "metaphysical" propositions, even though they are "without any logical content", may nevertheless be widely accepted because

---

44 *Economic Philosophy*, p. 1.   45 *Ibid.*, pp. 4 and 13.   46 *Ibid.*, p. 21.
47 *Ibid.*, p. 21.   48 E.g., *ibid.*, pp. 2–3.

they help to "justify the ways of Mammon to man".[49] This is the rationale of the virtual identification of "metaphysical" with "ideological" at the beginning of the book. The identification cannot be consistently adhered to, of course, if only because "metaphysical" propositions are not *necessarily* "ideological", but provided we bear this in mind it can serve as a useful heuristic device with which to start.

The first of "the leading ideas of the economists" which Mrs Robinson examines in order to illustrate her theme is the Classical concept of value:

> One of the great metaphysical ideas in economics is expressed by the word "value". What is value and where does it come from? It does not mean usefulness – the good that the goods do us . . . It does not mean market prices, which vary from time to time under the influence of casual accidents; nor is it just an historical average of actual prices. Indeed, it is not simply a price; it is something which will explain how prices come to be what they are. What is it? Where shall we find it? Like all metaphysical concepts, when you try to pin it down it turns out to be just a word.[50]

There follows an account, always interesting and often quite illuminating, of the way in which Smith, Ricardo and Marx grappled with the problem of value, and the way in which a number of the arguments they put forward were "taken up in ideological terms"[51] by their followers. The chapter ends as it began. "Value", says Mrs Robinson, "will not help. It has no operational content. It is just a word."[52]

Let us concede that "value" is in a way "just a word"; that it has indeed "no operational content", at any rate in the sense in which "saving", say, does have such content; and that it is a concept unlikely to appeal to that bluff and hearty common sense which demands of concepts, before they are passed as "true" or "scientific", that they reflect in a simple and direct way what is seen, heard and felt. Having said this, let us immediately add that there was nothing in any way mysterious or esoteric about the Classical uses of the term value.[53] To Smith and Ricardo, the statement that goods possessed "value" (short for "exchange value") meant simply that they possessed the power of purchasing or exchanging for other goods. The statement that under free competition goods would tend to sell "at their values" meant simply that their prices would in the long period tend to gravitate around their costs of production, including profits at the normal rate. And the "theory of value" was simply the theory which tried to explain why the level of these long-period equilibrium prices was what it was.

---

[49] Or, in the case of Marx and the Marxists, because they help to *condemn* these ways.
[50] *Ibid.*, p. 26.   [51] *Ibid.*, p. 32.   [52] *Ibid.*, p. 46.
[53] The Marxian theory of value is discussed separately above, pp. 98 ff.

One may, of course, if one wishes, object to the content of the Classical theory of value and propound some alternative explanation of prices, but it does not help much to insist on describing the very *concept* of value as "metaphysical". If one insists on doing so, it is "metaphysical" and not "value" which becomes "just a word".

Mrs Robinson's account of the actual content of Classical value theory is marred by two major errors of interpretation. First, she claims that Adam Smith's postulation of an "early and rude state of society" in which relative prices were regulated strictly by embodied labour ratios belongs solely to "the realm of myth".[54] Second, she argues that "among all the various meanings of *value*, there has been one all the time under the surface, the old concept of a Just Price".[55] Both these errors spring ultimately from the same source – her failure to appreciate that the early theories of value were vehicles for the presentation of the particular *economic methodologies* accepted by their authors, and that because of this the process of "testing" the theories cannot be simple and straightforward. But leaving this aside, it remains true and important, as Mrs Robinson says, that although "there does not seem to be any ideological overtones . . . in Ricardo's pursuit of *absolute value*", the argument was nevertheless "taken up in ideological terms" by his successors:

> His labour-unit as a measure of *value* somehow seemed to lead to dangerous thoughts. Was labour alone to have the credit for creating *value*? Does this imply that profits are an imposition on the workers? The corrections that Ricardo made in his search for a unit of *value* were taken to show that he admitted that capital also is productive, and the whole argument sailed off into a fog of metaphysics masquerading as analysis.[56]

It sailed off into this "fog of metaphysics", Mrs Robinson's argument can be taken to imply, because the post-Ricardian environment was one in which the "ideological overtones" of the theory of value began to assume much greater importance than they had done in Ricardo's time.

One of the results of the post-Ricardian debate was that in orthodox economics labour went out and utility came in. "*Utility*", says Mrs Robinson (italicizing it to indicate that it is really just as much a Bad Thing as *value*), "is a metaphysical concept of impregnable circularity".[57] It is "a mere word, that has no scientific content, yet one which expresses a point of view".[58] One of the interesting things about it is that "the ideological content of the *utility* approach to prices was curiously double-edged".[59] On the one hand, the doctrine of diminishing marginal utility "points to egalitarian principles, justifies Trade Unions,

[54] *Economic Philosophy*, p. 27. This view is criticized above, pp. 97–8.
[55] *Ibid.*, p. 46.   [56] *Ibid.*, p. 32.   [57] *Ibid.*, p. 47.   [58] *Ibid.*, p. 51.   [59] *Ibid.*, p. 51.

progressive taxation and the Welfare State". On the other hand,

the whole point of *utility* was to justify *laisser faire*. Everyone must be free to spend his income as he likes, and he will gain the greatest benefit when he equalizes the *marginal utility* of a shilling spent on each kind of good. The pursuit of profit, under conditions of perfect competition, leads producers to equate marginal costs to prices, and the maximum possible satisfaction is drawn from available resources.

This is an ideology to end ideologies, for it has abolished the moral problem. It is only necessary for each individual to act egoistically for the good of all to be attained.[60]

All that was needed, therefore, was to get rid of the egalitarian moral of utility theory by means of an "elegant conjuring trick",[61] and the justification of "the ways of Mammon to man" became pure and unalloyed.

Mrs Robinson undoubtedly protests a little too much in all this: sometimes she seems to speak as if it were inherently sinful to accept prices as a measure of satisfactions even as a very rough and provisional first approximation. But her account provides a very wholesome corrective to Schumpeter's view that the introduction of utility was "ideologically neutral", and there is only one point which may perhaps be added. Mrs Robinson mentions that "economics has profited enormously from the discipline that the marginalists introduced".[62] She might also have noted that with marginalism there was imported into economics the crucial assumption that consumers, as well as capitalists, engaged in some kind of "maximizing" behaviour. This may well have been an unrealistic assumption, but historically speaking it was a very important and valuable one – if only because it gave a great impetus to the general study of economic rationality, the first-fruits of which are today beginning to assume immense practical significance.[63]

When Mrs Robinson moves from the neo-classics to Keynes, the whole orientation of her discussion changes. Hitherto, when dealing with the great economists of the past, she has emphasized the presence in their work of certain "metaphysical" propositions which upon analysis could be seen to be ideologically motivated. Now, when dealing with Keynes's work, it is not the presence but rather the absence of such propositions which she emphasizes. Keynes, it seems, was the first great economist who was able to inoculate himself more or less successfully

[60] *Ibid.*, pp. 52–3.
[61] *Ibid.*, p. 57. Cf. p. 55: "The method by which the egalitarian element in the doctrine was sterilized was mainly by slipping from *utility* to physical output as the object to be maximized."
[62] *Ibid.*, p. 68.   [63] Cf. below, pp. 216–19.

against ideological infection. Keynes, says Mrs Robinson, blew up the whole elaborate structure of the metaphysical justification for profit by pointing out that "capital yields a return not because it is *productive* but because it is *scarce*".[64] By putting forward the notion that saving is a cause of unemployment, he cut down one of the arguments which the neo-classics had used to banish the egalitarian implications of the utility theory. And by diagnosing the cause of the enormous waste of resources of the 30's as a deep-seated defect in the economic mechanism, Keynes

added an exception to the comfortable rule that every man in bettering himself was doing good to the commonwealth, so large as completely to disrupt the reconciliation of the pursuit of private profit with public beneficence . . .

By making it impossible to believe any longer in an automatic reconciliation of conflicting interests into a harmonious whole, the *General Theory* brought out into the open the problem of choice and judgment that the neo-classicals had managed to smother. The ideology to end ideologies broke down. Economics once more became Political Economy.[65]

It is true, Mrs Robinson agrees, that in certain passages – notably the famous one about the classical theory coming into its own again[66] – Keynes defined a "diminished kingdom" in which "*laisser faire* can still flourish" and from which "it can make sallies to recapture lost territory":[67] but these passages are interpreted in terms merely of "moments of nostalgia for the old doctrines"[68] on Keynes's part. It is also true that there is one "great ideology-bearing concept"[69] in the *General Theory* – full employment itself. "The notion that Full Employment is attainable", Mrs Robinson writes, "has become, as Keynes in some moods intended it to be, the new defence of *laisser faire*. It is only necessary to remove one glaring defect from the private-enterprise system and it becomes once more an ideal."[70] But in spite of this, the "metaphysics" of the *General Theory* is "a weak infusion",[71] "thin and easy to see through",[72] etc. "Ideology" remains largely responsible (together, oddly, with a longing to return to the womb)[73] for "the survival and revival of pre-Keynesian ideas",[74] but the work of Keynes himself is relatively free from its baleful influence.

This change of orientation is if anything intensified when Mrs Robinson goes on to deal with the new theories of development and underdevelopment which have risen to such prominence since the war.

[64] *Economic Philosophy*, p. 75. The reference is to a passage on p. 213 of the *General Theory*.
[65] *Economic Philosophy*, pp. 75–6.   [66] Quoted above, p. 187.
[67] *Economic Philosophy*, p. 86.   [68] *Ibid.*, p. 85.   [69] *Ibid.*, p. 89.   [70] *Ibid.*, p. 94.
[71] *Ibid.*, p. 89.   [72] *Ibid.*, p. 98.   [73] *Ibid.*, p. 81.   [74] *Ibid.*, p. 83.

By and large these theories are presented as being relatively unaffected by "metaphysics" and "ideology": the general impression we are given is that in the face of these new developments the "orthodox economists" have "crept off to hide in thickets of algebra and left the torch of ideology to be carried by the political argument that capitalist institutions are the bulwark of liberty".[75] And in the last chapter of the book, too, where Mrs Robinson asks us to think about the "rules of the game" which ought to be laid down today, the continued presence in modern economics of certain "ideological" notions is again ascribed almost entirely to survivals of the past – "the old orthodoxy"[76] with its "*laisser-faire* bias",[77] etc.

Are we then witnessing the beginning of the end of the Age of Ideology? Is the new orthodoxy, as distinct from the old, in fact relatively immune from ideological infection? And does the same apply to the new Marxian orthodoxy which is emerging in the East? The great merit of Mrs Robinson's book is that it forces us to ask these questions. The great merit of Oscar Lange's *Political Economy*, to which we must now turn, is that it attempts a reasoned answer to them.

VI

"This book", says Lange in his foreword to the English translation, "is an attempt at a synthesis of my studies in various fields of economic science." The "synthesis", he explains, is based on the Marxian conception of political economy as a science which studies the processes of economic development, establishes the laws governing these processes, and shows how these laws can be successfully used to *shape* the processes consciously and purposively. The "synthesis", in other words, is oriented towards the problem of economic planning, which, as Lange emphasizes, is today of interest and importance not only in the socialist countries but also in underdeveloped countries and "even in highly developed capitalist countries".[78]

The first half of the book consists essentially of a "liberal" restatement of the basic methodology of Marxian economics, which largely revolves, as it properly should, around a presentation of the elements of the materialist interpretation of history. In spite of their orthodox appearance, these sections contain a certain amount of subtle softening-up for the "synthesis" which is to follow. For example, the definition of political economy is framed as broadly as the Marxist classics will allow, and a rather unfamiliar emphasis is placed upon that branch of

[75] *Ibid.*, p. 119. [76] *Ibid.*, p. 145. [77] *Ibid.*, p. 132.
[78] *Political Economy*, pp. xiii–iv.

P

political economy which deals with "problems which affect more than one social formation" and "general properties of the economic process which appear in all social formations".[79] Then again, the "super-structure" of a given mode of production is defined as "that part of social relations . . . and of social consciousness which is indispensable for the existence of that particular mode of production",[80] thereby trans-forming the so-called "law of necessary conformity" between super-structure and economic base"[81] into a tautology and preparing readers for the notion that certain important manifestations of "social con-sciousness" in capitalist countries today do not belong, at any rate in their entirety, to the capitalist "superstructure". And controllability of the economy no longer appears, as it used to do in Marxist textbooks, as the sole prerogative of a socialist economy: the concept of *gradations* of controllability, gradually increasing as we pass from *laisser faire* capi-talism through monopoly capitalism and state intervention to socialism, is substituted.[82] On the whole, however, Lange remains faithful in this part of the book to the traditional Marxist theoretical system, even in cases where one might reasonably have expected some criticism or development of it. Thus the particular method of abstraction which Marx employed is treated as a kind of absolute which *must* still be employed today, and there is no suggestion that this method itself might have been to some extent "relative" to the environment in which it was originally put forward. Less excusable, perhaps, is Lange's promulgation of the view that Marx's theory of pauperization was "formulated at a level of abstraction which does not permit [its] direct confrontation with reality",[83] and his tortuous and essentially apolo-getic discussion of the status of economic laws under socialism.[84]

The real "synthesis" begins when we pass to the chapter entitled "The Principle of Economic Rationality: Political Economy and Praxiology" – a chapter in which, significantly, the references to Marx's work become purely incidental. In pre-capitalist formations, Lange argues, economic activity is mainly traditional and customary. Under capitalism, by way of contrast, economic activity is divided into *house-hold activity*, in which the aims are still directly dictated by needs, and *gainful activity* (the production, sale and resale of goods, including labour-power), in which the aim becomes the obtaining of money income.[85] Gradually "gainful activity becomes an activity based on reasoning, a *rational activity*";[86] quantification of the ends and means of gainful

[79] *Ibid.*, p. 95. Engels is criticized in a footnote here on the grounds that he "did not fully appreciate the significance of this branch of political economy".
[80] *Ibid.*, p. 26.   [81] *Ibid.*, p. 30.
[82] See, e.g., *ibid.*, pp. 132 and 146.
[83] *Ibid.*, p. 115, footnote.   [84] *Ibid.*, pp. 80 ff.   [85] *Ibid.*, pp. 154–6.   [86] *Ibid.*, p. 157.

activity becomes possible, thereby facilitating the *maximization* of the aim of the activity (particularly in capitalist enterprises, where it is of course *profit* which is maximized);[87] and with the spread of "rational activity" in this sense it eventually becomes possible to visualize it as the result of "the application of a general rule of procedure which is called the *economic principle* or the *principle of economic rationality*".[88] This principle asserts

that the maximum degree of realization of the end is achieved by proceeding in such a way that either for a given outlay of means the maximum degree of realization of the end is achieved, or that for a given degree of realization of the end the outlay of the means is minimal.[89]

Behaviour guided by this principle is "a feature of a certain historical stage in the development of economic relations", and its operation under capitalism is more or less "restricted to private activity and antagonistic in character".[90] But in spite of this

the rationalization of economic activity within the capitalist enterprise, the practice of proceeding according to the principle of economic rationality, and especially the consciousness of this principle in human thought, all constitute an achievement of historic significance. This is an achievement on a par with the imposing advance in material technique made within the capitalist mode of production.[91]

The reason why it must count as an achievement of this magnitude, of course, is that it can readily be extracted from its private enterprise integument and applied in the *planning* of the economy. Social rationality may be radically different from private rationality, but it is still rationality. Capitalist book-keeping is followed by "the second great historic step in the development of methods of rational economic activity" – social accounting.[92]

But this is by no means all. The "economic principle" is obviously not limited to economic activity, but is applied in many other spheres of human activity, – in technology, for example, and in military strategy and tactics.[93] "Wherever activity is rational and the end is quantitatively measurable, or at least can be expressed in the form of a greater or lesser degree of realization, there the economic principle is at work."[94] The problem of discovering what all these fields of rational activity have in common has led to the emergence of *praxiology*, the general study of rational activity, of which the main branches are operations research and programming.[95] Praxiology thus becomes "a science auxiliary to political economy like logic and mathematics, economic statistics and

[87] *Ibid.*, pp. 160–6.   [88] *Ibid.*, p. 167.   [89] *Ibid.*, p. 167.   [90] *Ibid.*, pp. 172–3.
[91] *Ibid.*, p. 176.   [92] *Ibid.*, p. 186.   [93] *Ibid.*, pp. 186–7. [94] *Ibid.*, p. 187.
[95] *Ibid.*, pp. 188–91.

mathematical statistics, econometrics, economic history, economic geography and so on". It has a methodological significance for political economy, since "wherever economic activity is rational, praxiological principles of behaviour form part of economic laws".[96] And operations research and programming are of course of great importance in the planning of the socialist economy. "It may be", writes Lange at the end of this interesting chapter, "that after double-entry book-keeping and balance accounting and after social economic balances, they will form a third historic stage in the development of the methodological means of rational economic activity."[97]

Now one of the interesting and paradoxical things about "praxiology" in Lange's sense is that although it has now become an indispensable adjunct to Marxian economics it was in quite large measure the end-product of a trend in "bourgeois" economics which was violently opposed to Marxism – the so-called "subjectivist" trend, whose history Lange sketches (along with that of the "historical" trend) in his next chapter. The subject-matter of the subjectivist trend, as it appeared in the work of Jevons, was "the study of behaviour governed by the economic principle with the aim of maximizing the pleasure of possessing goods".[98] The trend thus rejected the Classical idea that economic analysis should start from the social relations between men in production, and substituted the idea that it should start from the mental relation between men and finished goods. It did not reject the Classical "economic principle", however: indeed, it took over this principle and extended it to cover the activity of consumers as well as producers.[99]

The thing which consumers allegedly maximized was "utility", which was interpreted first in terms of utilitarian psychology, and then, rather later, in what Lange calls "praxiological" terms. The praxiological interpretation "conceives utility as a degree of realization of the aim of economic activity, independent of the nature of the aim",[100] and leads to the gradual transformation of the subjectivist trend into a "logic of rational choice" aimed at the maximization of preference.[101] Then finally (for example with Robbins) comes "the assertion that political economy deals with a certain aspect of all rational human activity",[102] and the virtual transformation of economics "into a branch of praxiology, into a science of programming".[103] Lange condemns this development because it implies "the liquidation of political economy", and adds that for this reason "many economists brought up in the subjectivist school . . . are turning back to the traditional idea of political economy as the study of a particular field of human activity and the

96 *Ibid.*, p. 200.   97 *Ibid.*, p. 207.   98 *Ibid.*, p. 233.   99 *Ibid.*, p. 234.
100 *Ibid.*, p. 235.   101 *Ibid.*, p. 236.   102 *Ibia.*, p. 237.   103 *Ibid.*, p. 239.

social relations which result from this activity".[104] One of the main examples of this given in a footnote is Samuelson's widely-used textbook – an example which reinforces the impression that Lange is writing here with his tongue in his cheek. It is necessary for him formally to anathematize the "subjectivist trend", but he does this in a way which makes it clear (a) that very few economists now really accept the Robbinsian concept of economic science to which the trend eventually led, and (b) that historically speaking the trend performed the very valuable function of stimulating the development of praxiology. The moral which Lange overtly draws from this discussion is that "as political economy the subjectivist trend must be reckoned a failure".[105] The moral which he is really drawing, I would suggest, is that all roads lead to – the economics of control.

It is in the last chapter of his book, however, that Lange's main characterization of modern "bourgeois" economics is to be found. Here he is concerned with the problem of what he calls "the social conditioning and social role of economic science", and his main theme is the close connection between the development of political economy and the rise and growth of capitalism. Like Marx, he emphasizes the importance of the change which came over political economy after the death of Ricardo, when "the class conflicts peculiar to the capitalist social formation matured into the opposition of proletariat to bourgeoisie",[106] the "hired prize-fighters" took over in orthodox circles, and the high tradition of Classical political economy was carried on only by Marx. "The bourgeoisie", Lange writes,

lost interest in the further development of political economy. As political economy, now used by the labour movement, became inconvenient and even dangerous to the bourgeoisie, there developed a tendency to liquidate it as a science studying the economic relations among men and to substitute for it *apologetics, i.e.*, the justification of the capitalist mode of production.[107]

This is a familiar thesis, and Lange illustrates it in a familiar way by analysing the "basis and social function" of the subjectivist and historical trends.[108]

But, says Lange, "the bourgeoisie's liquidation of political economy . . . cannot be complete. For there are certain economic processes where the knowledge of economic laws is necessary for practical purposes in the implementation of economic policy. The number and scope of these processes increases with the growth of capitalism, especially in its last phase of development."[109] It is worth while listing these processes, as

---

[104] *Ibid.*, p. 249.　　[105] *Ibid.*, p. 264.　　[106] *Ibid.*, p. 288.　　[107] *Ibid.*, p. 297.
[108] *Ibid.*, pp. 297 ff.　　[109] *Ibid.*, p. 304.

Lange describes them, in some detail:

(*i*) Some elements of political economy dealing with the laws of money circulation, credit and the effect of custom tariffs, survive and may even in part be developed further. They are necessary as the basis of the administration of currency, especially the gold standard, and as the basis of tariff policy . . . Thus . . . certain parts of political economy connected with the study of market processes and especially of price formation, business conditions, money circulation and credit, international trade and international payments are maintained and even developed further. In these fields bourgeois economists make real, although fragmentary, scientific progress.[110]

(*ii*) Apart from these fragments of political economy economic sciences like economic history and economic statistics are cultivated in bourgeois circles.[111]

(*iii*) The amount of true economic knowledge required by the bourgeoisie increases in the monopoly phase of capitalism, because the scope of state economic policy expands and it becomes possible for private capitalist organizations to conduct their own economic policy . . . This requires . . . a knowledge of the economic laws operating in the market as well as the concrete numerical expression of the relations contained in these laws. At the same time the scope of state activity increases, both in the form of direct interference with the economic process . . . and in the form of economic activity based on the state ownership of some of the means of production . . . New branches of economic science are developed and existing ones are modified while new auxiliary disciplines appear as well. *Econometrics . . . social accounting . . . operations research* and *the science of programming . . . cybernetics* . . . [are new studies of this type].[112]

(*iv*) The problem of crises and business cycles and the mass unemployment which they cause have for a long time forced bourgeois economic thought to go beyond the conception of the subjectivist and historical trends and even beyond the old vulgar economy, and to take up the problem of capitalist reproduction and accumulation . . . [After the crisis of 1929–30] John Maynard Keynes produced his famous theory of employment which dealt with mass unemployment and economic stagnation as tendencies inherent in the modern capitalist system which the state ought to counteract by an appropriate policy of intervention. Partly under the influence of Keynes, partly independently of him, and in some cases even earlier, economic theories betraying similarities to the Marxist theory of reproduction and accumulation began to appear.[113]

(*v*) It became necessary to take an interest in the factors which determine the rate of economic growth. This resulted in the establishment of a new branch of economic study, the *theory of economic growth* . . . The theory of economic growth raises problems which are outside the traditional scope of the subjectivist trend, vulgar economy and the neoclassical school. It is forced to study the relation-

---

[110] *Ibid.*, p. 304.   [111] *Ibid.*, p. 305.   [112] *Ibid.*, pp. 305–7.

[113] *Ibid.*, pp. 308–9. A footnote to the last sentence refers to the mathematical models of the business cycle worked out by Frisch, Tinbergen, Lundberg, Samuelson, Hicks, Goodwin, Phillips and Kalecki. Kalecki's model, it is emphasized, is derived from Marx's theory rather than from Keynes's.

ship between the development of productive forces and the nature of the relations of production which determine both the possibilities and the incentives of capital accumulation. It must deal with the same questions as Marxist political economy . . . The theory of economic growth is forced to borrow its theoretical tools from Marxist political economy or else make its own – which look very much like those produced by Marxist political economy.[114]

And as if all this were not enough, Lange goes on to refer with (appropriately modified) approval to the "petty and middle bourgeois critique of monopoly" and "the critique of imperialism by the national bourgeoisie and its associated intelligentsia in colonial, semi-colonial or recently liberated countries".[115] And finally, and perhaps most important of all, he refers to "the professionalization of economic science" – *i.e.*, its increasing concentration in universities and scientific research institutes. This means that

the dialectic process of scientific research itself gains in importance. Engels noted that the professionalization of politics, law, religion, philosophy and so on, "creates special branches of the division of labour", which become independent of the social milieu which produced them. Applied to bourgeois economics this means that the dialectic process of scientific research in obtaining a wider field for its activity pushes economic thought beyond the bounds of the views and interests of the social milieu from which it arose.[116]

These essentially favourable characterizations of a great deal of modern "bourgeois" economics are of course subjected to frequent qualifications which it would be wrong to try to minimize, but even so the list of elements of "true economic knowledge" given by Lange remains a formidable one. One is therefore somewhat surprised when, at the end of all this, he describes these elements as "only fragments",[117] and goes on to proclaim – albeit in very carefully chosen words – that a fully systematic and unbiased political economy is possible only as a science linked to the labour movement.[118] So unexpected in the context is this stereotyped conclusion that Lange can hardly have expected his readers to take it seriously. Nor are the extended remarks about "conservative" and "progressive" ideologies which follow particularly helpful, except on a very general plane. One may agree that as a rule "conservative" ideologies have a tendency to obscure reality, and that "progressive" ideologies have a tendency to reveal it.[119] But generalities of this kind are not a very useful guide in the evaluation of current

---

[114] *Ibid.*, pp. 310–11. A footnote to the last sentence refers to Domar's *Essays in the Theory of Economic Growth*.

[115] *Ibid.*, p. 319.

[116] *Ibid.*, p. 314. Engels's famous letter to Schmidt of 27th October 1890, to which Lange is referring here, does not in fact go nearly as far as this.

[117] *Ibid.*, p. 319.   [118] *Ibid.*, p. 320.   [119] *Ibid.*, pp. 330–1.

trends in economics. For the salient feature of the present-day situation is that the tendency of "conservative" economics to obscure reality has been appreciably offset by the factors which Lange has already described, and that the tendency of "progressive" economics to reveal reality has been appreciably offset by the distorting factors which were operative in the Stalin period and which have by no means been fully overcome.[120] It is precisely because of this that for the first time in the history of modern economics some kind of "synthesis" has now become possible.

VII

The degree of agreement between the three writers whose ideas on economics and ideology we have been considering is much greater than we might have expected. All three, for example, agree that 1830 (or thereabouts) marked something of a watershed in the history of economics, although their *evaluations* of the different trends which began to separate out at that time are startlingly different. All three agree that a considerable portion of modern "bourgeois" economics is relatively free from ideological distortions, although their estimates of the *size* of this portion are different, and in the case of Schumpeter (as distinct from the other two) this ideological neutrality is regarded as no new thing. Finally, all agree that one of the most important proximate reasons for the emergence of ideologically neutral propositions in economics is the rigorous application of the ordinary rules of scientific reasoning. When Schumpeter speaks of the cleansing effect of "the rules of procedure that we apply in our analytic work", when Mrs Robinson speaks of science progressing by "trial and error"[121] and "the framing of hypotheses to be tested against the facts",[122] and when Lange discusses the way in which "the professionalization of economic science" enlarges the sphere of operation of "the dialectic process of scientific research", they are all really talking about one and the same thing.

But the rules of scientific reasoning have been available to us for a long time. Why is it then that over long periods in the history of economics (leaving aside the question of *which* periods) these rules were not fully applied in various sensitive areas, whereas in our own time, if we are to believe our authors, they are being applied so assiduously as to lead us to hope at the very least that we may be witnessing the beginning of the end of the Age of Ideology in our science?

---

[120] The tendencies to "transform political economy into apologetics" in the Stalin period are well described by Lange towards the end of his book (pp. 338–40).
[121] *Op. cit.*, p. 38.　　[122] *Ibid.*, p. 81.

Lange tries to explain this, as we have seen, in terms of the increasing need on the part of the bourgeoisie for "true economic knowledge" in the era of monopoly capitalism, State intervention and nationalized industries. A rather more plausible (and more general) way of putting this is to say that we are now living in an age in which, for better or for worse, the economic machine which formerly ruled our destinies is being increasingly interfered with. In some areas its influence has been suppressed altogether, so that new methods of performing the tasks which it used to perform have to be found. In other areas its influence is being modified and controlled by the state in what is regarded as the social interest. And economics is increasingly becoming subordinated to the task of implementing these new methods and directing these new measures of control. Mrs Robinson, it will be remembered, said in her book that "it is the business of the economists, not to tell us what to do, but show why what we are doing anyway is in accord with proper principles". Today, however, it *is* the business of the economists "to tell us what to do": they are far less concerned than they used to be with justifying "what we are doing anyway". And "telling us what to do", in an era when the replacement and control of the economic machine is the main item on the agenda, is not an unusually hazardous occupation, so far as the risk of ideological infection is concerned. The ends to be achieved are often given, as it were, from above; in many cases the problem to be solved reduces to a more or less technical one; and the process of "testing against the facts" is often not only relatively simple but also more or less obligatory, if only because the economists' employers are going to want value for money.

Nothing that I have said above, however, should be taken to imply that I believe that the securing of an ideology-free economics will be an easy task, or that a very great deal does not still remain to be done. So long as there are rival political ideologies in the world there are bound to some extent to be rival economic ideologies associated with them. And if we extend the word "ideology" to embrace not simply ideas conditioned by socio-economic forces but *all* unconscious conditioning (as in some contexts Mrs Robinson does), it becomes obvious that in this sense "ideology" will always be with us.[123] All we can do is to "go round about", to "see what we value, and try to see why".[124] But it seems a counsel of despair to say, as Mrs Robinson does, that "reason will not help";[125] that "no one . . . is conscious of his own ideology, any more than he can smell his own breath";[126] and so on. Surely, to a

---

[123] Cf. A. L. Macfie, *op. cit.*, pp. 216–17.
[124] Robinson, *op. cit.*, p. 14.
[125] *Ibid.*, p. 12.   [126] *Ibid.*, p. 41.

limited but significant extent, reason *can* help – and not least in making us conscious, even if only dimly, of our own ideologies. "The relativist", writes Professor Macfie in an impressive passage, "would not agree that individual reasoning is so determined by feeling or prejudice or conditioning that it is quite incapable of ever rising above them, of ever being to some extent impartial, of ever realizing bias and allowing suitably for it."[127] This may or may not be true. But we have to act on the assumption that it is true, if we are to act at all.

[127] *Op. cit.*, pp. 219–20.

INDEX OF PERSONS